PIANOFORTE

PIANO FORTE

A SOCIAL HISTORY OF THE PIANO

DIETER HILDEBRANDT

Translated by Harriet Goodman

INTRODUCTION BY ANTHONY BURGESS

George Braziller   New York

First published in the United States in 1988 by George Braziller, Inc.
First published in West Germany by Hanser Verlag, 1985.

For information, address the publisher:
George Braziller, Inc.
60 Madison Avenue
New York, New York 10010

Library of Congress Cataloguing in Publication Data:

Hildebrandt, Dieter, 1932-
  [Pianoforte, oder, Der Roman des Klaviers im 19. Jahrhundert. English]
  Pianoforte, a social history of the piano/by Dieter Hildebrandt; translated from the German by Harriet Goodman; introduction by Anthony Burgess.
    p. cm.
  Translation of: Pianoforte, oder, Der Roman des Klaviers im 19. Jahrhundert.
  Includes bibliographical references and index.
  ISBN 0-8076-1182-4: $19.95
  1. Piano—19th century—History.   2. Pianists—19th century.
3. Piano music—19th century—History and criticism.   I. Title.
ML650.H5313   1988   88-4314
786.1'09'034—dc19   CIP
                                                        MN

Typeset by Deltatype, Ellesmere Port, S. Wirral, England
Printed in the United States of America

First printing

PIANOFORTE

INTRODUCTION

CARL DAHLHAUS, reviewing this book in *Die Deit*, said '*Ein Thema hat seinen Autor gefunden*' – 'a subject has found its author'. The pianoforte has certainly found an author of the right race (and, whatever his race, certainly a very good author), for, despite its name and its origins, the piano, or *Hammerklavier* as Beethoven memorably called it, was one of the great implements of German romanticism. It had been preceded by various keyboard instruments whose charm we still recognise, but when strings began to be hammered, instead of delicately plucked, the soul of a turbulent era found the voice it needed.

A virginals, an instrument that our Virgin Queen played and played well, has a keyboard identical with that of the piano, though much shorter, and its successor the harpsichord also looks like an attenuated and very elegant piano, though sometimes it has, like an organ, two manuals. But both are thin-stringed, and the plectum that plucks the strings cannot sustain the sounds that are produced. The clavichord, which strikes instead of plucking, gives out an even fainter note than its elder sisters: it is a suitable instrument for a very small apartment with very thin walls and unmusical neighbours. All these instruments are played today, our era having been taught by Stravinsky, as well as by jazz, to reject romanticism and return to the dry pecking tone of the Age of Reason. Edward Heath showed the jazz pianist Oscar Peterson how to make use of the clavichord in a small combo (it would never do in a big band or an electronically amplified rock group), and the style of jazz piano – dry, sardonic, and with little use of the assertive sustaining pedal - owes more to Bach than to Liszt.

The piano begins its true career as the instrument of men and women who lived in the age of Napoleonic imperialism. If the harpsichord is the Alexander Pope of music, the piano is its Lord Byron. True, it was used by Haydn and Mozart, and the young Beethoven who followed Mozart, but much in the restrained spirit of the harpsichord. Its romantic possibilities only began to be exploited when a new philosophy came to Europe. The French Revolution looked forward to the collapse of all the old despotisms. It preached freedom, but this turned out to be freedom for a new despot. Napoleon Bonaparte may have pretended to liberate nations in the name of that revolution, but his liberations were really conquests in the name of himself and his hard-eyed Corsican family. The concept of the hero had come back into the world, and as Carlyle's *Hero and Hero Worship* reminds us, heroism did not necessarily have to take the form of the military conqueror. In Byron the hero is a man who detests war but glorifies his own ego. He loves largely, suffers from perturbations of the soul, is essentially solitary and tries to commune with Alps and rivers. He is an animated grand piano.

Technically, the pianoforte – so called because its tone could range from loud to soft, whereas the harpsichord always plucked the same number of decibels – owed its novelty to a capacity for sustaining notes and for damping them. Piano-engineering has not changed much since the time when Beethoven was given a Broadwood piano (which he called a Broadwood) and thanked the makers in horrible French. A harpsichord has, in its middle and upper ranges, a pair of stretched wires for every note, but a piano has three strings for each note, of great strength and tension, except in the lower stretches, where a single string as powerful as a cable tolls like a bell, and in the highest of all, where resonance does not matter. A padded hammer strikes. If the note is to be sustained, as a note in the orchestra is sustained, the right foot depresses a pedal. If an effect of muffled softness is required then, the left foot pushes down another pedal, and only one string of each trio of strings is struck. This explains the directions one sees in piano music – *una corda* (one string) for the soft pedal, *tre corde* (the whole three) when the pedal is released. At the same time, many dynamic gradations are permitted by the varied striking force of the hands on the keyboard.

This is clearly an instrument for the expression of a romantic personality, perhaps psychically unstable in the terms of the Age of Reason, quick to move from a whisper to a shout, capable equally of melting softness and frenzied noise. Its pitch range is greater than that of even the orchestra of Richard Wagner or Richard Strauss – it can go higher than the piccolo and lower than the double bassoon. Its effect is that of a one-man orchestra, and Franz Liszt demonstrated, by making piano versions of the Overture to *Tannhäuser* and the Prelude to *Tristan and Isolde,* that, though palpably inferior to the orchestra in tone-colour, it could easily attain its expressive range. Try playing the Venusberg music on a harpsichord.

Dieter Hildebrandt has a lot to say about the great nineteenth-century composers and performers, who were not, of course, all German. But we have to think of the romantic movement as a Teutonic phenomenon. It arose out of rejection of the imperial ambitions of the Corsican upstart, and, in defying Napoleon, Germany may be said to have found its soul. Germany certainly found that it was possible to be a nation instead of a parcel of principalities and duchies. And if Germany was not the Austro-Hungarian Empire, which produced Liszt, the same language was spoken in Vienna and Prague as in Berlin and Weimar. The Germanophone unity was finally decreed by Adolf Hitler, and this was, though perverted, a natural conclusion to the cult of the pan-Teutonic romantic ideal.

Certainly, the great monuments of the pianoforte repertoire, which have not been diminished in the age of Stockhausen and Boulez, have come out of Germanophonia. Chopin, leaving Poland to earn fame in the West, composed the lyrical poetry of the instrument, but the epics came from Beethoven, with the sonatas that demonstrate the whole gamut of pianistic possibilities and the five great concertos. It is the piano concerto which best expresses the romantic spirit, and, though Poland produced two, Norway one, and France (before Ravel) none worth talking about, the German-speaking territories, with Beethoven, Schumann, Liszt and Brahms, exhibited magisterially the heroic implications of a single man fighting, and being reconciled with, an orchestra of a hundred. Berlioz represented Childe Harold, who is really his author Byron, in a solo viola poeticising against an orchestra, but he should properly have chosen a piano. He did not, however, play the piano, and he is one of the two romantic composers who failed to exploit its power. (Wagner, of course, is the other, though even he has had, in certain productions of *Parsifal,* four grand pianos in the wings to simulate the chiming of bells.) Berlioz made up for his lack of pianism by employing bigger and bigger orchestras.

It is Franz Liszt who stands out as the great romantic hero of the instrument. Some say that his technique would easily be over-shadowed by some of the soloists of our day, but there is no living virtuoso who finds the most difficult of his piano pieces easy. In Liszt,

as in Chopin, the superb composer for the instrument is conjoined
with the superb practitioner. If Chopin took pianism far, Liszt took it
much farther. His hands were exceptional, and his management of
them such that he could hold glasses of water on both – even in
passages of great speed – without spilling a drop. But it was not just a
matter of developing technique; it was a matter also (and this applies to
Chopin as well) of finding in the sonorities of the piano new
possibilities for romantic music in general. Chopin breaks the
harmonic rules nearly a century before the academies give their
permission: he has consecutive fifths and sevenths, like any jazz
pianist. There is something in pianistic procedure which demands this
kind of unorthodoxy. In Liszt we find every possible harmonic
innovation – from the Scriabinesque dissonance to the Debussyan
whole-tone chord. The piano, being a romantic instrument, fore-
shadowed the breakdown of classical order in music. The hint of what
was to come in the twentieth century can even be heard in later
Beethoven.

With Claude Debussy, who liquidated, on behalf of France, the
long musical hegemony of Germany and the Austro-Hungarian
Empire, the experiments of Liszt reach their consummation.
Romanticism became impressionism. The piano ceased to be heroic,
and the poet of the keyboard expressed not himself but the essence of
external nature – water, mist, flowers, storm, heat, frost – as well as
unemotional artefacts like a picture postcard of a Spanish scene or
figures on a Greek vase. But the capacity of the piano to peck like one
of its tinny ancestors, to blur through use of the sustaining pedal, to
arpeggiate, to complement the great speed of scale work with the
solemnity of huge sustained chords, to wage war between the black
keys and the white (out of this came the polytonality of Stravinsky's
Petrushka) served modernism as well as it served the romantic heyday.
Nowadays, no composer is quite sure what to do with the instrument,
and the 'prepared piano' of John Cage is a sign of dissatisfaction with
what it always wishes to invoke, even when the cat walks over it or a
child bashes it with his tiny fists – namely, the spirit of Liszt. When
Cage makes his performer sit at the instrument and do nothing we have
reached the limit of dissatisfaction. To appreciate what the piano was
always meant to be about, we must go back to the heroic days which
Dieter Hildebrandt so ably chronicles.

He calls his book *Der Roman des Klaviers*. *Roman* means either 'novel' or 'romance' (which once meant the same thing: nowadays a romance can only mean a debased form of the novel, the speciality of Bills and Moon, to use David Lodge's inspired spoonerism). In that his survey is about a romantic instrument, *The Romance of the Pianoforte* is in order as a translation of his title. But I like to feel that the whole story of the instrument has the qualities of a novel – thrilling, with mercurial characters, an evocation of the erotic and the perilous. Whether there is a happy ending I do not know. But, though we lack a modern Liszt or Chopin, to say nothing of Beethoven, we do not lack brilliant interpreters to bring their wild-eyed century back again. The romance of the piano is probably not yet over.

Anthony Burgess
1988

THE UNSUNG HERO

How oft, when thou, my music, music play'st,
Upon that blessèd wood whose motion sounds
With thy sweet fingers, when thou gently sway'st
The wiry concord that mine ear confounds,
Do I envy those jacks that nimble leap
To kiss the tender inward of thy hand,
Whilst my poor lips, which should that harvest reap,
At the wood's boldness by thee blushing stand.
To be so tickled, they would change their state
And situation with those dancing chips,
O'er whom thy fingers walk with gentle gait,
Making dead wood more blest than living lips.
    Since saucy jacks so happy are in this,
    Give them thy fingers, me thy lips to kiss.

William Shakespeare
(Sonnet 128)

'The piano is the best actor in the company of instruments,' said the composer Ferruccio Busoni,[1] and Anton Rubinstein agreed with him: 'A piano is not just *one* instrument – it is a hundred.'[2] It has been called 'the most comprehensive musical instrument',[3] 'the most intellectual',[4] 'the most romantic',[5] while the social philosopher Max Weber declared bluntly: 'In its whole musical essence the piano is a domestic instrument of the bourgeoisie.'[6]

So what is it really?

It is probably the most paradoxical of instruments. Its proper name, pianoforte, appears to divide all music into loud and soft sounds, but that is too simple. Its keyboard appears to divide all music into black and white notes, which is also too easy, although a child was once heard to ask: 'So the black keys are for sad music and the white keys are for the funny parts?' One might add that it looks like a cross between an expensive piece of furniture, a lavish plant stand and an unmanageable sculpture. The piano is the most orderly instrument: it is a pending file of sounds. There, in seven and a half octaves, the whole of Western music lies in store, ready and waiting to be called up at the touch of a key. It has more to offer than a whole collection of records and cassettes, and between 'Mary Had A Little Lamb' and a full-grown sonata the possibilities are limitless.

The piano is the most athletic instrument: so much strength and momentum is required of the player that whole generations, not only of teachers but of anatomists, muscle specialists, chiropractors, orthopaedists and even masseurs have studied the art of playing the piano. The number of resultant publications is incalculable. Busoni once remarked of the young pianists he saw practising so obsessively: 'For them the piano is a sports field wrapped up in a musical instrument.'[7]

The piano is also the most inviting instrument: it not only offers up the range of its own musical possibilities, it also offers itself unreservedly. Touch a key and you hear a note. Use your fist and you are answered with a sort of chord. Use your whole forearm and you produce something very fashionable: a cluster. Flick the keyboard with one sweep of the duster and you have a glissando. This instant response is hardly something to be taken for granted, considering that most musical instruments are idiosyncratic and often downright stubborn. String instruments are notorious for responding to the novice with a fierce caterwauling – not to mention the wind and brass instruments, many of which, like the flute or the trumpet, can refuse to make any sound whatsoever.

The piano – this will be my last definition for the time being – is therefore most particularly democratic. Thus in 1800 the *Allgemeine Musikalische Zeitung* in Vienna could write: 'Everybody plays [the piano], everybody learns music.'[8] Around the middle of the century came Heine's groan from Paris: 'The reigning bourgeoisie must suffer for its sins not just the old classical tragedies and the trilogies that are not classic, for the heavenly powers have blessed it with an even more ghastly delight, namely that inescapable pianoforte that one hears tinkling in every house, in every company, day and night.'[9]

Again, about a quarter of a century later, the critic Eduard Hanslick raged at the 'common and pernicious piano-playing nonsense'. In a bluntly classic diatribe he went on:

Only if influential voices never tire of warning; if our conservatories work against the overproduction of men and women pianists, instead of frivolously encouraging it further; if finally every one of us sets himself against it in his own circle – then and only then will one be allowed to hope that the scourge horrifyingly known as 'piano fever' will gradually lose its virulence and claim fewer victims in future, both on the performing and the listening side.[10]

So had nothing changed in the course of a century beyond the intensity of complaints about the universal and all-too-common craze of the piano? Was there no progress to report aside from the fact that what could be dismissed in 1800 with the simple phrase 'Everybody plays the piano' was diagnosed in the era of hygiene as 'piano fever'? Must one conclude that the only constant throughout the dynamic nineteenth century, through all its technical and social revolutions, was the fact that people still played the piano, in 1900 just as well (or as badly) as in 1800?

In fact the general tenor of these complaints obscures the truth, which is in its way nothing less than sensational. Between 1800 and 1900 (not precisely on the stroke of the clock, but with considerable calendar accuracy) the piano underwent a development in its structure, its music, in the nature of public concerts and the education of a broad middle-class audience, even in the building of concert halls, so exciting that it is no exaggeration to describe it as the stuff of a novel. In fact the piano could be called the unsung hero of the nineteenth century – unsung, occasionally sinister, and often rather comic.

This hero conquered more of Europe than Napoleon and has occupied it much more permanently. It triumphed in the American civil war – on both sides – and rode out with the keenest of the pioneers to claim the Wild West. It united Germany long before Bismarck. It was a peaceful conqueror but often a tyrannical occupying force, exacting strict discipline with its loud commands. It soon terrorized whole cities, an omnipresent early Big Brother. No other general that century took so many prisoners. Over ten thousand young people were condemned to 'solitary confinement at the piano', children were chained to the instrument, and for young women in particular it was a pitiless chaperon. Some young people it frustrated in the worst sense of the word, for our hero was also a tempter, promising earthly fame and a route to immortality.

On the other hand this hero, like Don Quixote, was often obliged to concede defeat: it was bawled out, disembowled, martyred, abused, covered in scorn and beer many thousands of times. It heard curses such as Schumann's: 'I would like to smash my piano to pieces!'[11] It was thrown out of windows – in the March uprisings in Leipzig in 1830, for instance. It had its Waterloos, as when Franz Liszt broke its strings or Beethoven submerged it in his domestic chaos. Trivialized, caricatured and mocked, it none the less remained a hero able to defend itself against such attacks, as well as its own unfortunate disposition to go so easily and so deeply out of tune.

In the space of a hundred years this heroic instrument literally outgrew itself. Around 1800 it still travelled light: a player could happily pick it up, tuck it under his arm and carry it next door, or even as far as the next village. But soon it was able to withstand pressures of which no one had thought it capable, and by the middle of the century there it stood: a solid and unified whole.

As it grew bigger and stronger, so its confidence rose: the aristocratic music room it had long since abandoned; the patrician salon was soon too small for it; and before long it had ventured onto the true field of honour, the bold, vaulted concert halls, not a few of which were designed for it specifically.

The decisive defeat came at the end of the nineteenth century. Weary of conquest, celebrated almost unto death, the piano leaned its mahogany weight against the wall of the best room. It had become the victim of its own triumph.

Not forever. Every time a concert is given today, anywhere around the world, we are reminded how vital the piano still can be, both thundering and subtly intimating, as if to prove to us in black and white that its great past is still before it, at least for the next two hours.

There is nothing more exciting than the sight of a grand piano standing open on a concert stage in a hushed and expectant auditorium. The purpose of this book is to capture something of that unique excitement.

'I DO NOT PLAY FOR SUCH SWINE'
Beethoven

Beethoven is Lucifer's good son, the
demon guide to the last things.

Ernst Bloch

Let us start in Vienna.

At the beginning of the nineteenth century Count Moritz Fries was one of the city's richest men: factory-owner, landowner, proprietor of the bank that bore his name. He even bought himself a title. But Fries was one of the city's artistically-minded, music-loving aristocrats who were not just out to make money: their real talent lay in spending it. They were virtuosos of luxury, veritable magicians of opulence, grandmasters of showmanship. The Age of Enlightenment had taught them at least one thing: the importance of illumination. What will be brilliant must be well lit: in one year Fries spent 17,801 florins on candles alone. A quarter of a century later Fries & Co (bankers) was to go bankrupt.

The delight in splendid society was by no means limited to noble circles. Franz II was hardly noted for his benevolence; unsettled by the French Revolution and even more so by Bonaparte, he made it the duty of his minister Thugut to 'stamp out the revolt' in his own empire.[1] But the 200,000 inhabitants of the burgeoning capital city displayed a happy-go-lucky attitude that defied common sense.

'Everything here breathes light-heartedness and merriment. Thousands upon thousands crowd up and down the narrow streets from morning till night,' reported composer Johann Friedrich Reichardt,[2] and Berliner Friedrich Nicolai agreed, though his view was affected by a Prussian squint: 'The desire for pleasure, which is so common in Vienna, extends even to the lowest classes. But this persistent desire for pleasure, along with its attendant loss of time and distraction, cannot be conducive . . . to fruitful endeavour.'[3]

The cream of Viennese society (except the innermost circle at court) would assemble *chez* Fries for the evening: the Schwarzenbergs, the Kinskys, the Lichtensteins perhaps, the Lobkovitzes, the Lichnovskys, the Razumovskys, and certainly Count Palffy. These were music-lovers who knew all the endearing idiosyncracies of the business and who lived for cultural intrigue. They would plot to outdo one another, planning campaigns of extravagance, offering ever greater attractions.

The star attraction for some time had been a man named Ludwig van Beethoven, rumoured to be an illegitimate son of Frederick the Great. Since finally settling in Vienna in 1792, Beethoven had gradually established his fame and his notoriety with three strokes of genius: his impetuous virtuosity at the keyboard, his unprecedented talent for improvisation, and his rudeness, which must have reminded civilized Vienna of that archetypal character of the eighteenth-century novel, the noble savage. Cherubini had christened him the 'unlicked bear'.

'That young fellow must be in league with the devil,' Joseph Gelinek, an ordained priest and piano virtuoso, was said to have complained after a musical duel with the newcomer. 'I've never heard anybody play like that. I gave him a theme to improvise on, and I assure you that I've never heard anybody improvise so admirably. Then he played some of his own compositions, which are marvellous, really wonderful, and he manages difficulties and effects at the keyboard that one never dreamed of . . . He is a small, ugly, swarthy fellow and seems to have a wilful disposition . . .'[4]

Beethoven was indeed anything but beautiful: apparently he could be a fearful sight, and any association with him was bound to be nerve-racking. One lady, clearly no great admirer, described him thus:

Whenever he came to our house he used first to put his head round the door to make sure there was no one there he did not like. He was short and plain, with an ugly red face covered in pockmarks. His hair was very dark and hung shaggily about his face, his suit was ordinary, a far cry from the elegant fashion which prevailed at the time, and particularly in our circle. Furthermore he spoke in dialect, and had a rather vulgar way of putting things. Altogether he showed little evidence of breeding, his expression and behaviour being quite unrefined. He was very proud: I once saw Count Lichnovsky's mother, the elderly Countess Thun, kneeling before him as he sat back in the sofa, imploring him to play, but Beethoven would not do it.[5]

If his grooming was slovenly, his domestic habits were no better. Through a rapid succession of apartments – he moved as often as eighty times within Vienna alone – chaos prevailed. It seemed that every time he picked something up he either dropped it or broke it. Inkpots had a habit of tipping over into the piano. 'No piece of furniture was safe with him, least of all anything valuable. Everything was upturned, soiled or broken beyond repair.' He himself once admitted that his housekeeping was 'very like an *Allegro di Confusione*'.[6]

'A truly remarkable confusion,' one report agreed, and then went into detail:

> Books and sheets of music would be scattered in every corner – there the remains of a cold sandwich, here uncorked or half-empty bottles; there on the lectern the hurried outline of a new quartet, here the remnants of breakfast; there on the piano the beginnings of a magnificent work, the slumbering embryo of a symphony, here a printer's proof awaiting release. Personal and business letters would litter the floor . . . And despite this confusion our Maestro was wont to wax eloquent as Cicero about his love of order. Only when something simply could not be found, despite hours – days – even weeks of searching, then would he change his tune, and the innocent would suffer. 'Ja, ja!' was the pitiful cry, 'what a disaster! Nothing stays where I put it; everything has to be moved somewhere else; I am a fool to put up with it; oh heavens above!'[7]

Chaos breeds bad temper, and Beethoven was prone to violent outbursts of rage. 'But if I be provoked, at a time when I am more open to anger, then I burst out more fiercely than anyone' – so he excused himself to his student Ferdinand Ries, whom he had deeply and wrongly insulted.[8] And Beethoven had his scenes with everyone: friends, publishers, housekeepers, waiters, all suffered continually or at least occasionally from Beethoven's fury. Once he poured a bowl of soup over a waiter's head (because he had ordered something else),[9] and in some restaurants they made sure to let him leave without paying, lest he denounce them as frauds when presented with the bill.

We now have some idea of the man Count Fries would invite to entertain his music-loving friends. Let us take a particular evening – say the one on which Beethoven was to baptise a newly completed march in a four-handed ceremony. The once-insulted Ferdinand Ries is to join him for the performance. The pair take their places at the grand piano, open the music (on which the ink is not quite dry) and begin. The aristocracy of Vienna is transformed into an audience with the exception of two guests: a young count talks to a beautiful woman, standing by the door to the next room. Possibly the young man agrees with Kreisler, a conductor (who actually meant it ironically on the occasion he made the remark): 'Why should one be denied the opportunity, even in the middle of a concert, to strike up a conversation with one's neighbour about all aspects of politics and morality, and so achieve a dual purpose in a most agreeable fashion? On the contrary, this is to be encouraged, for music, as one will have occasion to remark at any concert or musical gathering, greatly facilitates speech.'[10] Perhaps the young count is speaking loudly, thinking to himself, well, how else am I to make myself understood with the noise these two musicians are making, much less have any hope of being heard by her?

More likely he thought nothing of it at all. For what was music for the surviving aristocracy of Europe around 1800 but table music, a foil for conversation, a melodic *mise en scène*? And above all, a balm to soothe the nerves of the card-player. Composer (and violinist) Ludwig Spohr reported from the court of Brunswick:

> These concerts at court with the duchess took place once a week and were most distasteful to the court musicians, the custom of the time being to play cards throughout the concert. Indeed, the duchess ordered that the orchestra always play *piano* so as not to disturb her game. The conductor therefore ignored any call for trumpets or drums and insisted that not a *forte* be heard. But because this was not entirely avoidable in the course of a symphony, however softly the orchestra played, the duchess further ordered that a thick carpet be spread under the musicians to muffle the sound. The result was that one heard 'I play, I pass,' etc. rather more clearly than the music itself.[11]

The arrangements were even more philistine at the court of the king of Württemburg in Stuttgart: there the concert stopped abruptly as soon as the card-play finished. When Spohr and his wife, harpist Dorette Scheidler, made it a condition of their appearance that the cards be laid aside, the king grudgingly agreed: the chamberlain then informed the violinist of the monarch's demand that in that case he and his wife should play what they had to without interval, 'so that His Majesty be not longer inconvenienced'.[12]

＊

That irritating feeling of being inconvenienced must have been foremost in the mind of the young count who went so far as to raise his voice. What happened then was not in the least musical: it was a revolutionary act, a verbal guillotine. Beethoven swept the hands of his young accompanist Ries from the keyboard, sprang up from the instrument and shouted at the festive company: 'I do not play for such swine!'

For seconds there was utter silence: the piano was mute, the chatterer struck dumb. According to Ries, the audience kept their nerve and tried to appease Beethoven: 'All attempts to bring him back to the piano were in vain, and he would not even allow me to play the sonata' – the next piece on the programme. 'So on a note of general discord the music stopped.'[13]

I do not play for such swine! A statement of impassioned rage, spoken in fury, yet also, at the beginning of the nineteenth century, a political protest, not just in the sense of an expression of revolt aimed at princes and nobility, but also as a bid for autonomy on behalf of music and music-makers. Music, having long since come of age, now expected to command the full attention of society. She was no longer content to be mere decoration, divertimento, accompaniment, 'aural ornament, donned by a room', as Blaukopf put it. She demanded that society be all ears and respectfully silent. Music would no longer frame a social event; she insisted on being the event itself.

But it was not just a question of denying princes their *divertissement*. Music now refused to serve any social function whatsoever, although this was just the period when the rousing power of the Marseillaise had shown that music could, or, as it may have seemed, should be called to the service of a cultural revolution. Lakanal, a member of the French Révolutions-Convents, had demanded no less: 'From now on music will no longer have the right to feel sufficient unto herself. She must take up her duty as a citizen, subject to official control. Music belongs in the public arena, among the people and on the battlefield.'[14]

But music wanted no Revolution. She was her own revolution, in that she was nothing but Music. Alongside the lodges of the Freemasons and the desks of enlightening writers like Voltaire, Diderot, Rousseau, Lessing and Beaumarchais, the music rooms of the palaces and villas and stately homes were among the revolutionary hotbeds of the period before 1800. A dilettante prince, in sitting down to make music with his servants, his hired musicians, established at least the 'aesthetic precedent' for other social relations. In playing the second violin part of a string quartet he was in reality playing nothing more than second fiddle. In hitting the wrong note more often than his professional hirelings, he tarnished the aura, violated the inviolability of his princely role. In obeying his musical instincts he flouted the rules prescribed by his rank. 'Characteristic . . . was the tendency, if not to abolish class divisions, at least for the time being to ignore them for the sake of the "musical dialogue", as Goethe called the quartet,' wrote the music historian Carl Dahlhaus.[15]

But the call for autonomy meant something even more concrete than this: music no longer wanted to serve a text, a liturgy, a message of any kind. She no longer wanted to be mass or oratorio, song or wedding hymn, chorale or dance; she wanted to throw off this ballast of speech and words and piety, and her greatest adversary around 1800 was no prince, no cultural revolutionary, no dogmatic priest – it was the human voice. It was that voice that would go on speaking words, singing songs, telling stories, saying prayers, describing scenes, assigning meaning. The autonomy of music meant: liberation from song, which meant: instrumental music.

Ludwig Tieck, writing shortly before the turn of the nineteenth century, described instrumental music as 'the highest form of musical language, which goes its own way and stops for no text, no lumbering lyric, making its own meaning and its own poetry.'[16] Tieck's friend Wilhelm Heinrich Wackenroder spoke of compositions 'whose notes – arranged by their composers like numbers in a calculation, or tiles in a musical mosaic, clearly ordered, but sensuous and in happy combination – when played on the instruments, speak a glorious and sensitive poetry . . .'[17] The complex and wilful structures of this music without human voice demanded a new way of listening: a silence not so much of respect as of necessary concentration. Wackenroder's fictional hero Joseph Berglinger would have made an ideal audience for Beethoven: 'When Joseph attended an important concert he would sit down in a corner without so much as a glance at the glittering audience and listen with complete devotion, as if he were in church – silent and immobile, his eyes fixed on the ground before him. The merest sound did not escape him, and by the end the strain of such attentiveness left him limp and exhausted.'[18] So the demand implicit in Beethoven's outburst could not be taken for granted, but could be seen as somehow inherent in the nature of an art that increasingly commanded respect, an art that intended to set the tone – in every sense. In Beethoven this demand assumed flesh, and it found in his works its systematic expression. Theodor W. Adorno explained: 'If he is already the musical prototype of the revolutionary bourgeoisie, he is also the prototype of a music that has thrown off its social obligations, a fully autonomous aesthetic, no longer in service to anyone. The essence of society . . . becomes in him . . . the essence of music itself.'[19]

The true 'instrument' of this musical and social revolution was the piano, which was steadily growing in power and influence. This happened in two ways.

First, as instrumental music became increasingly popular, the piano emerged as the tried and tested *universal instrument*. It could trace the outlines of a string quartet just as surely as it could probe the structures of a symphony. The poetic ideal of instrumental music was almost perfectly realized in the piano. The very keys looked like those 'tiles in a musical mosaic' which Wackenroder dreamed of for the new style of composition, and the discretion of the tone, the 'concrete illusionism' of the sound, was a further mark of that much-admired abstraction made perfect. And anyway, who looked more poetic? The sweaty, anxious, browbeaten players of a court orchestra? The string quartet hired by some nobleman for his stately home, where the cellist might be called upon to dig over the garden? Poetry, pure thought, music which made 'its own poetry and its own meaning' – were these not the rightful province of the individual?

And so, secondly, the universal instrument emerged as the *individual instrument* without equal, meaning rather more than that one person can play it alone. With the piano the individual player could assert himself, but he could also make a fool of himself; he could dazzle or bore, enchant or irritate. The solo pianist had to be master not only of his art but also of his own mind. The piano made a man of the 'player'. There is proof of this in any number of Beethoven episodes in which a piano played an important part, even when it was not played – as an instrument of refusal, a medium of protest, in effect a musical barricade.

Almost according to programme, just such a refusal occurred a few years later, in 1806. It was at this point that the challenge to aristocratic manners and morals was clearly formulated. In the autumn of that year

Beethoven travelled with his long-time patron, Prince Moritz von Lichnovsky, to the prince's estate at Schloss Grätz in Silesia. For various reasons he was not in the best of moods ('his mood is for the most part very melancholy, and, judging by his letters, the sojourn in the country has not amused him'). When he was not in the mood, Beethoven was not easily lured to his instrument; he frequently required a good deal of coaxing, and even after sitting down at the piano he often resorted to delaying tactics: 'Before he began to play he would strike the keyboard with the flat of his hand, run one finger up and down and altogether amuse himself heartily, usually laughing the while.'

No one was to laugh on this particular evening. There were guests, that is to say French officers, billeted on Lichnovsky's estate. Whatever it was that so irritated Beethoven – the presence of Napoleon's troops, their manner, the prince's less than tactful approach, his own private demons – what is certain is that patron and composer worked each other into a fury. The more obstinate Beethoven's refusal, the more imperious Lichnovsky's command that he play, and in the end it developed into a full-scale row, of which there are various versions on record.

One report has it that Beethoven was 'so sorely tried that he, now truly enraged, categorically refused to play, denouncing it as a servile task'.[20] The palace steward described the whole affair as a controversy only on paper and said that 'in his apartments' – Beethoven's quarters on the estate – 'a letter to the prince has been found in which he explained that he could not play for the enemies of his fatherland.'[21] But Ferdinand Ries's version is nothing less than drastic: '. . . Had Count Oppersdorf and one or two others not been there they would have come to blows, for Beethoven had already seized a chair, meaning to break it over the prince's head, after the prince had broken down the door that Beethoven refused to open. Spirits had been running high because the prince had prepared a fête for all the French quartered on his estate, and the guests, and one colonel in particular, had asked to hear Beethoven.'[22]

Whatever the precise details, most reports agree that Beethoven left Lichnovsky's land in a hurry that night, walked for an hour down the road to Troppau, and took the swiftest route available – the costly express-post coach – back to Vienna. Again one has a choice of three finales: 'To make good the insult, a bust of the patron was called upon to serve as scapegoat. It fell from the top of a cupboard and shattered on the floor.'[23] Then there is said to have been a letter: 'Prince! What you are, you are by birth and accident; what I am, I am by my own doing. There are and always will be thousands of princes; there is only one Beethoven.'[24] (Even if this letter, never found, is the stuff of legend, it does at least indicate the attitude and behaviour of which Beethoven is thought to have been capable.) We do however know that this final statement is authentic: 'It is good to mix with nobility, but one must have something with which to impress them.'[25]

After so much defiance and outright refusal it is time to write of an occasion when Beethoven did actually play. Vienna not only heard Beethoven explode, it also heard him improvise, and his extempore playing was the true source of his early fame.

In the year 1800 Beethoven let himself in for a musical competition, one of those parlour games so beloved at the time. Once more he revealed himself as a volcanic virtuoso, only this time he delivered not only the required improvisation but also that thing which Vienna most needed and most loved: a topic for conversation. Beethoven's opponent was Daniel Steibelt, one of the great piano virtuosos of his time and a highly popular composer. Piano concertos, sonatas, ballet music had flowed from his prolific pen, and had he not suffered from a chronic weakness for shady dealings, short of money as he always was to support his extravagant lifestyle, his reputation would have been more solid and his time in Paris and London more extended. Before coming to Vienna, Steibelt had just achieved another coup in Prague, appearing there with his English wife, who caused a furore with her tambourine-playing. He at once transformed himself from virtuoso to businessman, ordering a wagon-load of tambourines which he sold in the course of a few weeks to the ladies of Prague society.

In Vienna Steibelt encountered Beethoven: a well-travelled performer face to face with an eccentric, a virtuoso encountering a brute. No one was sure what would happen. There were, it was said, 'many friends of Beethoven who feared this man might ruin his reputation'.[26] At an evening gathering in Count Fries's palace the two met for the first time, and the expectant audience was not disappointed. Beethoven played the piano part of his Opus 11, the Gassenhauer Trio for Piano, Clarinet and Violoncello. 'The player cannot really show his mettle in that part. Steibelt listened with a sort of condescension, made

Beethoven a few compliments and was sure of his victory. He played a quintet of his own composition, improvised and made, with his tremulandos which were then something very new, a very great impression. Beethoven could not be persuaded to play again.'[27]

There is no doubt, according to this report, that the first round of the contest went to Steibelt. Eight days later there was another 'concert' *chez* Fries, a sort of return match. Steibelt opened with a virtually direct attack on Beethoven. Always a natural musician, he sat down to improvise at the piano, then played what was obviously a prepared improvisation (as if he were inventing it there and then), choosing to work from the theme of the variations movement from the Beethoven trio. The gesture was clear: listen – this is what you can really make of a theme like that.

Steibelt obviously meant to teach Beethoven a lesson. This time he could not escape. The contemporary account continues: 'He had now to go to the piano, to improvise; he made his usual, that is, his ill-mannered way to the instrument, half throwing himself upon it.'[28] But on the way he seized a page of the cello part of a Steibelt quartet (that had been played to start with), propped it up on the stand, and turned it, for all to see, so that it was upside down. With one finger he picked out a few notes from the upside-down page, impudently disconnected notes, provocative disharmony. Slowly but surely the bizarre sound began to take on some sense, the notes became a tune, and Beethoven plunged into one of his great extempore adventures. Such ecstasies and expeditions of invention sometimes lasted a full hour. Whether that was true on this occasion we do not know, only that Steibelt, truly out-played, left the company before Beethoven had finished. He refused to meet him ever again, and thereafter made sure, before accepting any invitation to a musical gathering, that Beethoven would not be present.

Do we still remember the young count who so infuriated Beethoven during his performance with Ferdinand Ries? He became, and remained for years, if not Beethoven's fiercest then certainly his most devious opponent in Vienna. He was Count Palffy, director of the royal theatre from 1805, and it was he who was instrumental in shutting down *Fidelio* shortly after it opened, and in presenting any number of difficulties to Beethoven. For instance, over the business of hiring a concert hall for a performance, Beethoven apparently cursed

Palffy 'in such excessively loud tones, while we were still inside his theatre, that not only the audience streaming out of the hall but even the count himself in his office could hear him'.[29] Later, when Palffy once agreed to let Beethoven use the hall, but only on unheard-of conditions, the latter mobilized his most highly-placed admirers, and the High Chancellor's office warned the director 'that such an excessive demand could only displease the very highest authority'.

Beethoven's comment on that occasion leads us back to the theme of autonomy: 'It is irresponsible, the way art is dealt with these days. I have to pay a third to the theatre management and a fifth to the prison [i.e. a workhouse for the poor]. Bah! Humbug. When all this is settled will I stop to inquire whether music is a free art or not?'[30]

THE WAR IN THE MUSIC ROOM (1)
On the Tradition of the Keyboard Tournament

> The only one whom I would like to see
> before I die, and who I would have liked
> to be, if I were not Bach.
>
> *Bach on Handel*

There is a rich tradition of duels at the piano. The keyboard makes an ideal shooting range, compact enough to be taken in at a glance, while at the same time the number of keys (even on the smaller early instruments) is so much greater than the number of fingers that any layman can readily appreciate how difficult it can be to hit them in the proper order to ensure a musical result. Even an onlooker with no ear for music can observe the sleight of hand that makes a mockery of any mundane accomplishment. It is human nature to want to look over other people's shoulders. Concert pianists to this day make their living from that psychological fact: there is always a run on seats on the left-hand side of the house, which have a view of the keyboard. Virtuosity at the piano is the most beautiful, the most difficult and the most sublime form of the conjuror's art.

Where there is a shooting range there will be shooting matches. So competitive concerts with rival pianists must be reckoned among the inevitable concomitants of the instrument. Even before Beethoven's day concert history is full of battling pianists. The chosen weapon in these duels was not the rapier but the improvisation, not the revolver but the sight-reading of an unknown piece, and usually both at once – in the form of an extempore variation on a theme first encountered there and then.

One of the most legendary of these competitions was arranged in the year 1717: Johann Sebastian Bach was to play opposite the Frenchman Louis Marchand. The novelist Emil Brachvogel included a somewhat fanciful version of the episode in his novel about young Friedemann

Bach, son of the famous court organist at Weimar. In Brachvogel's book, Friedemann accompanies his father to Dresden, whence he has been summoned by August the Strong.

'Today was the day,' Brachvogel begins:

> Marshal von Lemming had invited the court to a soirée to be attended by the royal family. The coaches rumbled along the Pirnaische Gasse and up the drive to the palace to set down their costly, diamond-studded contents, who flowed like a stream through orange-scented ante-rooms into halls blazing with light, where carpets, bronzes and vases were reflected in a hundred mirrors. The music room, destination of the guests, shone with its chandeliers and girandoles, its reddish-white marbled walls and its heavy gilt moulding in the glow of a thousand wax candles. What a proud gathering it was of all that Saxony had to offer in wealth, beauty, gentility and fame! What a host of happy, glowing faces!

Earlier in the novel the elder Bach writes a letter that is nothing less than a declaration of war:

> Honoured Sir!
> The undersigned Sebastian Bach, organist at Weimar, who, acquainted with your honoured self's world-famous renown as a piano virtuoso, is desirous of an opportunity to admire your skill in performance as well as in extempore composition, has come here from Weimar specifically for said purpose. Being also, after his modest fashion, a practitioner *in musica*, and desiring to know to what extent the French or German art is superior, he offers to compose extempore and fugato variations upon any theme which you shall choose for him, in two or more voices, himself expecting to meet the same willingness on your part, and bids you determine a time and place for the contest.
> Your humble servant Sebastian Bach

Somehow, at least in this version, the musical contest had turned into a political encounter. 'The company,' according to Brachvogel, 'had always been divided into two camps, two parties. On the one hand, admittedly in the minority, were the pillars of the old authority with their faith, their simplicity and their earnestness. They stood for the church, for time-honoured ritual, sacred music, the essential German character and the honour of the forefathers. They were in one word the church party.'

On the other hand, aligned with the Elector himself, one might have
expected to find a crowd of genial cosmopolitans who set less store in
the national honour of their forefathers than in the individual honour
of the living. But Brachvogel has a less positive view. Opposite the
church party, the novelist claims, 'strutted egotism in fine French
clothing.' Clearly, Marchand had no hope of victory in this version.

What a sight he was, the Frenchman, in his purple court dress! He
retired at once to an adjoining room with the affected remark that he
did not wish to 'amalgamate' himself with his opponent any more than
was necessary. But when they went to call him he was nowhere to be
found, and August had to content himself with the news that
Marchand had packed up and left Dresden for good. The German
language still preserves a ready expression for such a hasty retreat: one
is said to have left one's compliments in French.

Bach could so easily have played up to the occasion, but, heavy
earnest German that he was, he did not want to take advantage of the
situation. So he refused even to look at Marchand's work, 'farcical' as it
was, and asked Their Majesties for a theme on which he might
improvise. Brachvogel comes into his own here – handkerchiefs are
recommended.

The queen blushed faintly. 'When I was in Hamburg a year ago I heard
the old organist Reinken play a chorale on the organ in church. It moved
me so deeply that I can still remember it as if it were yesterday. I believe
that the song began: By the waters of Babylon.' Sebastian seemed to
shudder as if overcome by pious emotion.

'Yes, Your Majesty, I know the piece! And though I do not deserve
even to tie old Reinken's shoelaces I do thank Your Majesty most
sincerely for considering me worthy to play his composition. With
God's help I will attempt it.'

He went to the piano. With an impatient movement he swept
Marchand's chanson onto the parquet, closed the music stand and sat
down. Softly, solemnly, he began the chorale.

There was no applause, not a word of praise.

A shudder went through the gathering, and in each heart an
immeasurable something stirred, something that some of these people
had never felt before.

The queen and her ladies Kollowrat and Königsmarck sobbed
audibly, the king sat as if thunderstruck.

Johann Nikolaus Forkel, Bach's first biographer, reduced the occasion to a brief report on a single page. In his version we find that Bach was not the challenger but the challenged player; that throughout his life he studiously avoided making disparaging remarks about any fellow composer's work, and that, when asked the secret of his genius, he pointed not to God but to an altogether earthly virtue: 'I have had to work hard! Anyone who works so hard can achieve as much.'[1]

None the less it was an episode that fascinated his contemporaries and has continued to fascinate music-lovers and historians long after his death. It is no longer possible to reconstruct the exact details of the encounter from the historical records, some of which claim to be based on Bach's own account. But the very fact that the reports are so contradictory indicates that it must have been an exciting event, or possibly non-event. One account claims that Marchand, 'with no hope of victory, retreated humbly to his homeland, while the king and a great and distinguished gathering awaited him in the palace of Marshal Count von Fleming. He forfeited a payment of some thousand thalers and departed in the post-chaise.'[2]

More dramatic is this report:

Bach came and with the king's permission, but without Marchand's knowledge, was admitted as a guest to the next concert at court. When in the course of said concert Marchand performed, among other things, a little French song with many variations, and was greatly applauded, both for the talent exhibited in the composition as well as for his precise and fiery performance, so Bach, who was standing next to him, was called upon to try his hand at the piano. He rose to the call, played a short prelude, with masterful touches, and before one knew it he had repeated the little song Marchand had played, with variations of new genius, playing it a dozen times differently in a way that had never been heard before. Marchand, who up to that point had defied all rival organists [he was the most famous organist in France at the time] undoubtedly had to recognize the superiority of the present antagonist. For when Bach took the liberty of inviting him to a friendly contest at the organ, presenting him to that end with a slip of paper on which he had scribbled a theme, for extempore variation, at the same time asking him for the same, Marchand appeared so far from his familiar field of battle that he deemed it expedient to remove himself from Dresden by means of the post-chaise.[3]

Is it any wonder that encounters like these are told and re-told in infinite variations, in this case even blown up into a Franco-German musical war – and that the pattern is always the same, with the same dramatic gestures? One report has it that 'Bach took the Frenchman's composition and, although he had never seen it before, turned it upside down and played it with the greatest ease, to the astonishment of everyone present, including Marchand himself.'[4] So here it is already, that cocksure, startling, upside-down trick that is also supposed to have been the final scornful blow in Beethoven's skirmish with Steibelt. But the repetition of the episode does not make it more likely, in fact it leads one to suspect that the only thing – in both cases – that was ever turned upside down was the historical truth.

For all that, the 'war in the music room' may not be an inappropriate metaphor for the encounter between Bach and Marchand, as the choice of vocabulary of yet another contemporary report would indicate: 'Pompey was not therefore a bad general because he lost so soon to Caesar in the battle of Pharsus, and can every man be a Bach? I myself have heard the pious Capellmeister praise the skilfulness of this Marchand very highly . . .'[5] And by the way, one must remember that it was not the Bach of the cantatas and passions and certainly not the grand master of the fugue who travelled to Dresden in 1717, but the Bach of the toccatas. In that year of his alleged encounter with Marchand he wrote the Toccata in C Minor, his farewell to a musical form of enormous virtuosity, beguiling fugues (not always entirely in tune), and lyrical intermezzos – his farewell to a free and passionate, youthfully stormy, specifically piano-orientated (*toccare* implies 'touching' the keys) mosaic form of music.

There were by the way some good losers. One such was the English harpsichordist and organist Thomas Roseingrave, who visited Venice about a decade before the Bach–Marchand incident. While there he was invited to an 'academia' at the house of a nobleman and was asked, among others, to honour the company with – a toccata. Roseingrave later described the occasion to Charles Burney, a music historian:

> Finding myself rather better in courage and finger than usual, I exerted myself, my dear friend, and fancied, by the applause I received, that my performance had made some impression on the company.

But then, Burney goes on:

a grave young man dressed in black and in a black wig, who had stood in one corner of the room, very quiet and attentive while Roseingrave played, being asked to sit down to the harpsichord, when he began to play Rosy said, he thought ten hundred d____ls had been at the instrument; he never had heard such passages of execution and effect before. The performance so far surpassed his own, and every degree of perfection to which he thought it possible he should ever arrive, that, if he had been in sight of any instrument with which to have done the deed, he should have cut off his own fingers. Upon enquiring the name of this extraordinary performer, he was told that it was Domenico Scarlatti, son of the celebrated Cavalier Alessandro Scarlatti. Roseingrave declared he did not touch an instrument himself for a month; after this *rencontre*, however, he became very intimate with the young Scarlatti, followed him to Rome and Naples, and hardly ever quitted him while he remained in Italy, which was not till after the peace of Utrecht . . .[6]

Scarlatti himself reacted even more nobly when, a few years later, he met that '*caro Sassone*', the already famous Georg Friedrich Handel, in Cardinal Ottoboni's salon in Rome. The cardinal had determined to bring the two virtuosos together for a 'trial of skill'. 'The issue of the trial on the harpsichord,' reports Handel's first biographer Mainwaring, 'hath been differently reported. It has been said that some gave the preference to Scarlatti. However, when they came to the Organ there was not the least pretence for doubting to which of them it belonged. Scarlatti himself declared the superiority of his antagonist, and owned ingenuously that till he had heard him upon this instrument, he had no conception of its powers.'[7] And even later, when praised for a performance, Scarlatti is said to have invoked the name of Handel – and crossed himself.

Handel, Scarlatti, Bach – a sensational troika in the pre-history of the pianoforte. They were contemporaries in the strictest sense, all three of them born in the same year, 1685. Georg Friedrich Handel was born on 23 February, Johann Sebastian Bach on 21 March, and on 26 October came Domenico Scarlatti – the virtuoso who left baroque counterpoint further behind him than any of them, summoning romantic and even impressionistic sounds from the instrument, and whose short 'sonatas' with their confoundedly fast repetitive effects still count today among the most brilliant and most feared pieces in a pianist's repertoire (particularly since the loss of the second keyboard has redoubled the difficulties in some of these miniatures). But there is something even more remarkable about this coincidence of birthdays, and this is what really makes it significant: all three lived a very long time, given the average life expectancy of the period (about forty years), which means that they all had time to be epoch-making, each in his own way. Bach died in 1750, Scarlatti in 1757 and Handel, at the ripe old age of 74, in 1759. So they were all not just great musicians but also grand old men, proof that the fittest do sometimes survive.

The one trial of skill that musical Germans of the period most longed for never did take place: Bach and Handel never met. Forkel's version, if somewhat inaccurate in terms of dates, is relatively reliable:

> Handel he esteemed very highly and often expressed a wish to make his acquaintance. Handel being also a great player of the harpsichord and the organ, many music-lovers in Leipzig and the surrounding area desired to hear the two men together. But Handel could never find time for such a meeting. Three times he had come from London to visit Halle (his home city). At the time of the first visit, in the year 1719, Bach was still in Cöthen, just four miles' distance from Halle. He learned of Handel's arrival at once and wasted no time in arranging to pay him a visit; but the very day he arrived in Halle Handel departed once again. At the time of Handel's second visit (between 1730 and 1740) Bach was already in Leipzig, but ill. However, as soon as he learned of Handel's arrival, he sent his son Wilh. Friedemann to him, beseeching Handel most graciously to visit him in Leipzig. Handel regretted that he could not come. At the time of Handel's third visit, in the year 1752 or 1753, Bach was already dead.[8]

In fact this third visit took place in 1750, the year of Bach's death.

Whatever happened exactly, can a lifetime of such near misses be put down to mere coincidence? It is hard not to read something intentional into those dates, something that smacks of a careful policy of avoidance. One contemporary remarks critically: 'So Handel was not as curious as Johann Sebastian Bach, who once in his youth ran 50 miles on foot to hear the famous Lübeck organist Buxtehude. Thus it pained J.S.B. all the more that he had never met Handel personally, this truly great man, whom he so deeply esteemed.'[9]

It was not that Bach wanted to prove he was better than Handel; he was curious, he was after a musical dialogue, which is of course a form of comparison, but also an exchange. Those repeated overtures to a musical colleague should certainly not be interpreted as a publicity exercise, an urge to impress, but as one master's very natural interest in meeting another. In those days all one heard of one's contemporaries were their names and perhaps some echoes of their work; one might get hold of a dubious copy of a concerto or a suite, although Handel for one always made sure to omit the crucial part. A peek into another artist's studio – that is what Bach was after with his famous curiosity. He would have wanted to compare notes on such practical things as fingering, phrasing, legato technique, the registration of the organ; and he may also have hoped for a chance to swap a few virtuoso tricks.

Whether Handel did avoid Bach on purpose, whether he actually fled from him that first time (as Forkel certainly suggests), is an open question; however it seems more likely that Handel, with his ostentatious position in London, had far more opportunities for comparison than Bach could ever hope for in Weimar, Cöthen and Leipzig. He was simply not as curious about his colleague. The unconsummated rivalry between the two has been fanned all the more feverishly by admirers ever since – sometimes with all the fervour of a religious war – right up to the present day.

Our next scene is orchestrated not by a Saxon elector nor by a Roman cardinal but by Emperor Joseph II of Austria. The action takes place in the royal palace in Vienna. The time: January 1781.

A man enters the music room with a gentlemanly bow. He is twenty-nine years old, Italian born, now an itinerant piano virtuoso, and when at home, then in London. His name is Muzio Clementi, and for almost two hundred years that name has signalled, for students of the piano, the first venture into that dramatic musical terrain, the exciting field of the sonata. That first Clementi sonatine after about two years of lessons means that one is no longer an *absolute* beginner.

'I had only been in Vienna a few days,' Clementi later recalled, 'when I received an invitation to play before the Emperor on the pianoforte. On entering the music room I beheld an individual whose elegant attire led me to mistake him for an imperial *valet-de-chambre*. But we had no sooner entered into conversation than it turned on musical topics, and we soon recognized in each other, with sincere pleasure, brother artists – Mozart and Clementi.'[10] Mozart, who had only ten more years to live, was then twenty-five. Clementi was to survive him by more than forty years: he died in 1832.

The programme of this extended musical encounter has been

preserved. Clementi played, among other things, his great Sonata in B flat (Op. 47, No. 2) and a toccata, showing his virtuosity to advantage in its runs of thirds. Mozart improvised a prelude with several variations. Then both musicians moved onto neutral territory, sight-reading a series of short sonatas by Paisiello, taking turns phrase by phrase.

Finally each of them chose a theme from one of the Paisiello pieces, improvising freely while the other provided harmonic support on a second piano – a form of communal improvisation reintroduced only in the jazz age.

The Mozart–Clementi encounter might have been remembered as a rousing celebration of music, a delightful cooperation, but convention demanded a 'victor'. One account favours Clementi; another claims that the emperor won his wager, and that he had backed Mozart. Composer Karl Ditters von Dittersdorf recalled the occasion a few years later in conversation with the emperor.

EMPEROR: Have you heard Mozart play?
I: Three times already.
EMPEROR: How do you like him?
I: As any connoisseur must like him.
EMPEROR: Have you heard Clementi?
I: Yes, I have.
EMPEROR: Some people prefer him to Mozart ... What is your opinion? Be honest.
I: Clementi's way of playing is art alone. Mozart's is art and taste.
EMPEROR: That's just what I said . . .[11]

Mozart certainly considered himself the winner. In a letter to his sister written shortly after the concert he wrote dismissively: 'He is an excellent cembalo player, but that is all. He has great facility with his left hand. His star passages are thirds. Apart from that he has not a farthing's worth of feeling; he is a mere *mecanicus*.'[12]

The incident also sheds a curious light on the state of the imperial instruments. Mozart, who knew the problem, had borrowed a Stein piano from Countess Thun (whom we have already met, on her knees to Beethoven) for the evening. The court piano that had to serve for the communal parts of the programme was, according to Mozart, not only dreadfully out of tune but three keys were actually stuck. 'That doesn't matter,' the emperor is said to have declared to the musicians.

Clementi brings us back to Beethoven. Not that they played together; they did business with one another. Around 1810, when Clementi had long since bid farewell to his career as a virtuoso, having become a partner to the London piano maker Collard and a music publisher to boot, he secured the right to publish Beethoven's works in England. As soon as the agreement was signed and sealed he wrote to his partner in London, just as proud as if he had triumphed in a virtuoso competition: 'By a little management and without committing myself, I have at last made a compleat (*sic*) conquest of that *haughty beauty*, Beethoven . . .'[13]

NO. 7362
or: The Hammer in Question

Ein Schwachstarktastenkasten
Beethoven
(in search of a German name
for the pianoforte: literally,
'a weakstrongfingerkeybox')

To produce the so-called hammer leather for the instrument maker the very finest woollen sheepskins must be taken. These are softened in fresh water for four days, after which the undersides are spread with a mixture of chalk and ash and the skins then folded carefully into a pot with water. After three weeks they are taken out and the wool is removed before they are left again to soak in chalk and water for a further four weeks ... Thus prepared they are plunged into the lye, which is made of lukewarm water and corn husks, and are thoroughly tossed therein before being left to soak for three days, during which time they must be well stirred every day, morning and evening. The tanned skins are smoothed out and freed of all remaining husks and then laid in a lye of spruce tree bark, wherein they must be stirred every day morning, noon and evening, and the lye must be refreshed every eighth day for five weeks. In the sixth week a mixture of ash and tree oil is added to the lye and the skins are left to soak for a further eight days, after which they are washed out in sweet milk and then put out to dry ...

(from a description dated 1837)

On 27 December 1817 an imposing gift was packed up in London ready for transport: Thomas Broadwood, piano maker, was fulfilling a promise made to Beethoven during a visit in Vienna. The great composer was by this time almost completely deaf. Broadwood had asked to be allowed to present him with one of his powerful grand pianos. It was not the first instrument to be donated to him. In 1803

Sebastian Erard had sent him a grand piano from his workshop in Paris, and there are two notes recording the gift in his company files; in one case the addressee is given as 'Mr. Bethowen à Vienne', in the other as 'Mr. Bethoffen à Vienne'. (Even Beethoven was not always entirely sure how to spell his own name, particularly as a young man.)

Before the Broadwood number 7362 was packed into its deal and tinplate case, it was decorated with a few additional inscriptions. On the top above the keyboard is the donor's dedication:

Hoc Instrumentum est Thomae Broadwood (Londini)
donum, propter Ingenium illustrissimi Beethoven

On the front behind the keyboard the name BEETHOVEN is inlaid in ebony, with the names of the makers beneath it:

John Broadwood & Sons, Makers of Instruments to
His Majesty and the Princesses.
Great Pulteney Street. Golden Square. London.

And finally the names of five pianists, all of whom had tried and approved the instrument, were engraved to the right of the keyboard: Cramer, Ferrari, Kalkbrenner, Juyvelt and Ries.

So it was not just a musical instrument but a veritable historical document that was sent on its way that day from the Broadwood warehouse to the London docks. The destination registered there was Trieste. Beethoven's piano was to be sent, albeit in the off season, on a sort of Mediterranean cruise, via Gibraltar and Sicily. While the ship was still en route Beethoven sent his effusive thanks in bad French:

Mon très cher Ami Broadwood!
Jamais je n'eprouvais pas un grand Plaisir de ce que me causa votre Annonce de l'arrivée de cette Piano, avec qui vous m'honorès de m'en faire present, je regarderai comme un Autel, ou je deposerai les plus belles offrandes de mon esprit au divine Apollon. Aussitôt comme je recevrai votre Excellent Instrument, je vous enverrai d'en abord les Fruits de l'inspiration des premiers moments, que j'y passerai, pour vous servir d'un Souvenir de moi à vous mon très cher B., et je ne souhaits ce que, qu'ils soient dignes de votre instrument.

Mon cher Monsieur et ami recevés la plus grande consideration de votre ami et très humble serviteur

Louis van Beethoven

Vienne le 3me du mois Fevrier, 1818.[1]

It was a good three months before the transport overland from Trieste to Vienna could be effected; not because it took a horse-drawn caravan that long to cover the four hundred or so kilometres across the Alps, even with such precious cargo to slow the pace, but because Broadwood's agents in Europe had applied for special tax exemptions on Beethoven's behalf: it was hoped that he might be spared the usual duties. 'With especial generosity the imperial treasury waived the import duty to which foreign musical instruments were otherwise subject and thereby indicated in a fashion most welcome to all artists how concerned one was to encourage such rare musical genius with an equal measure of human estimation.'

Never before or since can the transport of a single piano have aroused so much public interest and concern. And of course the famous instrument was soon rumoured to have all sorts of miraculous powers. One newspaper boldly reported that

> everything about it is so lasting that in this respect it is quite without comparison. An indication of how long it will stay in tune is provided by the fact that even after its sea voyage from London to Trieste, and its journeys overland from there to Vienna and from Vienna to Mödling, it was not necessary to re-tune so much as a single note. In short, it is a true masterpiece, in its interior structure as much as in its outward form, which is chiefly distinguished by its unadorned simplicity, solidity and portability to any place whatsoever.[2]

That report was grossly exaggerated. The piano was painfully out of tune. There has never been and will never be an instrument that could arrive unscathed after such a monumental journey.

The complications of transport were at that time a new factor in the history of the piano; they provide the clearest indication as to how quickly the instrument was gaining stability and weight and volume. Gone were the days when musician and instrument-maker Andreas Stein could 'carry his piano under his arm for hours at a time, when he was due to play at a Sunday dance in a neighbouring town', or when composer Georg Benda 'carried his piano across the street late one night so that his librettist, who was already in bed, could hear him play the aria he had just composed with the first flush of inspiration still upon him.'[3]

With the Broadwood grand awaiting inspection in the storeroom of Viennese piano-maker Andreas Streicher – one of the Englishman's most famous rivals – it is time for us to define our terms and try to make some sense of a proper chaos of names. 'A rose is a rose is a rose' said Gertrude Stein in her famous poem. With the piano it is not so easy; on the contrary, the piano is no piano is no piano. The business of defining it is a real game of patience.

The German word *Klavier* can mean any form of keyboard instrument, the most important of which was originally the organ. The expression is derived from the Latin *clavis*, meaning key – hence the English 'keyboard'. In the alphabetical notation of medieval music each pitch was called a clavis. These pitch-letters were sometimes inscribed on the keys of the organ as a form of *aide-mémoire* for the player, so that clavis/key eventually came to mean the thing that is pressed to produce the desired pitch.

A positively astonishing range of instruments can rightfully claim to belong to the keyboard family, and many of their names are nothing if not picturesque. Who would guess that a *'Jungfrauenregal'* (literally 'virgins' regal') is actually a keyboard instrument, that an *'Apfelregal'* (literally 'apple regal') produces not apples but musical notes, that a *'Schlüsselfiedel'* ('key fiddle') has nothing to do with a violin, or that a *'Hackbrett'* or *'Hackebrett'* (literally 'chopping board') is not a butcher's or carpenter's tool but a sort of portable piano very popular towards the end of the eighteenth century (in English it was called a dulcimer). There are melodicas, glockenspiels, barrel-organs – all distant cousins, but family members all the same. One can of course create an exclusive inner circle by focusing not on the key but on the string hit or plucked by mechanical means as the crucial criterion of membership. That leaves one with clavichord, harpsichord, clavicytherium, clavicylinder, spinet and virginals – names that in each case evoke a different outer shape, a different inner mechanism, and a different application for public or domestic use.

In all this jungle of names the instrument which is really the subject of this book has not yet appeared: the pianoforte or *'Hammerclavier'*. As the German name implies the tone is produced not by blowing (as

in the organ and its offspring), nor by plucking (as in the harpsichord
or spinet), nor by pushing up little pieces of metal (as in the
clavichord), but by little wooden hammers cushioned in leather or
cloth or (nowadays) special felt. And as the Italian name implies the
tone thus produced can be loud or soft, depending on how hard the
player hits the keys; there is no need for the stops and couplers of the
organ, harpsichord or clavichord. The pianoforte was the first
keyboard instrument capable of a crescendo or decrescendo, an
increase or decrease in the volume of sound: the old 'terrace dynamics',
the either–or of keyboard volume, were suddenly obsolete.

In the nineteenth century, when the pianoforte began its triumphal
march, Gottfried Silbermann was hailed as the inventor of the hammer
action. Silbermann was a famous instrument maker who built organs
that are still places of pilgrimage for organists from all over the world;
he it was who delivered a quantity of grand pianofortes along with
some dozen harpsichords to Frederick II's Sanssouci. Music historians
have since established that Silbermann merely adapted and popular-
ized the invention of Bartolommeo Cristofori, the Italian curator of
Fernando di Medici's collection of instruments in Florence. He had
obviously come across a description of Cristofori's mechanism in a
work published in 1711 which tries to explain the sensational
importance of the new instrument:

> Every connoisseur knows that in music the play of soft and loud is like
> the play of light and shadow in painting, the secret source whence the
> experienced artist draws his power to delight his audience . . . Heedless
> of the fact that this supple variety of tone, in which the string
> instruments, among others, do so excel, is a quality entirely lacking in
> the clavichord, and that it would be thought a vain conceit for anyone to
> resolve to construct one with this peculiar power, none the less Mr
> Bartolommeo Cristofori of Florence, maker of instruments to the
> Grand Duke, native of Padua, has not only conceived this bold
> invention but has successfully brought it into being.[4]

Cristofori called his invention the 'gravicembalo col piano e forte'.
But it was almost a hundred years before the pianoforte really caught
on. Old habits of hearing, and the nature of the available music, which
often called for two manuals, ensured that harpsichords and clavi-
chords continued to take precedence for some time. There was also the
very practical matter of the old instruments being already in place.

Cristofori's expression soon appeared in any number of variants: from Pianoforte to Piano-Forte or Piano-Forté or of course in reverse, Fortepiano, each of which might apply to the grand or the square piano. The modern upright piano, which is what the Germans mean by the word *Klavier* when they use it in its strictest contemporary sense, was originally a pianino, with its mechanical equivalent, the pianola. The so-called '*grosses Klavier*' which sometimes appears in German fiction is simply a bad translation of the English 'grand piano', which is a '*Flügel*' in German. It is ironic to consider that '*piano*' in fact means 'softly', given the power and sonority of the modern instrument.

Not only the name but also the technical development of the piano soon followed divergent paths, the main routes being pointed out by the English action on the one hand and the Viennese action on the other. Again it is just another characteristic confusion in the history of the piano that the so-called English action was not invented by Englishmen but primarily by Saxon instrument makers, who had fled the continent during the Seven Years' War; and that the Viennese action was based on the so-called 'buffer action', which originated in Germany and was then further developed in Vienna by piano-makers like Andreas Stein, Gabriel Anton Walter and Andreas and Nanette Streicher.

In the Viennese instruments the tone travelled a relatively direct route from key to hammer to string; they were easy to play, but their volume was limited. The London pianofortes – usually in the square form so popular in England – had a built-in detour that allowed the hammer to swing more freely, thereby producing a fuller tone; but more force was required to produce the note.

Piano virtuoso, composer and teacher Johann Nepomuk Hummel wrote a vivid comparison of the two types of instrument:

The German (or Viennese) piano may be played upon with ease by the weakest hand. It allows the performer to impart to his execution every possible degree of light and shade, speaks clearly and promptly, has a round, flute-like tone, which, in a large room, contrasts well with the accompanying orchestra, and does not impede rapidity of execution by requiring too great an effort.

Hummel went on to praise the English action for its

durability and fullness of tone. Nevertheless this instrument does not admit of the same facility of execution as the German. The touch is much heavier, the keys sink much deeper, and consequently, the return of the hammer on the repetition of a note cannot take place so quickly ... As a counterpoise of this, however, through the fullness of tone in the English Piano-Forte, the melody receives a peculiar charm and harmonious sweetness.[5]

The significantly greater resonance of the English instrument explains why the Broadwoods went to the trouble of transporting one of their pianos to a city which could still be considered, despite the Erards' workshop in Paris, the piano-making capital of Europe. The powerful sound of the Broadwood was supposed to help Beethoven hear his piano again. Streicher however, who must have had rather mixed feelings about storing his rival's gift, encouraged a rumour among pianists in Vienna that the tone was indeed beautiful, but the action too heavy to be played on at all. Moscheles was said to have tried it, and others too, but apparently none of them could do a thing with it. The Englishman Potter, who was familiar with the English instruments, was the first one to get a good sound from it. He of course at once asked to tune it, but Beethoven protested: 'That's what they all say; they would like to tune it and spoil it, but they shall not touch it.'[6] So it may not be altogether wrong to suspect that he played it for years in its painfully travel-worn condition. A certain Mr Stumpff of London, who arrived with a letter of introduction from Broadwood, was finally allowed to tune it.

There is an old and no doubt still current supposition that the title of Opus 106 – 'Grosse Sonate für das Hammerclavier' ('Grand Sonata for the Hammerclavier') – was chosen by Beethoven after he began to use the Broadwood in the summer of 1818. In fact, although the work had already been sketched out in some detail, he did use the new instrument to complete the sonata, which is colossal in every respect. It is as if he were declaring possession in the prestissimo passage of the scherzo, which runs from an F below the bass clef to a top F four lines above the treble, spanning six full octaves – a range well beyond the capacity of any of his earlier instruments (so that in some earlier works the development of certain themes had to be cut short in the reprise).

However, the choice of the word Hammerclavier had nothing to do with the Broadwood; that was a product of Beethoven's linguistic pig-headedness, which surfaced periodically. In a letter to Andreas

Streicher, who was also one of his publishers, Beethoven had already raised the question early in 1817, when he was planning the publication of the A major sonata, Op. 101: 'In regard to the title a linguist should be consulted as to whether Hammer or Hämmer-Clavier, or, possibly, Hämmer-Flügel, should be inserted. – But be sure to let me see the title for my approval –'[7]

Then there is a so-called *Publicandum* dated 23 January 1817, announcing that: 'After individual examination and taking the advice of our council we have determined and hereby determine that hereafter on all our works with German titles, in place of pianoforte, *Hammer-Clavier* will be printed; our best Lt. Gen. [he means Streicher] as well as the Adjutant and all others concerned will govern themselves accordingly at once and put this order into effect. Instead of Pianoforte, Hammerclavier, – which settles the matter once and for all. Given etc. etc.'[8]

And in a further note from the time (in other words still a year before the arrival of the Broadwood), Beethoven explains:

Quite by chance I have hit on the following dedication – [for Sonata Op. 101]:

'SONATA

FOR THE PIANOFORTE

OR HÄMMER-CLAVIER

COMPOSED AND

DEDICATED TO

THE BARONESS DOROTHEA ERTMANN,

NÉE GRAUMANN,

BY L. V. BEETHOVEN'

... But should the title be already engraved, then I have the following two proposals to make, that is to say, either I shall pay for the new title, ie it will be engraved at my expense, or this title will be reserved for another new sonata which I shall compose. And indeed to bring another sonata into the world, all that is necessary is that the L(ieutenan)t G(enera)l's and First State Councillor's mines should be opened. [By that Beethoven means the publisher's cash box.] The title must first be shown to a linguist. Hämmerclavier is certainly German and in any case it was also a German invention. Honour to whom honour is due.[9]

But Beethoven's efforts in this case were in vain: not only was the sonata in question published with the title 'for the Pianoforte', but his

three last sonatas, Op. 109, 110 and 111, were given the same Italian
epithet. Even the Grand Sonata Op. 106, first published in England in
1820, was described as being 'for the Pianoforte'. Only in the first
German edition of 1823 was the piece announced as Beethoven would
have wished it: 'Große Sonate für das Hammerclavier'.

The solitary title reflects the uniqueness of the piece. It is by no
means the most beautiful of Beethoven's piano sonatas, nor the most
complex in terms of technical composition and development of motif;
it is however, with its forty-page score, the longest and technically the
most difficult of the sonatas, an insurmountable colossus for the
'clavier'. There is something almost lunatic about the dedication to the
Austrian Archduke Rudolf, his patron and student – rather as if a
sculptor were to dump a rough-cut block of granite at the door of one
of his masons. With earlier dedications it was possible to imagine that
the person so honoured might actually play the piece (or at least play
around with it), or else have it performed, but this Opus 106 was quite
impossible: not only for the son of the emperor but for any pianist far
and wide. The very difficulty of the work recalls a comment Beethoven
once made in answer to the violinist Schuppanzigh, who declared that
a certain new string quartet was quite beyond the capacity of his
instrument: 'What do I care for your miserable fiddle.' The conquest
of the Hammerclavier sonata was to be one of the great pioneer
ventures of nineteenth-century concert performance. And one of the
last pieces composed on the Broadwood no. 7362, considered
impossible for more than a hundred years, was left to the more daring
pianists of our century: the Diabelli Variations, Op. 120.

It sounds devilish enough; the man's name, however, was Diabelli, not
Diabolus, and he was no Lucifer, just a publisher – though there may
be many, then and now, who think the two amount to much the same
thing. This Anton Diabelli was once well on his way to becoming a
monk, but when the monasteries were secularized in 1803, he decided
to make the most of his earthly abilities: as a pianist, a composer of
sorts and a talented businessman. In about 1819, when he was on the
point of extracting his shares from Cappi and Diabelli to set up on his
own, as Diabelli and Co., he had a brilliant idea, which combined all
three of his gifts. He cobbled together a waltz of just three lines and
sent the piece to 'the most excellent composers and virtuosos of Vienna
and the imperial State of Austria', with the request that they should

each compose one variation on his little theme.[10] There was a threefold
calculation behind his request: at one stroke he more or less bound a
whole collection of contemporary composers to his publishing house;
he offered music-lovers an extensive and varied score; and at the same
time he provided them with what he himself described as an
'alphabetical dictionary of all the names, some of them long celebrated,
some still full of promise, of our illustrious epoch'.

The story of the Diabelli Variations is more than just a curious
chapter in the history of the piano; it is also a unique landmark in music
at the end of the first quarter of the nineteenth century. The second half
of Diabelli's collection, published in 1824 with contributions from 50
composers, provides an unparalleled cross-section of piano composition and performance in Vienna (and that means in Europe, and
that in turn means in the world) at the time. In those 50 variations on
Diabelli's impertinent theme you have a panorama of artistic skill and
technique, a resounding resumée of music on the threshold of
Romanticism.

The names run alphabetically from A (Ignaz Aßmayer) to W
(Johann Hugo Worzischek). For one of the contributors it was a last
work (Emanuel Aloys Förster), for another the first published piece
(Franz Liszt, then a child of eleven), and the ubiquitous Czerny is
there alongside the shy Franz Schubert. There is no lack of celebrities:
Joseph Gelinek, Johann Nepomuk Hummel, Anselm Hüttenbrenner,
Friedrich Kalkbrenner, Conradin Kreutzer, Ignaz Moscheles, Johann
Peter Pixis, Johann Wenzel Tomaschek, and even a Wolfgang
Amadeus Mozart – the great Mozart's son. Then there were the noble
dilettantes who did not need much persuading – the musical courtier
Count Moritz von Dietrichstein was happy to contribute, as was a
certain Ignaz Edler von Mosel and an Eduard Baron von Lannoy, and
the initials S.R.D. on Variation no. 40 masked Archduke Rudolf of
Austria himself. Diabelli proudly announced: 'The new firm A.
Diabelli and Cmp. considers itself fortunate to launch its career with
the publication of a musical score that is unique of its kind and that by
its very nature shall remain so . . . the outward presentation is in
keeping with the contents.'

The French writer Michel Butor considered why so many
composers should have agreed to participate:

Without being at all admirable in itself the suggested theme was necessarily interesting; proof of that is the fact that everyone else did accept. Each of them must have recognized a bit of himself in it. Its interest was therefore the opposite of what is commonly called originality; it was the fact that it was a sort of communal reflection of all the musicians he wished to publish, a crystallisation of contemporary music, and in particular of certain things in that music that Beethoven did not like; it was the fact that it was characteristic of the music of the publisher's time . . . Simple as it was, the waltz had, for Beethoven, an essential modernity.[11]

It goes without saying that Diabelli was both interested and diplomatic enough not to leave out Beethoven. The latter's first reaction was no doubt to refuse – he was notoriously unresponsive – but he soon set to work, and two years later, after repeated interruptions, he presented the publisher with not one but 33 variations. Diabelli intelligently decided to devote a whole volume to his work alone, which he published first – a daring move that music history has long and plausibly interpreted as Beethoven *v.* the rest of the world.

These '33 variations on a Waltz by A. Diabelli' are the most volcanic, bizarre, rugged, ironic, romantic and tempestuous compositions that Beethoven ever wrung from his Broadwood. He seized hold of the theme and transformed the waltz tempo to a march heavily accented with brassy chords, imperiously sweeping aside the trivial nature of the original with his '*Alla marcia maestoso*', as if to say, Make way! Butor tried to interpret the variations by giving each one a name: numbers 2 to 4 he pictured as scenes from a winter ball, beginning with 'Hoarfrost' and closing with an aristocratic waltz. The shrilly trilling variation no. 5 he called, rather curiously, 'Venus', envisaging the next three as a lovers' stroll, with the 8th variation entitled '*Valse tendre*'. But this tender waltz is so far the furthest removed from the original theme, a new musical character altogether, a piece of seductive romanticism, with chromatic caresses on the left that anticipate the hand-writing of a Chopin or Schumann. In the refractory staccato of no. 9 Butor heard a 'rustic march', followed, through three variations, by a 'country festival'. Later on in this poetic analysis he saluted 'Mars' (no. 13), the 'usurper' (in the violent variation no. 16, with its broken octaves reminiscent of boogie-woogie accompaniment) and 'Mercury'.

Is it permissible to conjure up such crowds of blessed and ill-fated figures in and behind these compositions, to dream up costumes for them, and even a script? The capriccio character of the whole work, that continual 'Didn't-you-hear?', might be said to encourage any listener's fantasy; and of course Beethoven himself, at least once, clearly suggested as much. The 22nd variation carries his own title, '*Allegro molto alla "Notte e giorno faticar" die Mozart*'. Here the composer breaks into the cycle with an operatic theme, Leporello's curse that he has no rest day or night: is this a musical joke, or a gibe at the publisher, or a way of announcing that Don Giovanni's record with the ladies ('*Aber in Spanien tausendunddrei*' – 'But in Spain one thousand and three') is now topped by a musical record – 'But for Beethoven thirty and three'?

Along with Michel Butor, the Belgian composer Henri Pousseur also puzzled over this number. Thirty seems to mark some sort of sound barrier for musical variations. Johann Sebastian Bach apparently broke through it with his 31 Goldberg Variations; apparently, but in fact the 31st is not a variation but a quodlibet, a little piece of fun, quoting the old folk song '*Ich bin so lang nicht bei dir g'west*' ('It is so long since I was with you') and thus recalling the theme that died out so long ago and now, at the end, returns to celebrate its own resurrection.

Although Beethoven himself spoke of '33 variations' both Butor and Pousseur tried to screw him down to 32 – in each case by tinkering with the composer's numbering as high-handedly as he himself dealt with Diabelli's theme. One of them counted out not just the theme, as is usual, but also the finale; the other fused numbers 16 and 17 into 'one variation in two parts'.

But why 32? Because that number is supposed to have held special significance for the later Beethoven. There are his 32 variations in C minor (with no opus number); but above all there are his 32 piano sonatas. Butor speculates that the Diabelli Variations are nothing less than an autobiography, a sort of lofty standpoint from which we may share 'the vision Beethoven himself may have had of his sonatas, and of the whole of his work'.[12] With the same bewildering boldness he calls the Diabelli Variations a coda to the piano sonatas, an abbreviated summing-up; and he goes on to claim that this abbreviation makes us dream of a more extensive work preceded, as it were, by variations chosen from Diabelli's second volume, and forming in itself 'a new spiral, considerably larger, even interminable, made up of contributions from the musicians of the future'.[13]

Even today the Diabelli Variations are rarely performed. Beethoven biographer Paul Bekker concluded in 1911 that they were unsuitable for public performance, and there are still critics who declare them unperformable when they have just heard the opposite proven in a concert hall. Beethoven himself never heard them. By the time he had composed them he was virtually deaf. 'The higher strings were all broken,' reports a visitor from that time. 'With all five fingers of his left hand Beethoven strikes the bass keys with all his might: "Listen how beautiful . . . !" He could no longer make out the notes, he was pleased enough with the rumbling. – Hauser could scarcely fight back his tears.'[14]

The Broadwood no. 7362 had one further reverent owner: Franz Liszt. Today it stands in the National Museum in Budapest, gleaming, polished and intact as it never was in Beethoven's day.

'. . . I SET OFF AGAIN, A STRANGER.'
Schubert

> Drink a glass of wine in Petersdorf
> on a star-bright evening in June,
> watch the glow-worms, listen to the
> crickets – then you'll know what a
> Schubert adagio is.
> *Anton Bruckner*

He was in terrible shape. He read terrible things. He read:

> . . . Magua buried his weapon in the back of the prostrate Delaware, uttering an unearthly shout as he committed the dastardly deed. But Uncas arose from the blow, as the wounded panther turns upon his foe, and struck the murderer of Cora to his knees, by an effort in which the last of his failing strength was expended. Then, with a stern and steady look, he turned to Le Subtil, and indicated, by the expression of his eye, all that he would do, had not the power deserted him. The latter seized the nerveless arm of the unresisting Delaware, and passed his knife into his bosom three several times, before his victim, still keeping his gaze riveted on his enemy with a look of inextinguishable scorn, fell dead at his feet.[1]

James Fenimore Cooper's novels – for all that the junior editions would have us believe – are one long death dance of knives and scalps and hatchet jobs, and Schubert never could get his fill of them. On 11 November 1828 he wrote to his friend and former flatmate Franz von Schober:

Dear Schober.
I am ill. For 11 days now I have eaten nothing and drunk nothing and I stumble weak and unsteady from arm-chair to bed and back. Rinna is

treating me. If I do eat anything I bring it up again at once. Be so good
then as to relieve me with something to read in this desperate condition.
Of Cooper's books I have read: The Last of the Mohicans, The Spy, The
Pilot & The Pioneers. Should you have anything else by him, I pray you
leave it for me with Frau v. Bogner in the coffee house. My brother, the
very soul of conscientiousness, will conscientiously bring it to me. Or
else some other book.

Your friend Schubert[2]

He never read another Cooper. The German edition, translated by C.
A. Fischer, was not completed until 1833, but that was not the reason.
Franz Schubert died a week after he wrote that letter, on 19
November 1828. 'As if dying were the worst that could happen to us,'
he had written to his father at the end of August.

On 1 September he had moved once again, out of the 'Blaue Igel' and
into his brother Ferdinand's rooms in Neue Wieden, Firmiansgasse
694, second floor on the right. Schubert had been suffering from 'hot
flushes and dizziness' throughout that summer; the fresher air of the
new Viennese suburb was supposed to do him good. He had always
liked moving – he moved almost as many times as Beethoven – but he
never settled down, preferring to sub-let rooms or stay with friends.
When he left Schober's flat it was a temporary move: he left his piano
and other personal effects behind him.

His piano? One of the many legends about Schubert would have it
that he was too poor ever to have owned a piano. Some decades ago
Otto Erich Deutsch gathered sufficient documentary evidence to
dispel this myth of poverty ('Schubert can never have gone hungry'),
and at least one of the many drawings of Schubert by Moritz von
Schwind features a dainty and clearly ageing Graf piano. In 1821, when
Schwind did the drawing, it stood in Schubert's rooms in the old
Theatiner convent (now Wipplingerstraße 21).

The Graf piano is said to have been a present from Schubert's proud
father after the première performance of his first mass. It is also said
that he left it with his brother Ferdinand at times when he did not need
it himself – when he was living with the Esterhazys or with Schober,
for instance, where there were instruments to hand. In any case there
can be no doubt that Schubert was surrounded by pianos: no other
nineteenth-century composer (barring one, himself a virtuoso – Liszt)
is so often shown in contemporary drawings seated at a piano with an
attentive audience looking on.

Early in his career Schubert set a poem by his near-namesake Christian Friedrich Daniel Schubart, 'Serafina to her Piano', to music, calling it 'To my Piano'. Shortened and slightly altered it read like this:

Sanftes Klavier

Sanftes Klavier
Welche Entzückung schaffst du in mir
Sanftes Klavier!
Wenn sich die Schönen
Tändelnd verwöhnen,
Weih ich mich dir,
Liebes Klavier!

(Gentle piano, what a delight you are to me, gentle piano! While beauties indulge themselves, dallying with trifles, I devote myself to you, dear piano!)

Bin ich allein
Hauch ich dir meine Empfindungen ein
Himmlisch und rein,
Unschuld im Spiele,
Tugendgefühle,
Sprechen aus dir,
Trautes Klavier!

(When I am alone I breathe my feelings into you, heavenly and pure, innocence at play, virtue speaks from you, beloved piano!)

Sing ich dazu,
Goldener Flügel, welch himmlische Ruh'
Lispelst mir du!
Thränen der Freude
Netzen die Saite!
Silberner Klang
Trägt den Gesang.

(When I sing along, golden piano, what heavenly peace you whisper to me! Tears of joy moisten the strings! The song is carried on silver tones.)

Sanftes Klavier,
Welche Entzückungen schaffest du mir,
Goldenes Klavier!
Wenn mich im Leben
Sorgen umschweben;

Töne du mir,
Trautes Klavier!

(Gentle piano, what delights you prepare for me, golden piano! When
my life is full of worries, sound in me, beloved piano!)[3]

For over a century these idyllic, teasing verses have helped to shape
the Schubert image, that image of the ardent dreamer, the sociable
entertainer, the tune-struck fellow at the piano surrounded by his
Viennese friends. In fact few other composers have so fiercely
contradicted this vision of the dear, beloved, gentle piano as the late
Schubert, sickening unto death. Innocence at play? Virtuous
thoughts? Heavenly peace? Tears of joy? Compare that with what he
actually composed in that summer of 1828 in the 'Blaue Igel' and the
Firmiansgasse flat: those three last piano sonatas, in the middle of
which all hell breaks loose.

But to return for a moment to that early song. It is as if Schubert had
intentionally arranged it to foster that idyllic image of the dreamy
composer, for he deliberately left out anything that might have echoed
of gloom or doom. Of the two verses in Schubart's original poem
which he did not use, one reads like this:

Melancholie
Dunkelt die Seele der Spielerin nie,
   Heiter ist sie!
   Tanzende Docken,
   Töne wie Glocken
   Flößen ins Bluth
   Rosigen Muth.

(Melancholy never darkens the soul of the player, he is gay! Dancing
chips, notes like bells, send a rosy spirit coursing through the blood.)

He called himself the 'most unhappy, most miserable man in the
world',[4] yet he chose to omit even this defensive invocation of the
melancholy spirit that so often 'darkened' his own soul (thereby
losing a Shakespearean allusion: those '*Tanzende Docken*' are the
'dancing chips' of sonnet 128.)

Who was this Schubert who worked so single-mindedly to encourage
the popular trivialization of the piano, only to torment the instrument

with his own mortal agonies in the last years of his life? He speaks for himself in this diary entry dated 14 June 1816, which was about the time of the 'Piano' song:

> Some months later I walked out again one evening. There can be few things more pleasant than an evening's stroll in the country after a hot summer's day ... In the uncertain light, accompanied by my brother Carl, my heart was content. How beautiful, I thought and called out, stopping for sheer delight. The proximity of God's acre reminded us of our dear mother. So we came, deep in solemn and congenial conversation, to the point where the Döblinger Straße forks. And as if from a heavenly home I heard a familiar voice call down from a carriage halting there. I looked up – and it was Herr Weinmüller, who climbed out and greeted us in his warm and worthy tones. – At once our conversation turned to the show of warmth in human voice and speech: how another man might have tried to express an equally friendly disposition in similarly warm and worthy sentiments, only to be laughed at for his vain attempt. It cannot be an acquired ability, it must be a natural gift.[5]

Hans J. Fröhlich, in his book about Schubert, takes care to interpret this passage, pointing out Schubert's curious desire to cover up the obvious fact that he and his brother had set out to visit the cemetery where their mother lay buried. He also notes that the point at which the two had arrived in their conversation was not a conversational point but a fork in the road, and that the heavenly home he mentions can scarcely be thought to imply Herr Weinmüller's carriage, but that he must mean the nearby graveyard. Fröhlich's detective instinct reveals some important clues.

This hallucinatory concreteness, this sleep-walking certitude, the voice calling down from a heavenly home with an earthly timbre of warmth and dignity, the carriage halting by 'God's acre' and that cry of 'How beautiful, I thought and called out' (as if one could call out something without first thinking it), then that incessant shift from sheer delight to the graveyard, from Herr Weinmüller to the hereafter, from the conversational to the geographical course – all this has its exact equivalent in Schubert's compositions. His music, like his diary, has a way of hovering between heaven and earth. Until hell comes into it at the end.

The shifting quality is neatly summed up in just two words from that entry: the 'solemn and congenial' (*'traurig traulich'*) conversation. For

Schubert that was not a contradiction in terms. For him it was a natural combination, a twilight mood of the soul: it was his minor key. Anywhere else in the musical world a minor key will mark a gloomy, threatening, ominous passage, but Schubert found comfort in that mode, just as he did on his evening stroll. A Schubert minor makes harmony with man 'in the darknesses of this life'. Here again he once wrote: 'Is there such a thing as cheerful music? I don't know of any.'[6] Beware of the moment when that harmony is shattered, when the minor consonance between life and music is abandoned and the piece suddenly shifts to a major key; then the pain really bites, and the sudden clarity is sheer torture. A verse from the *'Winterreise'* ('A Winter Journey') sums it up:

Ach, daß die Luft so ruhig!
Ach, daß die Welt so licht!
Als noch die Stürme tobten,
War ich so elend nicht.

(Ah, that the air so still! Ah, that the world so bright! When yet the storms did thunder, I was not so miserable.)

Just two weeks before his death Schubert composed a two-page inferno for the piano. There was no longer any question of major or minor, although one can just about pick out caricatures of key signatures. Suddenly he seemed to break out of his own musical style, abandoning any sort of structure or harmonic context, dispensing with the most basic piano technique: he simply raged, come hell or high water. In the middle section of the andantino of this late A major sonata there is a disaster, an explosion. 'The paroxysm in the andante,' wrote Alfred Brendel, left traditional ideas of form so far behind that the 'degree of anarchy' stood unrivalled until Schönberg wrote the third piano piece of his Op. 11.[7] Paroxysm in Greek means a sharpening, an intensification, and the dictionary defines it as an uncontrollable outburst of emotion, or the sudden intensification of a disease. Paroxysm indeed: these two sheets of music amount to no ordinary furioso or agitato.

To begin with there is a pale, furtive, cripplingly slow sort of order to the piece. Brigitte Massin describes it in the language of the musicologist:

The andantino prolongs the coda of the previous movement by means of the ostinato in the bass; the key is inextricably linked with that of the allegro: F sharp minor, the parallel to A major. In its character the theme of the andantino carries on where the adagio of the C minor sonata (which immediately preceded this sonata) left off; likewise in a 3/8 tempo, this again is a wanderer's lament about life on the road, but this time with a sense of painful weariness that recalls the tragedy of the 'Winterreise' . . . Here we have one of the last songs of the wanderer, and it is no less heart-rending for that. Everything is said very simply, the song soaring above the sluggish bass, balancing between minor and major; nothing happens, or almost nothing, apart from this heart-rending repetition, until at last the bass falls silent and the ever swifter tempo of the treble escapes from the obsessive lament . . .'[8]

Schubert's life-long devotion to music was itself nothing less than obsessive in the last decade of his life. 'I was brought into this world for nothing but to compose.'[9] Every day from morning to about midday he wrote music, played music, listened to music. He wrote hundreds of dances, all the rage in Vienna's Biedermeier period – they went in one ear and out the other, and in the end the Viennese still preferred Strauss. Then there are his 'moments musicaux', some of which sound so obstreperous that Robert Schumann claimed he could hear the 'tailor's bills' in them – bills 'he was in no position to pay, there is such a petty bourgeois frustration hanging over it all'.[10] Then the 'impromptu' pieces, piano pieces, marches for two and four hands, and the sonatas, the great wanderer fantasy. Also seven masses, not to mention countless choral works; eight symphonies, again omitting the orchestral overtures; and fifteen string quartets – as if the Quintet in C Major alone might not have sufficed as a claim to immortality. And through all those years he never forgot the lyrical form: in the end he composed more than six hundred Lieder. There was always that urge to speak in another man's voice, to take up another man's rhythm, brooding between the lines, making them his own. Again and again, on and on, day after day. Like the organ-grinder:

Und er läßt es gehen
Alles wie es will.
Dreht, und seine Leier
Steht ihm nimmer still.

(And he lets it go on as it will, grinds, and his organ never stands still –
from *Der Leiermann*, poem by Wilhelm Müller.)

There was always that barrel-organ staring up at him, the old piano
with its yellowed keys, those stinking stumps of teeth bared at him as if
sneering: compose us then. A keyboard after all is a huge, insane
puzzle, a puzzle with a million solutions, allowing infinite permutations of melody and modulation and harmony, a puzzle that a
composer will piece together a thousand times, only to be faced with it
afresh the following day like some primeval chaos, waiting for the
world to be created. For one moment – one brief instant – the dying
composer, a vomiting, sickly, broken mockery of a man, racked by
two diseases, syphilis and typhoid, for one moment he revolted against
this eternal torture at the keyboard.

If only he could escape that crippling lyric lament, just once, just one
single, last time. A modulating run begins, a cadence like a search for a
way out, a groping among the notes, tentative semiquavers, acceler-
ating into triplets, now an undisguised flight of demi-semiquavers, like
a passage from one of Mozart's late piano concertos, but so far the
movement is restrained, the fear contained, or at least denied
expression by the voice. Schubert does not mark a *sotto voce* here, but
the diminuendo after the pianissimo still holds, apart from one little
swelling of sound. The drama unfolding in the music has no real voice:
this is breathless anxiety, panting silence, a frantic, forceful back and
forth. But once again there is a pause, a last attempt to step back: an
extended trill, mezzo forte, hovering over the bass as it casts about for
a way out, and then, for the length of one bar, a double trill sounding
the alarm: SOS.

Now the attempt to escape, rising panic, as clashing discords shatter
the silence; chromatic harmonies in the bass against an ostinato in the
descant, reinforced in broken octaves, and then a desperate rush for an
exit, nowhere to be found, so the chromatics are carved up, the
ostinato made chromatic, until the music itself scarcely knows what is
going on here. Make that fortissimo! Surge on again in sheer frenzy, a
maniac raging, hammering against the wall of the keyboard, must it
still retort with notes, with sound. Don't give up now, hit it! And
again! What are you doing, poor Schubert? What is happening to you?
You are modulating again, not hammering, back in the strait-jacket of
harmony – you might be about to drift into the loveliest Ave Maria.

Gentle. That is how the world liked to see him, as Anton Schindler made clear in his letter: 'We all expect that you will act well and wisely, with none of this wilful behaviour . . .'[11]

Schubert was so much happier reading his Indian stories. There was that beautiful, soothing passage, as the old Mohican prepares to die:

'Let the bow, and tomahawk, and pipe, and the wampum of Mohegan, be laid in his grave; for when he starts 'twill be in the night, like a warrior on a war-party, and he cannot stop to seek them.' . . . Mohegan raised himself, as if in obedience to a signal for his departure, and stretched his wasted arm towards the west. His dark face lighted with a look of joy; which, with all other expression, gradually disappeared; the muscles stiffening as they retreated to a state of rest; a slight convulsion played, for a single instant, about his lips; and his arm slowly dropped by his side, leaving the frame of the dead warrior reposing against the rock, with its glassy eyes open, and fixed on the distant hills.[12]

Franz Schubert died on Wednesday, 19 November, at three o'clock in the afternoon, in the home of his brother Ferdinand in Neue Wieden, near Ronsberg – number 694, second floor on the right.

THE GLASS COACH
Solo for Clara Wieck

The pearl never floats on the surface;
it must be sought in the depths,
whatever the danger. Clara is a diver.
Robert Schumann

It was like a fairy-tale: the little girl waiting for the glass coach to roll up and sweep her away. She had only just turned nine, and that twentieth day of October, 1828, would be the greatest day of her life. Even as an old woman Clara would remember the occasion, and she improved the story each time she told it.

Clara Wieck had been thoroughly 'groomed' for the occasion, as her father put it; the black hair parted madonna-fashion, then twisted to a thick knot at the top of her head and crowned with a sumptuous bow; pendants drooping from her ears, and the little bony shoulders almost bare above the great puffy sleeves of the dress. She was a child transformed into a lady in miniature.

One can imagine her skipping back and forth from the mirror to the window she was scarcely tall enough to reach. Her father would have scolded her severely for such a display of vanity and curiosity, but he had gone on ahead, and her stepmother was not one to hold her back. To curb her impatience she may have sat down at the grand piano, gingerly arranging her skirts, to play a few études by Ferdinand Ries (the same Ries who studied with Beethoven, and who had long since started to compose his own work): such refreshingly up-and-down music to make the little hands run like rabbits.

Surely the coach was long overdue. She was expected – not by a prince in a fairy-tale palace, but by an audience in Leipzig's Gewandhaus, where she was to give her first public concert that very afternoon. It was to be a four-handed recital with an older girl, but Clara was not going to play the easier left-hand part with the bass accompaniment; she was to play the more difficult melody on the right.

She had always found it so much easier to express herself in music than in words. At the age of nine she played like a born musician, yet she could hardly talk. Even when directly addressed she often reacted like a deaf-mute. Her father worried that she might be hard of hearing and unfit for a musical career: an inaccessible, somewhat stupid, backward child. He failed to consider the fact that she had spent most of her young life with the maid, the good Johanna Strobel. 'She was not exactly talkative, and that must be the reason why it was only between the ages of four and five that I began to say a few words, and even then I understood little more. The piano on the other hand I heard a great deal, and my ears were therefore much more readily attuned to music than to speech.'[1]

The time had come. A voice called up the stairs: 'The carriage for Fräulein Clara is here!' Quickly she gathered up her gloves, bonnet and cape, and then climbed very carefully down the stairs and out into the Grimmaische Gasse, where the glass coach was waiting.

The glass coach? But it was hardly even a proper carriage, just a perfectly ordinary cart for several passengers, a so-called omnibus, and in it a whole crowd of giggling girls. Clara found a seat and perched on it unhappily as the carriage rolled off with a jerk, only to stop again a few streets further on to pick up another child, and then another, and then another. Was the Gewandhaus concert a sort of children's party, and was Leipzig populated by nothing but little girl pianists? Where were they headed anyway? Leipzig was looking more and more countrified. Little Clara finally managed to ask: 'Is this the way to the Gewandhaus?'

'To the Gewandhaus? No, we're going to Eutritzsch.'

And all her dreams of the Gewandhaus concert were drowned in bitter tears.

Then suddenly she heard the crack of a whip, the thunder of hooves, and a coachman calling out from the box of a carriage with gleaming windows: the glass coach from the Gewandhaus. The two Claras were swiftly exchanged: the daughter of the caretaker, on her way to a country fair, climbed into the omnibus, and the little pianist sank into the cushioned seat of the proper coach, all its fairy-tale elegance entirely lost on her now. The score of Kalkbrenner's variations on a march by Bellini, from his opera *Moses*, would be lost on her too. But surely her stern father would not expect her to play after such a distressing turn of events?

He was an unpredictable man. She had expected him to be furious (he had a terrible temper), but he greeted her as gently as could be, apparently not a bit annoyed at the delay. He even had a little bag of bonbons to comfort her: 'I quite forgot to tell you, Clara, that one is always mistaken for someone else the first time one plays in public.' After the concert Friedrich Wieck wrote in his daughter's diary, in her name: 'It went very well, and I made no mistakes, and was much applauded.'[2]

But even her worldly father, with all his experience of performance psychology – Wieck was an all-round man of the piano business (teacher, impresario and dealer in instruments) – was wrong about one thing: an artist is bound to be mistaken for someone or something else not just the first time she performs, but again and again throughout her career. She was often dismissed as a child prodigy, just because she was still a child. Even her dear and soon to be beloved friend had to be corrected on that point: 'No, Robert, when you call me a child, it sounds very sweet, but, when you think me a child, then I stand up and say: "You are wrong!"' Early in life the girl had learned the stubborn art of self-assertion. When a certain Count Kospoth invited her to perform with his wife, who was quite a well-known pianist herself, the nine-year-old replied: 'I would be happy to come, but can your wife really play?'[3]

There were times when she was not just mistaken for someone else but abruptly sent packing. In the autumn of 1831 Friedrich Wieck and Clara, now twelve years old, arrived in Weimar. They had made no preparations; they simply trusted to luck to guide them through the famous musical capital. But if the ambitious Wieck thought that his daughter's reputation had spread from Leipzig and Dresden as far as Weimar itself, he soon learned that Weimar was fully occupied with its own claims to fame. 'The order of the day here is culture, but also enormous egotism and narrow-mindedness, a certain stiff courtly pride and etiquette; narrow-mindedness in art, but above all in piano music; recent compositions for the piano are not known here, even by name.'[4]

Wieck wrote that resigned entry in the diary after several days spent fruitlessly waiting in the antechambers of the court. Oberhofmarschall von Spiegel had ushered father and daughter straight out again after a very brief audience: he was offended by Wieck's suggestion that he should smooth their way in Weimar, and there could be no question of a concert in the court theatre – what would one be coming to? Actor and director Genast simply pretended not to be there when they called. And because he had no heart for further embarrassments, Wieck never even went to see *Hofkapellmeister* Johann Nepomuk Hummel, the piano virtuoso who had just published, as a sort of pedagogical legacy to future generations, his 'Studies for the Pianoforte'.

On their first day in town the Wiecks had made their way to the Frauenplan to gaze worshipfully at the house where His Excellency himself, the venerable Goethe, was said to live. They did not meet Minister von Goethe that day, but they were introduced to such local worthies as a certain Mister Schmidt and a Mister Töpfer, and others with comical names like Froriep and Petersilie (Parsley) – Clara had had to stifle her giggles. It was well worth the effort, because most of these people did own pianos themselves, and they often arranged little gatherings where Clara might be invited to perform. Coudray, the court architect, was also there, and he said he would mention her to Goethe, who was a friend of his. Whereupon that great curiosity-seeker promptly summoned the travellers to call on him the very next day.

Clara's father recorded the event in her diary: 'On the first of October at noon we had an audience with His 83-year-old Excellency, Minister von Goethe. We found him reading, and the servant led us in without further ado . . . He greeted us very warmly; Clara had to sit with him on the sopha (*sic*). Shortly thereafter his daughter-in-law came in with her very intelligent-looking children of 10–12 years of age. Clara was then asked to play, and because the piano stool was too low, Goethe himself fetched a cushion from the adjoining room and arranged it for her. She played "La Violetta" by Herz. More visitors arrived, and she went on to play bravura variations by Herz, Op. 20.'[5] A few days later Goethe wrote to his friend Karl Zelter, the composer and director of the singing academy in Berlin: 'Yesterday a curious phenomenon was brought to my attention: a father presented his piano-playing daughter, who, on her way to Paris, performed various new Parisian compositions; the style was also new to me, it demands great skill in performance, but is always spirited; one follows easily and it is very pleasant. Since you know about these things, do enlighten me.'[6]

Suddenly the dismissive city, arrogant, courtly Weimar, seemed to have changed beyond recognition; the people at the hotel and in the streets behaved quite differently, and the landlord's cold nod was replaced by a friendly salute. It was as if the place had suddenly decided to smile. And all because the whole town seemed to know about their visit to Goethe as soon as it happened, and the old man's enthusiasm was no secret either – he was even said to have been moved to tenderness (yet again!).

Then the Lord Chamberlain himself, von Spiegel, the very man who had virtually thrown them out of his office only a week before, came to call on them in their modest hotel. This time he oozed civility, winningly suggesting that they all forget that little misunderstanding of the other day, it being the burdensome nature of his position to be overwhelmed by incessant and impossible petitions; he now had the honour of delivering an invitation: please to come to a concert at court, that very evening.

And that evening, at the request of the Grand Duke, Clara was obliged to play for almost two hours. The lord of Weimar sat down next to her, enchanted, and eager to experience the little miracle from close at hand. The following evening, on 7 October, she played her next concert, in the town hall, sitting on the podium surrounded by a circle of music-loving ladies. The keen interest fired her performance; the improvisation went particularly well; five hundred listeners applauded and even cheered.

Once more she was allowed to play for Goethe, this time her own composition, her first variation. Goethe thanked her father, in writing, 'for the masterful musical entertainment'. Clara herself received a bronze medal with a portrait of the poet, wrapped in a piece of paper on which he had written, 'For the artful Clara Wieck'. The proud father recorded Goethe's spontaneous exclamation: 'The girl has more strength than six boys together.'[7]

Goethe had always suffered the little children to come unto him. Ten years previously, in October 1821, the then twelve-year-old Felix Mendelssohn, accompanied by Zelter, had been so warmly welcomed that he wrote this giddy letter home to his parents: '. . . Now listen all of you, *all* of you! On Sunday the sun of Weimar, Goethe, came . . . He is very friendly, but I do not think any of the portraits are like him

... One would take him for a fifty-year-old, not seventy-three ...
Every morning the author of *Faust* and *Werther* gives me a kiss, and
every afternoon my friend and father Goethe gives me two kisses.
Think of it! In the afternoon I played for Goethe for over two hours,
and partly I improvised.'[8]

Music critic Ludwig Rellstab recorded the occasion, at which he was
also present, with as much detail as sympathy. He described how
Goethe himself opened the Streicher grand that he had specially
ordered; how it was agreed that Felix should begin by improvising;
how the unfortunate Zelter came to suggest that he take as his theme
the song 'Ich träumte einst von Hannchen' ('I once dreamed of little
Hannah'), a hit song from the Rococo period that the boy had never
heard; how Zelter therefore had to pick out the melody and triplet
accompaniment with his crippled fingers; and how the twelve-
year-old then sat down at the piano.

> Felix first played it right through ... bringing his fingers so to speak
> into line with the main theme ... But suddenly he broke into the
> wildest allegro. The gentle melody became a thundering motif that he
> carried now into the bass, now into the treble, using beautifully
> contrasting figures, in short he created a fiery stream of gushing fantasy
> ... Everyone was struck with astonishment; the small boyish hand
> swept the notes before it, mastering the most difficult combinations, the
> passages rolled, bubbled, flew by like a breath of ether, a stream of
> harmonies poured out, bridged by unexpected bars of counterpoint –
> only the banal melody was somewhat neglected, finding little to say for
> itself in this brilliant parliament of sound.[9]

Zelter hid his pride in a dry cackle: 'So, you must have dreamt of
goblins and dragons. That was a trifle excessive!' But Goethe was
excited, wanted to hear more, a fugue by the 'old master' Johann
Sebastian Bach, of course, and the minuet from *Don Giovanni*. The
boy flatly refused to play the overture, saying it was no task for the
piano. The old man grew greedier than ever, went to his cupboards,
pulled out one handwritten score after another, including a Mozart
adagio. Finally he said, 'Now here I have something that will trip you
up. Take care!'

Rellstab recalled the scene:

> With these joking words he reached for another sheet and propped it on

the stand. It looked very odd indeed. One hardly knew if it was a sheet of music or a piece of lined paper, spattered with ink and smudged in various places. Felix laughed in astonishment. 'What sort of writing is that! How is one to read it?'

'Guess who wrote it.'

Zelter had gone to the piano and looked over Felix's shoulder. 'That is Beethoven's hand! One can see that a mile away! He always did seem to write with a broomstick and as if wiping his sleeve across the score . . .'[10]

So Mendelssohn set to under the eyes of the impatient Goethe:

Felix began to play at once. It was a simple song, but to find the true notes among the blots and smudges a rare swiftness and sureness of eye was required. The first time he played it Felix often laughed and pointed a finger at the right note, which he had found somewhere quite other than where it ought to have been, and the occasional mistake was corrected with a cry of 'No, thus!' Then he cried: 'Now I will play it for you!' And the second time not a note was wrong.[11]

Goethe called an end to the cruel game after that, but during the two weeks the boy was in Weimar he opened that piano again and again, saying, 'I have not heard you yet today, make a little noise for me.'

Despite Goethe's compliments the Wiecks' visit to Weimar ended on a sour note. The wife of privy councillor Schmidt, impressed as she was by Clara's performance, worried what price she must have paid for her precocity. She accused Friedrich Wieck of making his daughter a slave to the piano and allowing her no space to run about, no time for other games, and no company of her own age. For Wieck such criticisms were familiar, and therefore doubly irritating. At the beginning of that year Clara had appeared in Dresden, and rumours were rife. The poor little girl was said to be forced to practise twelve hours a day, and of course she was not so little either – no less than sixteen years old, for all her father said, and not yet able to read or write. When the lady in Weimar added her voice to the fray, Wieck was furious. He was obviously still smarting from her accusations when he wrote to composer Ludwig Spohr in Kassel, where they also intended to stay a few days, to assure him '. . . that I would not presume to ask for your kind protection were I proposing to introduce you to a mere child prodigy taught by means of forced and tedious repetition to play a few concert pieces . . . and I furthermore assure you that in the judgement of all the many philanthropists who have become acquainted with Clara, I appear to have succeeded in keeping her character and her childlike innocence free of any excessive precocity.'[12]

Even fifty years later Clara still found it necessary to clear her father on that point. In a letter to the then famous woman journalist La Mara she declared her support for his pedagogical style:

> People have simply no idea how different one's whole education, one's whole career must be, if one is to make a significant contribution as an artist. My father kept a close eye on the physical aspect of my musical training: as a child I never practised more than two hours a day, and later never more than three, and every day I went walking with him for as many hours, in order to strengthen my nerves; furthermore, until I was fully grown, he always took me home from any gathering at 10 o'clock, because he considered it vital to sleep before midnight. He never allowed me to go to balls, saying I needed my strength for other things than dancing, on the other hand he never denied me a good opera, and beyond that, from very early girlhood, I was used to the company of the most distinguished artists. Those were my childhood pleasures, rather than dolls, although I never lacked for those. People . . . thought it all an exercise in cruelty, convinced that my achievements, which may indeed have seemed beyond my childish years, were impossible, unless I was forced to practise day and night . . . I will thank him (Wieck) all my life for his so-called cruelty . . .[13]

Mrs Schmidt's accusations are still very topical. In recent years the issue has been revived with particular intensity. It would seem that the piano, more than any other instrument, is particularly susceptible to the danger of mechanical drilling and mindless endurance training. Artur Schnabel once said: 'I should ban the word "practice" from the vocabulary, because it has become a nightmare for children. I would ask: Have you made any music today? . . . If not, then go home and make some.'[14] A piano teacher from East Germany recently complained 'that the creative imagination of the pupil, the love of music and the joy of making music are often too little emphasized in the lesson, in fact considerably more time is devoted to learning the names of the notes and keys and how to position one's hands and fingers, so that the natural interest in music and the first seeds of a desire to create are slowly but surely killed off.'[15]

Also in that vein is Grete Wehmeyer's temperamental attack against 'solitary confinement at the piano', which she describes using the example of the life and teaching of Carl Czerny. She challenges a concept that she sees as characteristic of the achievement-orientated society of the nineteenth century. 'The industrial work ethic steered even art and artists onto a path that led inexorably to the perfection we now hear in every recording. For over two hundred years instrumentalists have embraced this ideology of work and career, honing their training methods. Because the capitalist work ethic is still fully accepted in the marketplace, in industry and in science, it is still in full force in the artistic arena.'[16]

Friedrich and Clara Wieck left Weimar on 12 October 1831. Many months later, in mid-February 1832, they arrived in Paris, the final destination of their long winter tour. The last leg of the journey from Mainz seems to have sapped what strength remained to them: 'God, what a journey, what a strain those four nights en route to Paris! and how difficult it is now that we are here, unable to speak a word of French!' The city of light greeted them with a cold glow: 'Everything other than what we expected.' They hid themselves away, freezing, in their rooms in the Hotel de Bergère on Montmartre. This was much worse than the day the glass coach failed to come, much more off-putting even than Weimar. People could not even pronounce the name of their home town. 'Leppsic', they would say, knowing only that it was somewhere to the east. And child prodigies? *Mon Dieu*, they had more than enough of those.

Even the people they had counted on to be friendly and supportive treated them at first with arrogant reserve. Piano virtuoso Friedrich Kalkbrenner, who himself came from Germany but had been trained in Paris, where he had lived for the past two and a half decades, listened to a few of Clara's own compositions and called her *'le plus grand talent!'* but then added, 'What a pity, in Germany she will perish as a pianist.' He interrupted her father's protest: 'Begging your pardon, sir, in Germany they all play in the one style, the Viennese hop or Hummelesque crawl, thus Czerny, Ciblini, Pixis, Hiller, in a word, all who come here from Germany.' Despite Wieck's assurances that he would never teach Clara either to hop or to crawl – to play, that is, with fingers firmly crooked – Kalkbrenner retreated into his scepticism like a crab into its shell.

Father and daughter threw themselves bravely into Parisian life. Wieck sneered at himself in a letter to his wife:

You should see me at the soirées with my yellow gloves and white cravat, my hat ever in my hand, half German and half French and half despairing, flaunting myself from 10 o'clock in the evening to 2 o'clock in the morning . . . Also my broad boots and shoes (built rather like the ferry one used to take from Wurzen across the Mulde), the blue frock coat with the velvet collar and the little yellow buttons, the black leggings that fit so snugly. I look like a young oak tree in Rosenthal.[17]

Two weeks passed before Clara was given a chance to perform, at a *grande soirée* on 2 March in the home of the Princess Vandamore. 'What a place!' her father exclaimed as they entered the palace. An imposing hall had been designated for the concert, but it looked less like a music room than a china shop: everywhere there were vases, cups, animal figurines, ballerinas, floral lids. Then there were stuffed birds with monstrous beaks, and a wealth of silk hangings and drapes certain to muffle the music.

The assembled company was so illustrious that it hardly mattered that the names meant nothing to the two Leipzigers: those who were not princes were ambassadors or at least government ministers. This was not just foreign territory, it was another world, fantastic, mocking, and deeply *décolleté*.

The ladies scarcely had eyes for the ill-matched pair that called themselves father and daughter, preoccupied as they were by a virtuoso performance on the guitar, in other words by a passionate guitarist. The young man with the curly black hair knelt before the ladies, throwing himself at their feet, languishing and lascivious, and when he plucked the strings it was like the wildest and most intimate tickle. He had no need of his Andalusian national costume: the smouldering Latin eyes, the supple boldness of his gestures, the seductive nonchalance of his posture said enough – a cold-bloodedly hot-blooded Spaniard. Wieck realized that this was not to be an occasion devoted purely to music.

When Clara's turn came she found herself struggling less with the indifference of the audience than with the contrariness of the instrument, every key of which jerked and stuck. It was a routine experience: the more elevated the company, the shabbier the piano. Now and then a player would be humiliated with an outdated instrument that had nothing but black keys, the upper ones impossibly narrow. But Clara played her piece with bravado, and Kalkbrenner's enthusiastic applause indicated to the rest of the audience that they had been treated to a respectable artistic achievement, so they joined in with an obliging show of clapping, somewhat muffled by their gloves. 'Bravo,' Kalkbrenner cried; 'Good girl,' the princess chimed in.

When the vocal numbers were finished Clara was asked to play again, but Wieck refused, explaining to Kalkbrenner that one could not expect the child to take on that 'tough old bone' of an instrument a second time. Anyway he was quick-witted enough to have noticed that the company was beginning to disperse. One must learn to control one's vanity, he thought (and later wrote in the diary), and beware of overdoing it. The Spaniard was already fingering his guitar.

And yet the evening did pave the way to Clara's first big public appearance in Paris. The *Constitutionnel* printed a friendly little piece about the girl pianist, and a room was booked in the Hôtel de Ville, the city hall, for the 9 April 1832. Invitations were printed and sent out; it was hoped that all the very best people, including musical friends and perhaps even virtuoso rivals, would attend.

Then cholera broke out in Paris, and no one had further thought for a concert. Even the smaller room which Wieck hastily booked was empty when Clara sat down to play. She played for the first time without sheet music, and she improvised for longer than she had ever done. The evening might have been called a success, had there been people there to notice as much.

There is no more vivid description of that sudden outbreak of the epidemic than Heinrich Heine's portrait of a city rashly celebrating its feast of fools:

> Owing to the vast misery prevailing here, to the incredible filth, which is by no means limited to the lower classes, to the excitability of the people and their unrestrained frivolity, and to utter want of all preparation and precaution whatever, the cholera laid hold more rapidly and terribly than elsewhere.
>
> Its arrival was officially announced on 29 March, and as this was the day of *Mi-Carême*, and there was bright sunshine and beautiful weather, the Parisians hustled and fluttered all the more merrily on the Boulevards, where one could even see maskers, who, in caricatures of livid colour and sickly mien, mocked the fear of the cholera and the disease itself. That night the balls were more crowded than usual; excessive laughter almost drowned the roar of music; people grew hot in the *chahut*; all kinds of ices and cold beverages were in great demand –

when all at once the merriest of the harlequins felt that his legs were becoming much too cold, and took off his mask, when, to the amazement of all, a violet-blue face became visible. It was at once seen that there was no jest in this; the laughter died away, and at once several carriages conveyed men and women from the ball to the Central Hospital, where they, still arrayed in mask attire, soon died. As in the first shock of terror people believed the cholera was contagious, and as those who were already patients in the hospital raised cruel screams of fear, it is said that these dead were buried so promptly that even their fantastic fools' garments were left on them, so that as they lived they now lie merrily in the grave.[18]

It was more of a flight than a departure: on 13 April 1832 Friedrich and Clara Wieck left Paris. We will stay put and let Clara go on without us, but we will see her again, a good twenty years later, as the wife of Robert Schumann, who was already breaching the frontier of 'genius and lunacy', and again almost half a century after that as the grand old lady of the piano, at home in every concert hall in Europe.

PARIS, OR THE ROMANTIC RÉUNION

> The great poem of the shop windows
> sings its colourful verses from
> the Madeleine to the Porte-Saint-
> Dénis.
>
> *Honoré de Balzac*

> . . . and the great city, with all its
> voices, resounded like a
> vast orchestra around her.
>
> *Gustave Flaubert*

On 12 December 1831, an observer wrote:

> Paris is everything one could want. In Paris one can amuse oneself, bore
> oneself, laugh, cry, do whatever one has a mind to do. No one takes any
> notice, because there are thousands of others here doing the same, each
> in his own way . . . There is the greatest luxury here, and at the same
> time the greatest filth, the greatest virtue and the greatest vice. Posters at
> every turn about venereal disease – noise, din, racket and filth, more
> than one could possibly imagine. One is lost to the world in this
> paradise, and that is very convenient indeed: no one cares how anyone
> else chooses to live . . . One day you pay two hundred sous for the most
> lavish meal in a gaslit restaurant full of mirrors and gilt decoration, and
> the next day you are served a sparrow's portion and asked to pay three
> times as much for it. At the beginning I had to pay dearly to learn my
> way about . . .[1]

Is the musical hand of the writer apparent in that eager, anxious,
impecunious letter? Surely not: his name, in fact, was Frédéric
Chopin.

Another man, also a newcomer to Paris, wrote this just one week
later:

Yesterday I was in the Chamber of Deputies; I must tell you about it. But what do you care about the Chamber of Deputies? That is a political song, and you would rather know if I have written any wedding hymns. But that is the trouble: the only songs composed here are political; I think I have never spent two such unmusical weeks in all my life. It seemed to me I would never again think of composing; all because of the *juste milieu*, and when you are with the musicians it is even worse, for they do not even *argue* about politics, they *moan* about it all. One has been stripped of his position, another of his title, a third of his money, and it is all, as they say, because of the milieu. Yesterday I saw the 'milieu'; it wore a light-gray frock coat, looked noble, and sat at the top on the ministers' bench. It was however under fierce attack from Mister Mauguin, who has a long nose. Seriously, you think this is no concern of yours, but that will not help you in the least . . . Paris is irresistible, and because above all I must see Paris now, this is how I see it.[2]

Is the musical hand of the writer apparent in that letter full of political satire and journalistic observation? Unlikely: his name, in fact, was Felix Mendelssohn.

Paris is irresistible. Behold this Paris, the 'enchanted city' (as Heinrich Heine called it), this fairy-tale metropolis newly transformed, this dream world, where the true marvels were marvels of merchandising. For the first time luxury had come down to earth in the hundreds of shops, boutiques, *magasins de nouveautés*. For the first time the fairy-tales of magic wands and golden geese were there within reach, in shop windows and displays. There was no cholera now, and the new disease was shoppers' fever, a libertarian mania for consumption and self-decoration. Proper married women waited in their thousands for a lover like Frédéric Moreau (from Flaubert's *Education Sentimentale*), who wanted to buy up everything in sight for his beloved: 'He looked at the cashmere shawls, the laces, the jewelled pendants in the shops, and imagined them draped about her waist, sewn on her corsage, flaming in her black hair. On the flower-women's trays, the blossoms opened only so that she might choose them as she passed; the little satin slippers, edged with swansdown, in the shoemaker's windows, seemed to await her feet . . .'[3]

The storming of the Bastille had become the storming of the pastille, of confectionery and corsages, lace, ostrich feathers and genuine parakeets. The gentleman with the floppy hat and the umbrella, and the friendly but not altogether sociable face that looked so remarkably like a pear, was that well-known figure of fun, Louis Philippe, the bourgeois king, formerly Duke of Orléans, elected after the revolution of July 1830. Somehow, now that one could afford so many magnificent things, it seemed a pity to deny oneself a king, as long as he made no trouble and did not try to run the place and certainly kept well out of any war. Lafitte, the banker, made all that quite clear immediately after the election of the new monarch: 'From now on the bankers rule.'

This Paris after 1830 was literary territory par excellence. Never has there been a city so hot, so wild, so relentless in its pursuit of writers, literati, romanciers. Their novels, often serialized in the newspapers, portrayed that 'capital of the nineteenth century' in all its political and social reality. The despicable consequences of an unbridled money economy, the grotesqueries of the nouveaux riches, the absurd social duels between Carlists, Bonapartists and Philippists, between republicans and revolutionaries; lives, careers, ruinous falls from grace; entrepreneurial spirit and pensioner mentality, the transition from the individual fate to the decline and fall of whole groups – all this was the stuff of the great novels of the time, churned out by writers like Balzac, Stendhal, later Flaubert and the brothers Goncourt, still later Maupassant and Zola.

Stendhal identified the common denominator: 'I am of the opinion that at an income of over 50,000 francs private life is no longer a matter for the four walls of home ... The personalities are charming, when they are true and not exaggerated; but this charm could easily rob us of all we have come to see over the past twenty years.'[4] Until the end of the century, until Zola, there was scarcely a French novel written in which inheritances, pensions and capital yields, auctions and unexpected wills, bribes and provisions for maintenance, sales of property and mysterious bequests did not play some part – and no minor role at that, but an important part in the dramatic action, if not the central vehicle of the plot. The rule of money became a significant motif in the literature of the time. (The same is true by the way of the English novel, except that the result was much more melodramatic – viz. Dickens.) Balzac, the epic reporter of these conditions, was at the same time a prime example of the problem. Would his *Comédie Humaine* have stretched to such interminable length had he himself not been so desperately short of money that he simply had to go on writing? What he owed to his contemporaries was first and foremost not the epic but the rent.

The great fashion of the moment was the philosophy of Saint-Simon and his new socialism – which was soon reduced by his followers and imitators to a sort of emporium of happiness, an all-purpose supply of virtues, abilities, claims to fame. 'One cannot imagine,' Mendelssohn wrote,

> what they hope to achieve when they tackle the thing from the outside in this way: promising honour to one man, fame to another, an audience and applause for me, and money for the poor – when they destroy any further desire to achieve with their cold appraisal of ability. And then to top that their idea of universal love, of disbelief in hell, the devil and damnation, of abolishing egotism – . . . how they want to redesign the world and make people happy.[5]

By the time Mendelssohn wrote that, Saint-Simon's social ideal had given way to a substantially pragmatic concept of state provision, his utopia transformed to a land of milk and honey:

> *Oui, quand tout le monde entier, de Paris jusqu'en Chine,*
> *O divin Saint-Simon, sera dans ta doctrine,*
> *L'âge d'or doit renâitre avec tout son éclat,*
> *Les fleuves rouleront du thé, du chocolat;*
> *Les moutons tout rôtis bondiront dans la plaine,*
> *Et les brochets au bleu nageront dans la Seine;*
> *Les épinards viendront au monde fricassés,*
> *Avec des croûtons frits tout au tour concassés.*
> *Les arbres produiront des pommes en compotes*
> *Et l'on moissonnera des cerricks et des boites;*
> *Il neigera du vin, il pleuvera des poulets,*
> *Et du ciel les canards tomberont aux navets.*[6]

From the early 1820s this land of milk and honey was increasingly vaulted by a new, concrete heaven. The god of conspicuous consumption had brought forth more than shop windows, showcases, boutiques; it had built its own horizon, a firmament of iron and glass, a radiant shield of daylight, with its own profane uses. The new covered streets were 'places of refuge for anyone caught in a sudden downpour, offering a secure if somewhat confined promenade, with undeniable benefits for the shopkeeper' (from a guide to Paris published in 1852). But the most remarkable thing about these glass streets was their name.

They were called not *galleries* (as in Italy, somewhat later), nor *promenades couvertes*, as they were often advertised: they were called *passages* – a name borrowed from virtuoso performance.

The passage after all was the raw material of brilliant display at the piano. Passages were made of rapid scales and broken chords, glissandos and breathless thirds, *jeux perlés* and pianistic acrobatics. Surely the word had musical rather than architectural connotations, recalling for instance Walter Georgij's recommendations, from his *Little Book of the Piano*, as to useful basic equipment for the sight-reader: 'One must acquire a fund of musical formulae, a solid stock of figures one is liable to come across wherever one goes, particularly in classical and romantic music ... Mozart's passage technique in the allegro movements consists almost entirely of scales, arpeggios and certain ornamental refinements.' Beyond that there are some 'simple sequences that are as common in classical music as sand on a beach'.[7]

Passages meant Mozart indeed with his garlands of trilling tones, those chains of notes now bright, now sombre, rising sharply, falling sharply, supply twisting from melancholy to serenity, skipping from rococo to romantic. Passages meant Haydn too, and the early Beethoven, through to the fifth piano concerto, that begins by crashing about in a powerful, imperious E flat major cadence, rather the way people do when trying out a new piano. There are passages like that, blissfully long, in Schubert's sonatas. As the vehicle of virtuoso display the passage lent itself to vulgarization: it was the lifeblood of the Cramer-Clementi trade of music publishing, exploited by Hummel and Moscheles for their finger exercises, no doubt irresistible given the geography of the instrument: up and down, back and forth, over and under, running together and scurrying apart.

That is what was so extraordinary about the new Parisian passages: not just that they adopted a musical term, but that they did it at just that time, when the musical equivalent was losing ground, stretched to its theoretical and practical limits through over-use and popular availability – a time when the passage, in music, had been sent out into the streets. (This was such an obvious and exciting turn of events that it is impossible to understand how Walter Benjamin managed utterly to overlook it in his *Passage Work*.)

Of course the new horizon of glass and iron incorporated the piano itself, for a piano is also a piece of merchandise. Mendelssohn described the clustered confusion of goods for sale:

> . . . the day before yesterday I paid a musical visit or two to the grumpy Mr Cherubini and the friendly Mr Herz. There is a big sign on the house: *Manufacture de pianos par Henri Herz, marchand des modes et de nouveautés.* I thought they went together, having failed to notice that there were two different signs, and went in downstairs to find myself surrounded by crêpe and lace, and had to ask bewildered for the pianos. Upstairs a crowd of girls waited with earnest little faces; . . . then dear Herz came out, and granted his pupils an audience . . . All of his pianos have a plaque: *médaille d'or, exposition de 1827*; that impressed me. I went from there to Erard, tried the instruments there, and noticed a sign in big letters on each of them: *médaille d'or, exposition de 1827*. Back home I went straight to my Pleyel, opened it, and there was another sign in big letters: *médaille d'or de 1827*. The thing is a sort of honorary title; but it is indicative.[8]

Mendelssohn's account requires a little explanation. We have seen how Clementi covered his back, as his virtuoso career began to wind down, not only by teaching but by becoming a partner in a music publishing house and a piano factory – Collard's factory, to be precise. The same was true of Henri Herz, a virtuoso of the smoother sort who had founded his own piano factory in Paris, after his plans to join forces with Klepfer were dashed by the latter's declaration of bankruptcy. The interesting thing about Herz's activities, and the same is true of Clementi and Kalkbrenner (a partner in Pleyel's firm), is the combination of pedagogy and production, of virtuosity and manufacture. And it was not just a question of business acumen and financial security. The point was that virtuoso experience was to be passed on not just to students but also to instrument-makers. Teachers were as much concerned with the mechanics of the piano as with techniques of positioning and fingering. This close connection between theory and practice, between piano-playing and piano-making, demonstrates more clearly than anything else that the pianoforte was the communal product of a great number of interested minds – a favourite field of experiment for amateur tinkers and professional virtuosos, for mechanics and musicians, for salesmen and teachers. In the first quarter of the nineteenth century the piano underwent a full-scale revolution. Czerny acknowledged as much in his speech to the students of August Eberhard Müller's piano school (1825):

> Even the fortepianos themselves are every year refined with new inventions and improvements, and it is as yet impossible to predict when this complicated instrument will finally be perfected; and at the same rate the virtuosi of our time, in their playing as well as in their compositions, have brought a perfection to the handling of the instrument, and a versatility to any performance, that one could not have imagined possible.

That versatility in turn affected the design of the instrument.

For example, the most important invention of those years was a mechanism which for the time being improved neither the tone nor the volume of the instrument, serving only in a very particular situation: the rapid repetition of one note. Such repetitions are one of the traditional attractions of virtuoso piano music, but they are also an integral part of the living, breathing, vibrating sound of the piano. One of the most famous examples is the '*beben*', the quivering passage from Beethoven's Opus 110, when the semiquaver on A is repeated 27 times – a sort of trill on a single key. This effect, easy enough to produce on the old clavichord with its tangent mechanism (whereby the string is pressed from below), was a bit of a problem on the pianoforte: in the English action the free-swinging hammer fell too far back, and in the Viennese action it was too stiffly fixed to allow for such rapid repetition. Sebastian Erard, who had built the first French pianoforte in 1777, invented the '*double échappement*' as a solution to this problem: in his action the hammer was caught by a little lever as it fell, so as to be poised for a new stroke even before the key was released. This solution (subsequently simplified and thereby improved by Herz) was the first of three significant innovations which the nineteenth century contributed to the perfection of the piano. The other two were the introduction of overstringing, whereby one group of strings was made to cross the other, and the full iron frame.

The piano may have given the 'passage' to architecture, but it got its own back by taking over one of the most important building materials of the time: namely iron. In the first half of the nineteenth century iron became the indispensable raw material. It was subject to a course of development, as Walter Benjamin wrote, 'the tempo of which accelerated through the century. The trigger to that development was the discovery that the locomotive . . . must run on iron tracks. The railroad track became the first iron part produced for assembly, the forerunner of the girder. Iron was avoided in domestic buildings but used in passages, exhibition halls, railroad stations – buildings serving transitory purposes . . .'[9] Iron soon came to serve the same function for the piano as it did for the passage, spanning the strings as it had spanned the glass horizon. At this time, piano-makers in Europe had got as far as experimenting with iron struts to support the old wooden frame; in America Alpheus Babcock of Boston made the first square piano with a full iron frame in 1825, and in 1840 Chickering made the first grand piano with a full iron frame.

Newcomers Chopin and Mendelssohn had their own reasons for coming to Paris: it was the Mecca of the Romantic period, with Victor Hugo its leading light. The Romantic atmosphere remained impervious to the political situation, indeed the economic fantasies of the day may have encouraged the Romantic feeling. Paris was busily grooming itself to become the capital of the nineteenth century (as Benjamin called it). The letters of Mendelssohn and Chopin from that year of 1832 – the year of Goethe's death – lead us up and down the town, to the glittering celebrities and the tiny cafés, to the *Opéra-Comique* and the most obscure local theatres, because according to Mendelssohn, 'the whole life and people of France are reflected there . . . There is an extraordinary bitterness in all these comedies, a deep sense of antipathy . . . Everywhere politics plays the leading role. Politics and lechery are the two key points of interest, and for all the plays I have seen, not one has lacked a seduction scene and an attack on the ministers of state.'[10]

Chopin got the same impression when he visited the grand old men of the Parisian musical scene: 'Cherubini [talks] of nothing but cholera and revolution. These gentlemen are desiccated dolls to be treated with respect, for indeed one can learn a great deal from their works.'[11] Chopin's account of an opera produced at the *Opéra-Comique* is an all-too-grotesque indication of the extent to which this old guard attempted to influence and to dominate the musical life of Paris. The opera was called the *Marquise de Brinvilliers*, and no less than nine desiccated dolls had collaborated on it. The story of Marie Madeleine de Brinvilliers, a poisoner burned at the stake in the seventeenth

century, called together the collective skills of Auber, Boieldieu and
Cherubini, as well as such forgotten (or never particularly famous)
composers of opera as Berton, Blangini, Carafa, Herold and Paer, and
a mysterious musician by the name of Batton, who moved on to the
manufacture of artificial flowers, and is said to have ended his days as
an inspector at the Paris Conservatory.

Chopin realized that the musical life of Paris was at a turning-point:
'A dozen talented young people, students at the Paris Conservatory,
are patiently awaiting public performances of their operas, symphonies, cantatas . . .'[12] And he points, half in shock, half in envy, to
the case of Meyerbeer, who languished in Paris for three despairing
years before he was able to organize a production of his opera *Robert
der Teufel.*

The situation was no different for the phalanx of piano virtuosos:
the tone was still set by a generation whose ideal was brilliance and
bravura. Among the many visits made by Chopin, Hiller and
Mendelssohn were calls on these technical masters of the piano – Pixis,
Hallé, Herz and Kalkbrenner. The latter was considered the greatest of
them all, a vain, almost unbearable man, but a performer of
magnificent serenity, delicacy, clarity. When Chopin visited him he
was so impressed that he refused to compare him with Paganini. 'I have
to admit to you that I have played like Herz, but I would like to play
like Kalkbrenner. If Paganini means perfection, then Kalkbrenner is
his equal, but so entirely different. It is hard to describe his calm,
enchanting touch – the unheard-of regularity revealed in every note –
he is a giant trampling people like Herz, Czerny etc. in the dust, and
me as well.'[13]

But when Kalkbrenner offered to take Chopin under his wing and
make him his student for three years, Chopin refused with a sure
instinct: 'Three years is a lot, too much . . . nothing will be able to blur
[my] will and plan, all too bold perhaps, but noble none the less, to
create a new world for myself . . .'[14]

And in the middle of the Romantic Réunion, with Berlioz, Liszt,
Meyerbeer, Delacroix, Delaroche and Vernet, and the cluster of
writers around Victor Hugo – Alfred de Vigny, Emile Deschamps and
David d'Angers – in the middle of this fantastic society, this social
fantasy, Chopin stayed to become one of the city's most singular
figures, a gentle autistic, while Mendelssohn went on to complete his
worldly education in London.

ETUDES FOR THE SALONS
Chopin

The piano is my second self.
Frédéric Chopin

He was five and a half feet tall, and he weighed just 110 pounds: he always looked delicate, brittle, almost transparent, and not quite of this world. George Sand later called him her 'little one', and Mendelssohn, no heavyweight himself, dubbed him 'Chopinetto'.

He was always suffering from something. 'Chopin has been dying his whole life long,' said one malicious Parisian lady, and another: 'He has such a charming cough.' Foul odours he found intolerable, noise was anathema, and if a servant came into the room suddenly his hair stood on end. Once, in the notoriously wet winter of 1838/39 on Majorca, he really did fall ill, and he wrote with the sarcasm of a patient doomed to die: 'The three most famous doctors on the island have examined me; the first sniffed what I spat out, the second pummelled me where I spat, and the third felt and listened how I spat. The first said I was dead, the second said I was dying, and the third – that I am going to die.'[1] One of the names George Sand thought up for him was 'my little complainer', and also, 'my dear deceased'.[2]

His disgust at the world around him affected him physically. Once he had to spend a night on a boat with a cargo full of swine, but he was equally offended by any audience in a large concert hall. 'I was not made to give concerts; the audience makes me shy, I feel suffocated by their breath, paralysed by their curious stares.'[3] It was not really stage fright, just that he could not bear the steamy atmosphere of communal enthusiasm, the smell of sweat from an excited crowd.

Alfred Cortot reckons that he gave no more than thirty concerts in a large auditorium in his whole life – about as many as Franz Liszt would have given, at his busiest times, in a single month. In the nineteen years which Chopin spent in Paris he gave exactly nineteen public performances, usually in the company of other pianists, as well as singers and orchestras or chamber-music ensembles. If a pianist's success is usually measured in the number of public concerts and the volume of applause, then there was only one pianist less 'successful' than Chopin in the whole of the nineteenth century – namely Robert Schumann. But none the less – or possibly *because* he was so elusive – Frédéric Chopin was a legend in his own time. People went to his last concert as if it were a séance. Early in his career he was called the 'Ariel of the piano', a spirit of the air.

As the epithet implies, Chopin's aversion to public performance was not just a physical and psychic condition, but had something to do with his style of playing and the subtlety of his tone. To put it bluntly, he played too softly. 'Chopin knew that he had no effect on a crowd; he compared an audience to a sea of molten lead, whose tides can indeed be harnessed in the forge, but are no less difficult to stir for all that, and need a muscle-bound worker.'[4] This according to Franz Liszt, who was in a position to know.

The Chopin works played today as pieces of explosive drama – the *Révolution étude*, the *Grande Polonaise brillante,* the furious second motif of the F Major Ballade, the scherzos – must have sounded rather muffled in Chopin's hands. Almost every contemporary critic mentions his lack of volume.

Chopin himself reported to his parents about his first concert in Vienna, in August 1829: 'The general feeling is that my performance was too feeble, or rather too delicate, for those who are accustomed not only to hear, but also to see the artists who play here almost bang their pianos to bits.'[5] The Viennese aristocracy however had 'greatly praised the delicacy and elegance of my performance'.[6] In Warsaw, half a year later, the rear stalls 'complained about the quiet per-formance',[7] and the *Kurier Polski* newspaper advised him to put 'more energy into the finale'. His 'enchanting delicacy of touch'[8] was appreciated by the Munich newspaper *Flora* after Chopin's guest appearance there in August 1831. In Paris music critic and pianist Fétis remarked that for all he admired Chopin's performance and com-position, 'the volume of tone he extracts from the piano is very small'.[9]

Gottfried Benn's famous poem 'Chopin' makes an anatomical happenstance into an echoing metaphor:

Nie eine Oper komponiert,
keine Symphonie,
nur diese tragischen Progressionen
aus artistischer Überzeugung
und mit einer kleinen Hand.

(Never composed an opera, nor a symphony, only these tragic progressions [made] out of artistic conviction, and with a small hand.)

Everyone noticed Chopin's small hands. They were wiry and well-trained, however, and Cortot describes the fingers 'well separated from one another where they join the hand'.[10] George Sand spoke of Chopin's 'velvet fingers'. Those small hands were extraordinarily supple, and admirers were given to exaggerated praise: 'It was a wonder to behold one of those small hands stretching to master a third of the keyboard. Like the jaws of a snake preparing to swallow a rabbit,'[11] said composer Stephen Heller.

Yet this thin, delicate, sensitive man with the touchingly small hands and the soft, restrained style succeeded in conquering the metropolis of music – despite his fear of concerts and his aversion to people. He conquered Paris in his own way, discreet, reserved and intimate, but so completely and lastingly that his fame far outshone the glitter of public performance. Chopin was at home in the grand and worldly salons of Paris, where careers and marriages were made and broken, and much of it to music. Alfred Cortot describes

that atmosphere of jealous exclusiveness that enveloped Chopin to the point of becoming a cult. Admittance to this aristocratic circle was reserved for 'the happy few' whose monopoly it was. When he appeared on the artistic horizon of the French capital, he was debarred from acquiring an immediate popularity. He was, nevertheless, able to secure those social amenities most pleasing to him as a lover of elegance and essential to the development of his art. Without the aid of high-pressure publicity, a tacit understanding was gradually established, a kind of 'confidential' fame which circulated only among the chosen few . . . 'One does not merely love him; one loves oneself in him,' remarked one of the regular visitors to the happy musical gatherings that resulted from this mutual understanding.[12]

Chopin's entrée into the world of the salons was facilitated by his Polish friends, as well as by the fact that he was himself a Pole driven

out of Warsaw by the political circumstances of the day. He was also
lucky. According to the Chopin legend he bumped into Valentin
Radziwill one day out on the boulevards. Radziwill, a relation of
Prince Anton Radziwill of Warsaw, took him along to a soirée given
by James de Rothschild. Once there he sat down at the piano, played,
and by the time he stood up again he had arrived. He became the
protégé of such influential men as Prince Anton Czartoryski, Count
Apponyi and Marshal Lannes, and the ladies came to him for lessons:
Baroness de Rothschild, Princess Marcelline Czartoryska, Princess de
Chimay, Countesses Potocka, Kalergis, d'Est, Branicka, Esterhazy,
and countless others.

After a year in Paris Chopin wrote home to Warsaw about his
success in high society, and the letter is a characteristic mixture of pride
and scorn, cunning and distance:

> I am acquainted with all the best people, sit between ambassadors,
> princes and ministers, and I do not even know what miracle has worked
> this wonder, for I have never pushed myself forward. For me this is the
> most important thing at the moment; one's talent is inestimably greater,
> immediately one has been heard in the English or the Austrian embassy;
> you are a better player, immediately you have been the protégé of
> Princess Vaudemont – I cannot write that I am her protégé, for the
> woman died a week ago; and that was a lady who entertained the court
> in her salon, and who did a great deal of good, offering sanctuary to
> many aristocrats during the first revolution; the last of the old race of the
> Montmorency (mistress of a vast number of white and black bitches,
> canaries, parrots, and the most amusing little monkey in all the world,
> that used to bite the other countesses here of an evening) . . . Today I
> have five lessons to give, think of it, I earn a fortune; but the cabriolet
> and the white gloves, without which one cannot cut a good figure, cost
> more. I love the Carlists, cannot endure the Philippists, am myself a
> revolutionary, so that the money means nothing to me.[13]

He was indeed a revolutionary, though not in the political sense. He
had, for a start, a revolutionary attitude to his instrument. In the rough
draft of an unfinished book on teaching the piano there is a paragraph
reminiscent of Karl Marx's determination to stand Hegel on his head:
'Many futile methods have been tried to teach pupils to play the piano,
methods which have no bearing on the study of the instrument. They
are analogous to teaching someone to walk on their hands in order that
they may go for a stroll.'[14]

No one had ever touched a piano the way Chopin did. He saw the keyboard as an anatomical construction in perfect accord with the form of the human hand. 'No admiration can be too great for the genius who was responsible for so cleverly adapting the keyboard to the shape of the hand. The black notes, intended for the long fingers, make admirable points of purchase. Could anything be more ingenious? . . . Thoughtless people, knowing nothing of piano playing, have frequently suggested levelling the keyboard.'[15] His anatomical understanding of the keyboard went so far that he claimed, were the keyboard to be levelled in such a way, it would be necessary to remove a joint from each of the long fingers in order to play an effective staccato. The C major scale, in his view, was the most difficult of all to play, despite being the easiest to read – simply because it has no black keys to act as supports.

The basic position for the right hand that Chopin recommended to his students was E, F sharp, G sharp, A sharp, B. When he asked them to practise scales, he always began with the easiest, as he saw it: B major, in which the long fingers are consistently supplied with black keys. Many of the less decipherable keys in Chopin's works are there not just for musical reasons, but for technical purposes of convenient fingering. They are not so much keys for the ear (and the characteristics of different keys are hotly disputed), but above all for the hand.

Chopin did not believe in playing with the hands alone, as older pianists like Kalkbrenner still did; he insisted that the wrists and forearms, indeed the whole of each arm, must be called into play. But in this theory and practice he concentrated above all on the fingers. Among his notes is a short speech to a girl he had taught: 'Dear child – you have had excellent music lessons. You have been taught to love Mozart, Haydn and B. (Beethoven or Bach?) You can read the great masters at sight with ease. You have a feeling for them and understand them to the full . . . All that you need is a fluent technique in order to express in your playing that feeling for the great masters, whom you have grown to love.'[16]

As an older man he once wrote that he had never managed to rid himself of his two arch-enemies, 'a huge nose and a disobedient third finger'.[17] But as a teacher he never believed in the sort of drill intended to train every finger to the same strength and readiness. His attitude was more like that of a mother with a motley brood of children:

The strength of each finger is relative to its shape. The extremities of the hand are formed by the thumb, which is its strongest member, and by the little finger. While the third finger has a greater freedom as a point of support . . . the fourth finger is bound to the third by the same tendon like a Siamese twin and is the weakest. One can try with all one's might to separate them, but this is impossible and, thank heavens, useless. There are as many different sounds as there are fingers. Everything hangs on knowing how to finger correctly.[18]

Fingering, technique and composition went hand in hand, in Chopin's view, and he was always generous with his markings. The most distinctive characteristic of Chopin's fingering is a sort of gliding system. The elegiac and lyric melodies of many of his compositions depend on the use of the third, fourth and fifth fingers in the descant. And Karol Mikuli, one of his students, reported Chopin's use of an utterly new and heretical technique: 'With one and the same finger he often played two keys one after the other (and not just when sliding from a black key down to the next white one), without allowing the slightest interruption in the sound.'[19]

But Chopin was also revolutionary in a far more spectacular sense. Granted, he was inclined to ingratiate himself with the ladies and gentlemen of the Parisian salons with intriguing little pieces, mazurkas and nocturnes (a genre made popular by John Field), always useful for a gallant dedication tailored to the occasion, and usually simple enough to be played at home by the cream of Parisian society. But when Chopin set out to conquer the salons, overpowering princes, diplomats and cardinals, subjugating nobility and money and politics and beauty, he used – the études. He expected them, in other words, to listen to lessons – rather like Brecht. He broke the old bounds of the genre: technical, musical and social. People may have found occasion to practise the occasional étude in those grand reception rooms, but it was unheard of for a pianist to present such a piece as a virtuoso performance. Chopin made the étude socially acceptable, musically expressive: he made it a new art form.

What had the étude been before his time? It is tempting to call it a sort of miserable Cinderella in the service of pianistic technique, suddenly ushered into the palace by the prince Chopin and crowned as his wife, while its arrogant sisters, the sonata and fantasia, languished in the corner. Tempting, and to some extent true. The function of the étude had been to serve as a 'helping hand' to childish beginners, to ladies who wanted to play 'brilliant but not difficult' pieces, even to advanced students daring to attempt a little bravura. In eighteenth-century Germany they were in fact called *'Handstücke'* or *'Handsachen'* (pieces or things for the hand), mere gymnastics, technical exercises. Even in Chopin's time people were still publishing this sort of pure exercise; their chief proponent, Carl Czerny, will appear later in this book, but even a man like Henri Herz published an endless series of finger exercises, which are as hard to play as they are to bear.

But in fact the étude had a rather different geneology. Oscar Bie describes its origins in a masterfully impressionistic passage from his book on the piano: 'It is there *in nuce* in Bach's work . . . In a Bach *"inventio"* or *"sinfonia"* a motif will be worked and re-worked for all voices and all fingers. In a prelude elaborating any basic theme, in a fugue with its strict codex of canonical sequence, the same thing is happening: the motif is being exploited for all it is worth.'[20] And they had all played Bach's 'Well-Tempered Clavier', not just as a study in counterpoint, but also as an exercise: Mozart, Beethoven (when he was still with Neefe in Bonn), Schumann and of course Chopin, whose students testified that he knew many of the pieces by heart and frequently used them as teaching material. Around the turn of the nineteenth century a weighty work was published for students of the piano, the title of which indicates where the étude was intended to lead: the *'Gradus ad parnassum'* by Muzio Clementi. That was followed by Cramer's études, which were full of technical obstacles but which did exhibit a new pre-Romantic style behind the exercise. And then there were Johann Nepomuk Hummel's études. Oscar Bie hails him as the 'inventor of the modern pianistic phrase', and says that 'Hummel made the delights of the Hammerclavier and the effects of the seven octaves available to all. What our dilettantes ascribe to Chopin, the rich, full tone, the burning coloratura, is all there in Hummel's work . . .'[21]

The étude may have become socially acceptable, but who could play it? When Chopin's Opus 10, the first collection of twelve études, was published in June 1833 (he was already working on the second cycle, Opus 25), a wail of protest went up from critics and pianists alike. Ludwig Rellstab was one of the leading voices in the fray; he published this richly sarcastic piece in his music review, *Iris*.

As long as he [Chopin] goes on hatching such deformities as the above-mentioned études – a source of much amusement for all my friends, including the pianists among them – we will go on laughing at them . . . Let us spare ourselves a special review of each of the 12 apostles, which Mr. Chopin has sent into the world in these 12 pieces, and content ourselves with the more useful remark that a person with crooked fingers may well find the means to straighten them in these études, but that a less handicapped person ought to beware, and refrain from playing them except in the company of Messrs. von Gräfe or Diefenbach [two Berlin doctors], who may indeed find, if this sort of piano playing comes into fashion, that a whole new practice will open up to them as assistants to famous piano teachers.[22]

He had similar feelings about the piano concerto opus 11: '. . . in most cases it would be madness to practice Chopin's passages, which are not written because they were conceived thus or thus to sound magnificent, but because the composer has determined that they are more difficult this way.'

Rellstab was not talking entirely through his hat: certainly Chopin thought of these pieces as a form of provocation, and he indicated as much by dedicating the first cycle to Franz Liszt. The first étude alone is a veritable obstacle course for the fingers, and the fact that it is written in C major makes it no easier, by Chopin's own theory. Walter Gieseking admitted that at one time he spent six hours a day practising this one piece.

Chopin seems to have had a particularly intimate if mildly athletic relationship to this first étude. One of his best students, pianist Frederike Streicher, remembered that Chopin advised her to practise it very slowly every morning. This particular étude, he told her, would do her good: it would broaden her hand so that the scales of chords would sound like strokes on a string instrument. Unfortunately, he added, it did not help every student, and seemed to encourage some to forget all they knew. 'I know very well,' the young lady wrote, 'that it is widely believed, even today, that this étude can only be played by a very large hand, but this is not true; what is needed is a supple hand.'[23]

Chopin did not choose a particularly hasty tempo for this first étude (marked 'allegro'); but it is one of the first pieces in the history of piano music whose speed has nothing to do with bravura or virtuoso wizardry, and everything to do with the richness of the tone and the unfolding polyphony. 'Although never more than three keys are pressed at any one time, the sustaining pedal enrichens the sound to as many as thirteen or fourteen parts,' according to Harthmut Kinzler, who admires 'a polyphony not normally realizable in a two-handed piece for the piano'.[24] Robert Schumann noticed the same effect in the first étude from Chopin's second cycle (Op. 25): 'It would be wrong to think he had meant every little note to sound distinctly; it was rather a surging A flat major chord, heaved upwards now and again by the pedal; but through the little harmonies one heard the greater melody . . .'[25] Chopin jealously guarded his études. In the spring of 1839, on the way back from Majorca, he heard that Clara Wieck had played the fifth étude from Opus 10, and that in Paris; he wrote back that he was pleased at the news, but in a later letter he asked indignantly: 'Did the Wieck girl play it well? And how could she choose that étude, the very one least likely to interest anyone who does not know it is just for the black keys. It would have been better to sit still.'[26]

The étude, after all, was his Cinderella, his only queen. Chopin at least would have agreed with Oscar Bie's pronouncement: 'There is no more "genuine" piano music than the étude. The very essence of the piano becomes music in that form.'[27]

THE WAR IN THE MUSIC ROOM (2)
Liszt v. *Thalberg*

> Thalber has three parts feeling to one part
> skill.
> But Liszt has three parts skill
> to one part feeling.
>
> *Gioachino Rossini*

One of the contemporary accounts of the Bach *v.* Marchand tournament grandly concluded that 'Pompey was not necessarily a bad general merely because he lost the battle of Pharsalus to Caesar'. In the nineteenth century martial vocabulary returned with a vengeance to haunt the piano. On 26 March 1837 the Parisian *Gazette musicale* announced a forthcoming concert with the following words: 'The greatest interest ... will be without question the simultaneous appearance of two talents whose rivalry at this time agitates the musical world, and is like the indecisive balance between Rome and Carthage. MM. Listz [*sic*] and Thalberg will take turns at the piano.'[1]

Tournaments of this kind were part of the tradition of the instrument, but the evening of 31 March 1837 was a climactic event, the *non plus ultra* of a musical ritual, and a high point of Parisian social life in the nineteenth century. Rival fans had been disputing the point for years, and now, at a soirée in the salon of the Princess Belgiojoso, a gathering in aid of Italian refugees, it was to be decided: who was the greater pianist, Liszt or Thalberg? Liszt was the ecstatic player, while Thalberg was admired for his magnificent calm and nobility of bearing. His fame has faded, but Heinrich Heine recalls it in a portrait that at the same time indirectly criticizes Liszt for his behaviour at the piano.

> Thalberg enchants me, I would almost like to say through his musical behaviour: his playing is steeped in harmony ... his performance is so gentlemanly, so noble, so decent, so entirely without grimaces and

affectations of genius, so entirely without that braggardly boyishness that so thinly disguises an inner despair, which we have so often remarked about our musical success stories. The women are particularly fond of him, although he does not seek their sympathy with epileptic fits at the piano, although he does not play on their overexcited sickly nerves, although he neither electrifies them nor galvanizes them: he simply delights them with his soothing sound, his measured mildness.[2]

Heine's portrait tallies pretty well with Thalberg's own ideal:

> In broad, dramatic passages a great deal must be demanded of the instrument and as much sound as possible drawn out of it, but this not by pounding the keys but by touching them briefly and firmly, pressing them down with strength, decisiveness and warmth. In simple, gentle passages the keyboard must be kneaded, so to speak, worked over with a hand of pure flesh and fingers of velvet; in this case the keys should really be felt rather than hit.

Thalberg had a particular attraction: he was the man with three hands. Not that he was deformed, but he was a very special sort of pianist. When he played, his right hand did all that a virtuoso's right hand was expected to do, runs and scales and resounding arpeggios, but his left hand was no less busy, thundering out accompanying octaves, dashing off tremolos, clambering down to the booming depths. His own compositions were designed to allow both hands ample opportunity to show off their finesse.

That was the moment for the Thalberg miracle, when both hands seemed fully occupied with their virtuoso tricks up and down the keyboard: somewhere in the middle one would begin to hear a tender, expressive melody, massaged into the keys. Virtuosity may never have been nearer to the magician's skilful bluff, the acrobatic passages serving not just to decorate but to distract attention from the musical secret: Thalberg's third hand consisted of his two thumbs, which carried the burden of the melody over long stretches of the piece.

The thumb really deserves a chapter of its own in the history of the piano. The 'emancipation of the thumb', as Bernard Gavoty called it, was inevitable as early as the eighteenth century, as technique became increasingly complicated. Such emancipation was essential to the development of the virtuoso passage, with its rapid runs across the entire keyboard and its broken chords, one following hard on the heels of the next.

Bach's son Philip Emanuel recorded his father's attitude to the problem of the thumb:

> My late father told me that in his youth he had heard great men who never used the thumb unless a great span was required. Because he lived at a time when musical taste was undergoing a very significant change, he was compelled to devise a far more complete use of the fingers, and particularly the thumb, which aside from other good services is above all quite indispensible in the more difficult keys, where it must be used as Nature intended. In this way was the thumb raised from its previous inactivity to the position of the chief finger.[3]

But this was by no means common practice in the eighteenth century. D. G. Türk, in his *Clavier Schule* [*Piano School*], criticizes a habit prevalent at the time: 'The thumb . . . must never be allowed to hang down or to rest on the base-board, because these two above-mentioned errors lead to other inevitable gaps (erroneous division of thoughts), before the thumb can be brought to its place.'[4] In the old fingering technique the thumb and little finger were considered inferior instruments to be ignored wherever possible: they were called into action only in the playing of chords, and at the ends of passages. In piano-playing parts of Europe there were various schools of teaching, but all of them more or less agreed in their contempt for the thumb, usually marking the fingering for scales as 2323 or 3434 or even 234234. In English texts the thumb was dismissively referred to as 0 or X, so that the index finger appeared as 1. (For modern players it is important to know where Bach and his contemporaries may have changed position in order to avoid the thumb or little finger, for that will have affected the phrasing. Only one of Bach's numerous compositions – from the '*Notenbüchlein für W. F. Bach*' – has been passed down with its original fingering.)

Carl Philip Emanuel Bach campaigned enthusiastically for the use of the thumb: 'Nature made no other finger more nimble than the thumb, which can so bend under the others, busying itself with its suppleness and its advantageous shortness at places and times when the other fingers cannot reach.' But he does not allow complete license: moving the thumb under the little finger, or the little finger over the thumb, he decries as 'reprehensible' moves.

The Romantic period removed these last restrictions. Chopin sometimes made altogether eccentric use of the thumb, for instance in the mazurka-like A major prelude, when he extends an octave chord downwards by a third, which is possible only because the extra notes (A sharp and C sharp) fall on black keys and can be struck by a thumb laid crosswise. Or there is Schumann in the first of his *'Nachtstücke'*: four times in a row he recommends the use of the thumb in the tenor part, so that the low F may be held in the bass. In the *'Reconnaissance'* of his *'Carnaval'* the right-hand thumb has plenty of hard and swift work to do, as if to make up in one go for a hundred years of sleep.

The Liszt–Thalberg rivalry was by no means confined to the salon of the princess; in fact the encounter on 31 March was the last round in a duel carried on up to that point largely in the pages of the Parisian press.

At the beginning of that year, 1837, Liszt had published an article in the *Gazette musicale*, which the paper printed with some reluctance (as was indicated in an editorial preface to the piece). In that article Liszt scornfully wrote that he had taken the trouble to look through all of Thalberg's compositions – the work, he said, of one afternoon. He then went on to describe one of the pieces:

> In all seriousness: it seems to us impossible, with the best will in the world, to find anything in the twenty-one pages of this fantasia that could be called the product of a heightened aesthetic sense combined with inventiveness, colour, character, nerve or enthusiasm. Nowhere is there life or vigour. Impotence and monotony – in the final analysis, that is all we find in Thalberg's work.[5]

At the time that was written not even Liszt's most ardent admirers could claim that he had distinguished himself as a great composer (the B minor sonata was not to appear for another fifteen years). The critique could only be interpreted as a malicious attack against a rival pianist, a piece of pure spite. It broke all the rules of etiquette, and the fact that it contained a good deal of truth may not have been entirely clear even to Liszt himself. The result was that virtually every music-lover in Paris, including all the aristocratic circle, was won over to Thalberg's side.

François-Joseph Fétis, who edited the *Gazette musicale* from

Brussels, where he had founded the Royal Conservatory in 1833, made himself the spokesman for the outraged musical public. In a long reply Fétis recalled Liszt's beginnings, spoke of the 'frequent changes in his performance technique', the 'mechanism of his fingers', and called his early works 'profanations'. For Thalberg he had nothing but praise: 'What greatness! What richness! In his hands the instrument was transformed into a magnificent orchestra, as if he had more than five or six hands at once! He mastered the piano as if by magic, the secret of which will never be discovered . . .'[6]

Fétis also asked why none of Liszt's friends had stopped him from publishing his unfortunate article, why he himself had forgotten 'that nothing is more vulgar than this eruption of foul temper against a more fortunate colleague', and that 'the wisest critic is incompetent when he attempts to comment on his own work or a rival's'. An honest friend, according to Fétis, would have taken Liszt aside:

> . . . What do you mean by this article? Do you hope to destroy a reputation that is inconvenient to you? The judgement of a person involved means nothing; people will see nothing in your criticism but an attempt to hurt a man you fear; they may even conclude that his talent must be greater than yours, and you will have achieved the very opposite of what you intend . . . And whatever do you mean by all these spiteful remarks . . . are they not simply proof of your contempt, indeed your hatred for him?[7]

In his vehement reply to Fétis, Liszt admitted that the editor was not alone: 'You yourself are a pianist, so everyone tells me, therefore you may not judge other pianists; you compose pieces for the piano that do not appeal to us, therefore you may not say that other composers' works are bad. What deep and admirable logic!' Was he supposed to make himself an expert critic of fantasias for violin or concern himself with the harmonics of the timpani and the perfection of pegs for the double bass? 'What! When any schoolboy is allowed to assess composers and performers through the ages, can it be that my eighteen years of study have not earned me the right to express my opinion about good and bad works for the piano?!' Then he turned bitterly to the chief accusation: 'Jealousy . . . envy. Yes, it is true, this foolish, odious accusation has been thrown at me – and – I admit – much as I was prepared for it, it did wound me to the quick – nothing could have preserved me from the accusation that I am envious of Mister Thalberg, whose loyal character no one has ventured to doubt. So I am a jealous man and envious of Mister Thalberg, that is a foregone conclusion, and it could not have been otherwise.'[8]

The urge to compare virtuoso performances (an urge so easily satisfied today with the mere flip of a record) was no longer just a pastime for princes and archbishops, emperors and kings, as it had been in the eighteenth century. The whole of bourgeois society had taken up an interest in the piano, and the great virtuosos no longer awaited a royal invitation to display their talents; they sought out their own audiences in the major cities of Europe. The age of the concert tour had dawned.

In Vienna, a favourite destination for pianists of the day, one critic drew up a sort of score sheet, which he attempted to justify: 'Risky as it is to draw comparison between pianists, one finds oneself almost forced to do so given this rash of recent concerts . . .' He started by listing the general characteristics of the pianists he had heard and observed: Clara Wieck, Adolph Henselt, Franz Liszt and Sigismund Thalberg. Liszt was notable for the passion of his expression, Thalberg for his refined sensuousness, Clara Wieck of course for her rapturous enthusiasm, and Henselt for his genuine German lyricism (whatever that may be). Thalberg was delightful, Liszt demonic, Clara inspirational and Henselt wonderfully exciting. Then he compared the four pianists according to various criteria, for instance:

Clarity of performance:
1. THALBERG
2. CLARA WIECK
3. HENSELT
4. LISZT

Feeling of Warmth:
1. LISZT
2. HENSELT
3. CLARA W.
4. THALBERG

Other criteria in the list, published in the Viennese *Neue Zeitschrift für Musik*, included: '*Improvisation*: Liszt, Clara W. *Deeply artistic nature*: Liszt, Clara. *Towering spirit*: Liszt. *Versatility*: Clara, Liszt, Thalberg, Henselt. *Musical scholarship*: Thalberg, Henselt, Clara,

Liszt. *Musical judgement*: Liszt, Thalberg. *Beauty of Touch*: Thalberg, Henselt, Clara, Liszt. *Boldness*: Liszt, Clara. *Egotism*: Liszt, Henselt. *Willing to recognize others' achievements*: Thalberg, Clara. *Good examples*: Thalberg, Clara. *No grimaces in performance*: Thalberg and Clara.'[9]

There was no lack of build-up to the long-awaited Liszt *v*. Thalberg confrontation in Paris. First Thalberg gave a matinée performance in the auditorium at the Conservatoire, where he played his Moses Fantasia and a paraphrase of 'God Save the King'. The audience was not large but musically informed and beside itself with enthusiasm. Liszt got his own back in grand style: he leased the Paris Opéra, an enormous hall commonly used for lavish musical spectacles. The risk was not small: savage the keyboard as he might, the grand pianos of the time were still limited in terms of volume of sound.

He was risking the impossible, in fact, but the scheme did not backfire. One critic wrote: 'When the curtain rose and we saw that slim young man . . . a sort of awe came over us. All our sympathies were with this fool – for only fools achieve great things. The whole audience shared the dramatic tension, and every ear strained fearfully for the first note. By the fifth bar the battle was half won; under Liszt's fingers the piano throbbed . . .'[10]

Around this time Liszt wrote to his friend George Sand:

Social art is no more and is not yet. Whom are we most likely to meet in our day and age? Sculptors? No, manufacturers of statues. Painters? No, manufacturers of paintings. Musicians? No, manufacturers of music. Everywhere artisans, nowhere artists. And this is agony for a man born to art with all the pride and savage independence of a true child. He sees himself surrounded by this crowd of manufacturers, attentively devoting their services to the moods of the masses and the imagination of the uneducated rich . . .[11]

It sounds almost as if it were Thalberg, not Liszt, who had leased the great opera hall; as if Liszt, not Thalberg, had played in the exclusive auditorium at the Conservatoire.

After all the build-up and all the gossip the actual encounter in the salon of the Princess Belgiojoso was something of an anticlimax. The illustrious setting, the exclusive audience, the prohibitive entrance fee of 40 francs for a worthy cause, and then the long programme including various other artists conspired to dampen the antagonistic flavour of the evening. Liszt was first to perform, playing his Niobe fantasia, then Thalberg followed with his fantasia on *Moses in Egypt*. Both artists refrained from insulting gestures or speech. They greeted one another with such perfect politeness that Liszt afterwards felt compelled to explain: 'But: must they be enemies, when one artist denies another a value ascribed to him by an overly enthusiastic public? Are they then reconciled, when they continue to respect and admire one another in all other respects?'[12]

But who won? There is a sort of judgement in the epigram which Liszt ascribed to his mistress, the Countess d'Agoult, but which legend attributes to his hostess, the Princess Belgiojoso:

'Thalberg is the best pianist in the world.'

And Liszt?

'Liszt – he is the only one.'[13]

MUSIC AS BODY LANGUAGE
Schumann

Our senses are like so many keys on a piano that are struck by our
natural surroundings, and often enough they strike themselves.
Denis Diderot

Music achieved by the fingers alone is sorry work; but music that echoes
from within resounds in every heart, and outlives the brittle body.
Robert Schumann

As a young man Schumann was addicted to his diary. He kept a record
of his debts, his beer consumption and the resultant hangovers; he
noted down the books he had read, his comments on Shakespeare's
characters, and writing ideas of his own. He made a note of something
as concrete as the 'purchase of the Melzer grand piano for 225 thalers'
on 15 June 1831,[1] continuing two days later with a piece of pure
fantasy: 'Two entirely new persons enter my diary as of today – two of
my best friends, although I have never seen them – Florestan and
Eusebius.' He then explained that 'Florestan and Eusebius are the two
sides of my dual personality, whom I would like to melt together to
one man.'[2] This dual personality troubled him: 'It seems to me
sometimes as if my objective self would like to part altogether from my
subjective self, or as if I were somewhere between my appearance and
my reality, between my figure and my shadow. My genius, why have
you forsaken me?'[3] He wrote: 'I am sinking, I am sinking back into the
slime; is there no hand come down from the clouds to hold me? I must
be the hand.' And also: 'Where there is genius, it matters little in what
form . . . it is apparent, be it in gravity, as in Bach, or in ease, as in
Mozart, in warmth, as in Beethoven, or in darkness (. . . not the right
word) as in Schubert, or in nothingness, in me. Stop! There I have
something – nothingness, endless nothingness.'[4]

He kept the diary – and he practised the piano like a man possessed.

For years he had wavered between literature and music, and his family had persuaded him to study law. Then when Friedrich Wieck accepted him as a student early in the 1830s he devoted himself to the piano, determined to become a virtuoso. The diary testifies to his eagerness and his frustrations: 'The Moschele étude nervous and uncertain – how can that be? Worked on it for fourteen days, studied doggedly . . . the dry, cold keys.' Or: 'New beginning – new resolve – started well as usual; eight hours studying Chopin – with fire and purpose.' Sometimes he recorded a whole programme of work:

In passing a schedule of my studies, as followed for the past nine days: from 7–10 solitary work on Chopin with the hand as steady as possible; I follow my plan from page to page but lift out certain passages to practise. At 11 o'clock I usually start on Czerny's trill exercise that cannot be played loosely, softly and lightly enough. Then Hummel's finger exercises in their four classes according to the interval range, to which I add five new ones each and every day. The afternoon I leave entirely to my mood, but am sure to continue with the F sharp minor sonata by Hummel. – Do not be discouraged, dear Robert, if it does not always trip and trill lightly as in the last eight days; practice patiently, lift the fingers gently, hold the hands still and play slowly: and everything will come right again.

The two invented friends contributed their criticism. Eusebius for instance admonished him:

You must practise more. The scales are all right. If only you could control your style, your touch: it is different from day to day. Yesterday you had the one I liked: I'll describe it – your hand rested gently on the keys, the foremost joints curving inwards, the finger striking the key like a little hammer powered by its own strength, the arm and hand remaining still, the finger hardly lifting itself, mostly pressing down.

Then on 8 May 1832 he wrote a brief entry that reads like an alarm signal: 'The third [finger] is coming on reasonably well through use of the cigar mechanism. The movement is independent now.' Behind Wieck's back Schumann had invented a procedure or apparatus intended to perfect his fingering; it is not clear exactly what he did to himself. Artificial gadgets for binding the hands were in fashion at the time, but it seems that Schumann used some method of his own, devised in collaboration with his friend Töpken, a fellow student in Heidelberg. Apparently this involved binding the index finger in some way, so that the middle finger was encouraged to function more independently. At first it seemed to work: 'The third is a little stronger,' according to his entry on 13 May. But just ten days later: 'The third really seems incorrectible.' Then between 14 and 22 June 1832 comes a single succinct comment: 'The third finger is completely stiff.'

Robert Schumann's career as a pianist was finished before it began. He would not accept it at first. On 9 August he wrote to his mother: 'My whole house has turned into an apothecary shop. I had got rather worried about my hand and deliberately put off asking an anatomist, because I was afraid I would hear the worst, that is I was afraid he would say it could not be healed. I made all sorts of plans, was quite decided to take up theology . . . Finally I went to Prof. Kühl, asked him in all conscience whether it would be all right.' The professor prescribed baths in animal extracts: 'The treatment is not attractive, and I worry that something of the bovine nature will rub off on me.' He was advised to play the piano as little as possible.

In 1833 he made one last appeal to a homeopath, although he had virtually abandoned hope: 'I play the piano but little now – do not be shocked – (even I am resigned and think of it as a stroke of fate) on the right hand I have a lame, broken finger; the damage, insignificant in itself, was so exacerbated by neglect that I can hardly play with the hand at all.' By the following year this resignation had given way to an enterprising decision, and he could write to his mother: 'Do not worry yourself about the finger! I can compose without it just as well, and I would hardly be happier as a travelling virtuoso – home has spoiled me for that sort of life. I am even brave enough to improvise in front of other people, as I used to . . .' But when he travelled (which was rarely) and met people who asked to hear him play, the old trouble would flare up like an open wound. In 1838 he wrote to Clara Wieck from Vienna:

Sometimes I feel so miserable with this painful hand, and never more so than here. And I can tell you something: it is getting worse. How often have I cried out to heaven, asking: 'God, why have you done *this* to me?' It would be so useful to me here, with the music so alive and ready within me that it should rush out of me like breath, but as it is I must coax it out so painfully, stumbling with one finger over the other. It is all so dreadful, and has caused me so much suffering.

In the autumn of 1833 his despair deepened when he fell ill with what Henri Pousseur speculates may have been the first outbreak of a venereal disease. There were crises of anxiety, a psychotic phase during which he attempted suicide several times, only to be crazed with grief at his own behaviour, often losing all sense of his identity. In 1827, the year in which he lost his sister Emilie (through suicide) and his father, he had wondered: 'I go through my whole life asking myself: is that you or isn't it? did you do that? – could you have done that? – the whole of the past year flew by me like a dream.' In 1833 again two close relatives died: in October his sister-in-law Rosalie, to whom he was deeply attached, and then a month after that his brother Julius. He wrote to his mother: 'For the past weeks nothing. I was little more than a statue, neither cold nor warm; only a furious spate of work has brought me slowly back to life. But I am still too timid to sleep alone ... Terrible blood pressure, unspeakable fears, loss of breath, momentary spells of fainting ... If you have any conception of this sunken sleep of the soul you will surely forgive me for not having written.'

The trouble with the hand made him abandon his diary. Five years later he came upon the old notebook while staying in Vienna, and he summed up that autumn of 1833:

'Torments of the most agonizing melancholy from October to December – an idée fixe of going mad had come over me.
    '... moved from the fourth floor, where I could no longer bear it, down to the first with Günz.
'Günther as bedmate.'

There is a Schumann legend that one night – 'the night of 17 October – the worst of my life – Rosalie's death the day before' – he tried to jump from the window of his apartment in the Burgstraße.

But it was another twenty years before he actually made the fatal leap.

For all his fear of heights, his dread of going mad, and his recurrent melancholy, the 23-year-old Schumann was a clear-eyed journalist with his wits about him, and he was interested in writing more than a private diary. He was keen to contradict the impression that he only lived in the provincial town of Leipzig, and then mostly in a cosy corner near the fire in the *Kaffee-Baum* coffee house (still as popular as ever); he wanted the world to know that he had his feelers out all over Europe. He saw himself as a man of the future, just like his Florestan: one of 'those rare men of music who seem to anticipate everything new and extraordinary'.[5] Eusebius himself was no slouch in this respect: he was the one Schumann playfully credited with the discovery of Chopin – 'Hats off, gentlemen, to a genius!'[6] It was hard to find a place for such enthusiastic outbursts in the pages of the *Allgemeine Musikalische Zeitung*, a very routine publication: 'But the reviewers are always the same! Have you ever recognized a future maestro – you oxen! What do you say to Beethoven! – how you tremble now to have to allow anything similar . . . Oh if only I could stuff you down a cannon, to get you used to false fifths.'[7]

In April 1834 Schumann and several of his friends – including Clara Wieck's ageing father – founded the *Neue Zeitschrift für Musik*. It was soon the leading musical journal in the German language, and it still exists. At the start of the journal's second year Schumann proudly proclaimed: 'Our convictions were clear from the start. The idea is simple: to remind the world of past ages and their works . . . , to denounce the recent past as an unproductive period, devoted only to the forcing of superficial virtuosity, and finally to prepare the ground for a new poetic age.'[8] The poetic age, poetry itself, had nothing to do with solitary confinement in an ivory tower, not as far as Schumann was concerned. Poetry to him meant mobilization. Harald Eggebrecht summed up his vision: '. . . Schumann's conception of poetry was as a battle cry against all that was stiff, dry and reactionary in academia and society.'[9]

Schumann's imaginary companions were of very practical service to him in producing the journal. Many of his original collaborators soon fell away: Wieck for instance left, and Schumann's talented friend Schunke, also a composer, died in the first year of publication. By using the names of his invented friends Schumann was able to create an impression of many reviewers at work. Twenty years later he was still chuckling at his clever camouflage: 'And here again I refer to that society that was more than secret, in that it existed only in the mind of its founder, the 'Davidsbündler' ['League of David']. It appeared to allow a number of critical attitudes to art to have their say, inventing opposite but not irreconcilable artistic characters, of which Florestan and Eusebius were the most prominent, with Maestro Raro mediating between them. This secret society was the leitmotif of the magazine, combining "Truth and Poetry" in humorous fashion.'[10] (Schumann was certainly fond of codes: Raro is not so much a combination of Florestan and Eusebius as of the names Clara Robert.)

Schumann's games of hide and seek, which he often used as a means of avoiding people, led to some curious episodes. His friend Krägen remembered the time he arrived from Dresden and went to call on Schumann. He pulled the bell, but no one answered. He could hear someone playing the piano in Schumann's room, so he rang again, long and loud. Finally a little window over the courtyard opened, Schumann looked out, said gruffly: 'Oh Krägen, it's you – I'm not at home.' Then he shut the window and went back to his piano.

He did not hide from reality. His magazine was always alive to the currents of the future, in politics as much as in music. Music was presented as a social phenomenon.

> Radical changes in music are as significant as radical changes in politics. In music the new influence is apparent there where the art is most sensuously linked with life, in dance. With the gradual disappearance of the contrapuntal monopoly miniature forms like the saraband and the gavotte faded away, hoop skirts and beauty marks fell out of fashion ... Shortly thereafter Beethoven burst upon the scene, breathless, embarrassed and distraught, with dishevelled hair, his chest and head uncovered like Hamlet, and no one knew what to make of him; but it was too stifling and dull for him in the ballroom, and he stumbled out into the dark ... Now a new generation is growing up ...[11]

Somewhat later Schumann wrote a piece about the true 'instrument' of the new musical generation: the piano. According to his magazine:

> Piano music marks a significant stage in the recent history of music; it was in this music that the first signs of the new genius appeared. The leading musicians of our day are pianists; a comment that has been made in previous times ... The instrument itself has reached a high degree of perfection. As players have progressively improved their technique, and composition, thanks to Beethoven, has become increasingly bold, so the instrument too has grown in range and importance, and if it comes (as I think it will) to the use of a pedal as in the organ, a new range

of possibilities will open up to the composer, and the piano will gradually free itself of the supporting orchestra to become a yet richer instrument, fully mature and independent . . . It would surely be seen as a loss, were the piano concerto with orchestra to fall completely out of fashion; on the other hand we can scarcely gainsay the pianists when they declare: 'We have no need of other support, our instrument is most effective on its own.'[12]

That was a significant observation on Schumann's part: the piano, with its progressively improved mechanism, its increasing volume, and the greater subtlety of its tonal nuances, was fast becoming the new solo instrument. Composers and pianists were beginning to make extraordinary use of its orchestral possibilities, but above all they were beginning to discover its true medium, that peculiarly pianistic territory between full booming sound and profound intimacy – a supremely individualistic domain. The piano sonata was as it were the skeleton of a symphony, but in the 1830s the piano piece as such came into being. All of Schumann's compositions from this period, from Opus 1 (the Abegg Variations) up to Opus 23 ('Nachtstücke' – Nocturnes) are pure piano pieces, a grand phantasmagoria of the instrument's new, inward-turning possibilities, as revealed by the Romantic period. More than ever before the keyboard was a fantasy world, a sound laboratory, an echo chamber of the tortured mind. Romantic composers used the piano to express their passions, their ecstasies, their frenzied rage, their fears and their obsessions. And there is an unprecedented physical aspect to this music. Composer Dieter Schnebel explains:

> In that Schumann – unlike Beethoven, whose work was idealistically aimed at the musical structure – always considered the physical realization of any piece, he could be said to have composed beyond the notes into the fingertips, seeing music as he did – very forward thinking – as a vital and human process. So that his music grew beyond the ideal superstructure of the constructed sound to become a more comprehensive human activity.[13]

Actually one ought to take a much more prosaic approach to Schumann's piano work. Disgruntled contemporaries liked to think of him as a music critic who happened to compose as well. Liszt, never entirely friendly, wrote to Berlioz: 'Our ingenious Schumann has written some enchanting scenes of children! Schumann is a soulful poet and a great musician.' Schumann himself consciously used his literary inventions, and his *doppelgänger* fantasy, in his music as much as in his journalism. Opus 1, the Abegg Variations, is snobbishly dedicated to 'Pauline Comtesse d'Abegg'. There was no such person (though he did know a certain Meta Abegg, not a titled lady but 'an old bag of 26').

Schumann's passion for a verbal masquerade is very evident even in the title of his *Carnaval*, which he composed between 1834 and 1835. The work is full of the classic Comedia dell'arte characters – Pierrot, Harlequin, Coquette, Pantalon and Colombine – all of them rubbing shoulders with figures from Schumann's real and fantasy lives. 'Chopin' and 'Paganini' are there; the ghost of Schubert is conjured up in the 'Valse noble'; even Clara Wieck ('Chiarina') is among them, as well as Ernestine von Fricken ('Estrella'), to whom Schumann was engaged for a time. It goes without saying that there should be a 'Reconnaissance' and then a 'Promenade'. But the 'Sphinxes' are a riddle: minimalist pieces of just four notes, in one case only three – this is music frozen in the form of a picture puzzle. The brief 'Pause' towards the end, on the other hand, is anything but restful: one imagines the whole company in a mad whirl, rushing wildly for the window to watch the final march of the *Neue Zeitschrift* conspirators against the Philistines.

The subtitle of the work is '*Scènes mignonnes sur quatre notes*' – four notes expressly named in the dancing letters passage: 'ASCH–SCHA'. Asch was Ernestine von Fricken's home town, and Scha the four letters of Schumann's own name which can be expressed in musical notes. In *Carnaval* the verbal riddle becomes a musical structure that appears in every piece. These notes, according to Dieter Schnebel, are 'the unifying principle behind this overabundance of tonal images. In almost every one of the 22 pieces they are as it were the serial substance, not really consciously heard but ever present and forming a more or less subconscious unity.'[14]

Opus 6, composed in 1837, is Schumann's last monument to the secret society of his imagination. Its title: 'Davidsbündler – Tänze'. One must resist the temptation to interpret Schumann's works too literally according to their titles, but at first glance this composition does look very much like a lively argument at the *Kaffee-Baum* transcribed for the piano, or a musical debate between Eusebius and Florestan. The movements are initialled almost exactly like articles from the magazine: the first marked jointly Florestan and Eusebius, then alternately F or E. Number 9 is headed 'Hereupon Florestan concluded with a painful twitch on his lips,' and at the end there is this: 'Quite superfluously Eusebius added this, and his eyes shone with happiness.' In a later edition Schumann deleted all such stage directions.

The conceit of the musical debate is in any case only the first layer of meaning in this composition. Schumann intended his beloved Clara Wieck to hear quite a different story in it. On New Year's Day 1837 he wrote to her in Vienna: 'The dances are full of wedding thoughts – they were written in the most wonderful state of excitement I can possibly imagine.'[15] In his next letter he wrote: 'My Clara will know what is in the dances . . . The story is in fact a whole eve-of-wedding party, and now you will be able to fill out the preface and conclusion for yourself. If I was ever happy at the piano, it was while I composed these dances.'[16] Right at the beginning a 'motto' of Clara is written into the music, and the end dies away in the lowest bass notes available in Schubert's piano, a pianissimo outbreath, while a ritardando halts all movement – all the rapture a piano can possibly achieve is there in that finale.

But in the middle of the piece pandemonium breaks out in every movement ascribed to Florestan. The markings only hint at what actually happens – 'ungeduldig' ('impatient') is marked at one point, or 'sehr rasch und in sich hinein' ('very fast and inward-looking'), then 'frisch' ('fresh'), 'balladenmäßig sehr rasch' ('very fast and like a ballad'), and 'wild und lustig' ('wild and merry'). Pounding heartbeats, racing pulse, a breast full to bursting: this is a music of the body, a trance-like state of ecstasy and desire played out on the piano. As Roland Barthes wrote: 'The Schumannesque body will not hold still . . . It is not a meditative body . . . It is an impulsive body, always fidgeting, moving on to something else – thinking of something else; it is flighty, intoxicated, absentminded and impassioned all at once.'[17] Barthes was writing there about the 'Kreisleriana', but what he says applies equally well to many of the 'Davidsbündler' dances: 'In Schumann (to my taste) the keys are struck with too much timidity; the body taking possession of the keyboard is almost always a mediocre body, trained and drained by years of conservatory or career . . . what the virtuoso displays, therefore, is the platitude of his own body, which is incapable of "striking". It is not a question of strength but of fury: the body must do the hammering, not the pianist.'[18]

Schumann certainly paid a price for the novelty of his music: much of his work for the piano was long considered too provincial and peculiar to be taken seriously. In later life Liszt apologized for having neglected Robert Schumann in his many concerts. Frédéric Chopin, whom Schumann so enthusiastically publicized very early in his career, never played a single piece of his, not even the 'Kreisleriana', which was dedicated to him. He did at least reciprocate by dedicating the F major ballad to Schumann, but none of his students ever learned anything by the Leipzig composer.

Another composer who had little time for Schumann was Richard Wagner. In the latter 1840s, when both of them were living in Dresden, they carefully avoided one another. Eduard Hanslick told a revealing little story about the two of them: asked whether he enjoyed Wagner's company, Schumann answered, 'No, as far as I'm concerned Wagner is impossible; he is an ingenious man, but he talks too much.' And then the crosscheck: 'Wagner came to talk about musical conditions and personalities in Dresden, including Schumann: "we are on good terms, but one cannot spend time with Schumann: he is an impossible man, he says nothing." '[19]

The grimmest misjudgement was pronounced by Friedrich Nietzsche, who spoke of 'emotional drunkenness', claiming that 'with him German music was threatened with a deadly fate, that of losing the voice of the European soul and sinking to the level of mere patriotism'. He was fiercely contradicted by Tchaikovsky, who anticipated the contemporary assessment when he wrote: 'Schumann's music strikes chords that his great predecessors never touched. It echoes the secret processes of our souls. Those doubts, depressions and glimpses of the ideal that move the heart of every man today. History for Schumann has not yet begun . . .'[20]

In the end Schumann paid for his music with his sanity. At the end of February 1854 he threw himself off a bridge in Düsseldorf into the wintry Rhine, only to be pulled out and rescued by the crew of a passing boat. Shortly afterwards he voluntarily retired to a sanitorium at Endenich, near Bonn, where he lived on for two and a quarter years, occasionally manhandling a piano set up for him especially.

The agonies of his music afflicted his very soul.

CARL CZERNY: OPUS 500
or: How do I make my entrance?

Czerny is much more sensitive than
all his compositions.
Frédéric Chopin

In Czerny I have always admired
the full-blooded musician much
more than the eminent pedagogue.
Igor Stravinsky

'When the pianist is to play in public (for example in the theatre), it is all the more important that he make a proper entrance, in a decent black suit, as even a small oversight may easily give rise to embarrassing remarks.'[1]

Carl Czerny, the piano teacher par excellence of the nineteenth century, concerned himself with every detail of the pianist's art. His ideal of 'fluency' did not begin and end with pianistic technique: the aspiring pianist, in his view, should be equally fluent in the art of making an entrance, respecting the ceremonial of the concert. His Opus 500, the Pianoforte School, accordingly includes a little manual of etiquette about how to deal with an audience, and with one's own stage fright.

After the three requisite bows (first to the principal box, then to the opposite side, and finally to the centre) he [the player] takes his seat, removes his white gloves, and gives the sign to the orchestra. All preparatory preludes are to be strictly avoided. The player must take care to keep his fingers warm and supple in readiness for his appearance.

Most young artists do not stop to consider how important that first appearance in public will be. The future fortune of the artist depends entirely on whether he was successful, that very first time, in gaining the attention, the admiration and the good will of the audience. The successful débutant assures himself of an attentive future audience, so that no single finesse, no particularly satisfactory passage will go unnoticed . . . It is in the nature of things that a large and therefore mixed audience must be surprised with something extraordinary, and the surest, indeed the only means to that end is: accomplished bravura combined with good taste.[2]

Easily said, but nothing could be more difficult: that moment of entering onto a stage, any stage, never ceases to be one of the trickiest times in a virtuoso's life. In those few steps from the dressing room he will undergo the most terrifying and at the same time most magnificent metamorphosis – the piano standing out there so stolidly is suddenly surrounded by an almost visible aura of expectation, the pianist himself encircled in a whispering, rustling, rumbling silence, and the tension physically manifested in the crackling spark that leaps across to him from an 'electrified' audience. Suddenly the piano seems to belong to the auditorium rather than to the pianist, whose first job must be to recapture the instrument, its familiar keyboard now nothing less than the 'giant black-and-white teeth' (Alberto Savinio) of the public creature out there. (The pianist is always at a disadvantage compared with any other soloist, in that he is forever playing on unfamiliar instruments. There is in fact nothing more understandable than the notorious insistence of certain pianists that their own piano accompany them on any tour, whatever the complications of transport.)

But to continue: it is not just the piano that is transformed, but the pianist's own body. The sudden dizziness, the momentary loss of sight are only the mildest symptoms of stage fright. It's the hands that worry him. Suddenly they seem to be no good to anyone – stricken with cold, bone white, the fingers trembling or frozen stiff. 'Warming up' – just like a football player – is all very well, but those few seconds or minutes until the first chord are as good as a bout of frostbite. Experienced pianists have any number of ways of dealing with this crippling situation: some fidget endlessly with the piano bench, others pull out black or white handkerchiefs to be deposited in strategic places, another may twitch his cuffs or coat-tails, where a lady will pat down or puff up her hair, arrange her skirts, or simply sit still, visibly pulling herself together. Vladimir Ashkenazy has a way of surprising the audience by plunging into the music before the welcoming applause has died down, thus covering any initial nervousness in the clapping of many hands.

Carl Czerny – who himself performed in public – has a word of comfort for the aspiring pianist:

> Many students, when asked to play before an audience, exhibit an almost childish anxiety and awkwardness, and make a sorry mess of all that they have learned. This evil habit . . . is in most cases easily cured:
> 1. A student who has mastered the basic principles of my teaching, a calm, firm touch, correct fingering, and proper posture, will not be so susceptible to anxiety.
> 2. A student who takes care not to play a piece before an audience until he knows it so well that he can play it in private at least ten times in succession without a single mistake – such a student will be less likely to fall prey to any glaring awkwardness.
> 3. It is also important that a student take time to learn which pieces are suitable for performance . . .[3]

There are two significant insights in Czerny's dry three-point programme that most pianists would still accept in principle. Firstly, that confidence in performance has to do with self-confidence (including confidence in one's technique) and individual perfectionism. Secondly, that one can practise the art of appearing before an audience just as well as one can practise scales – it's a simple matter of performing in public as often as possible. One can learn to control one's nerves.

Another interesting point in Czerny's Opus 500 is his recommendation that the piano be positioned with the treble keys nearest the audience, as is usual nowadays. At the time this was a relatively novel suggestion. For concerts in aristocratic music rooms and salons the audience usually sat in a circle around the piano, so that its positioning depended only on the proportions of the room. The problem did not arise until concerts came to be held in large public halls. Apparently it was the Bohemian virtuoso Jan Ladislav Dussek who first placed the piano sideways on, not for any musical or acoustic reason, but because he had a remarkable profile.

As music historian Harold C. Schonberg noted, Dussek

> was the first to sit with his right side to the audience. This way two ends were accomplished. Dussek was able to exhibit his noble profile and the

bow of the piano; and the raised lid of the instrument could act as a sounding board, throwing tone directly into the auditorium. Johann Wenzel Tomaschek, himself a pianist from Prague and a countryman of Dussek, later was to boast about Dussek's revolutionary achievement. Nobody can take *that* away from him, Tomaschek pointed out, and added that all other pianists hastily followed suit, 'although they may have no very interesting profiles to exhibit'.[4]

Eduard Hanslick, that famous and much-feared critic, frequently sounded forth on the posture or attitude of a pianist. (Aspiring pianists nowadays are advised to practise with the aid of a mirror.) Here is Hanslick on the undesirability of distracting behaviour:

> It may seem harsh to tell a young artist that it would be best to hear him when he is out of sight, – but one day he will know to thank us for it. Mr Treiber loves – perhaps without knowing he does it – to mime the whole course of his effusive emotions throughout his performance. Now we know of nothing more disturbing than that habit of lifting the eyes to heaven at every fermata, painfully shaking the head at every minor chord, or nodding six times at a figure of six accentuated notes. If this is, as we gladly believe, nothing but an unconscious expression of heartfelt emotion, then Mr Treiber must learn to control his unconscious. It is by no means a matter of indifference how a player conducts himself in performance. True feeling flows through the *sounds* alone surely and directly into the soul of the listener; no one will pay him a penny for all he expresses with his eyes, head and shoulders.[5]

Such melodramatic mimicry has by no means entirely died out, as one can easily see by glancing at a few contemporary record covers. Whoever is responsible for all those embarrassing expressions of rapture and tragedy – be it photographers, record publishers, or consumers – one cannot help wishing that the artists themselves would refuse to have any part of it.

Then there is that new tendency to conduct one's own performance, as it were: arms thrown up at the end of a dramatic passage as if vaulting the heavens, or the whole element of surprise robbed from an attacca transition, fortissimo to sudden pianissimo, by the pianist's cowering posture. Not that there is much to be said for a performance entirely lacking in temperament; it is just that this sort of affected over-emphasis should be discouraged before it comes back into fashion.

Dussek may have determined the positioning of the piano, but it seems that Clara Wieck was responsible for another innovation introduced at about this time. There is no definite proof, but contemporary reports would indicate that she was the first virtuoso to perform from memory. In the spring of 1837 she appeared in Berlin: Rellstab called her programme 'monotonous' and spoke of 'half-empty halls', and various other listeners were positively irritated by the fact that she dispensed with sheet music and page turner. Bettina von Arnim called her 'one of the most insufferable artists I have ever known. How pretentiously she sits at the piano, and now *without* a score. How modest Doehler seems beside her . . . !'[6]

In order to understand why Bettina found this habit of Clara's so insufferably pretentious one must remember that, up to that point, pianists had played without scores only when they improvised, relying then on their imaginations alone. Apparently it was the custom to refer to a score even when playing a piece of one's own composition – and no wonder, given the prolific genius of the great composers of the period. Clara must have given an impression of coyly pretending to improvise, or of pretending to play a piece of her own (she had composed one or two things), or even of taking liberties with another composer's work. No one will have believed that she could possibly remember every note. (There is in fact reason to believe that her version of the 'Appassionata', as she played it in those years, was only an approximation of the original.)

Czerny also has something to say on this point, and again it is surprisingly practical advice. 'It is a very useful thing to be able to play a number of pieces from memory, so that one is not forever encumbered with heaps of music, and it is an ability which does credit to the pianist. How often it happens that one comes across a fortepiano unexpectedly, and how unpleasant it is on such occasions to have to apologize, after a few stumbling attempts, that one knows nothing off by heart.'[7] He advises every one of his better students to be confident of at least a dozen pieces at any one time, always including one or two fugues.

On the other hand Czerny is not unaware of the drawbacks of this useful habit: 'There are students who have such an excellent memory for music that they continually embarrass their teacher by playing any piece from memory after just a few attempts and thereafter preferring not to look at the score. The unfortunate result is that the student thus accustoms himself to an inexact performance and neglects his sight-reading skills.'[8] In such cases Czerny simply moved the student onto something else, and soon afterwards onto something else again, so that he was forced to practise the precise art of reading a score.

This Carl Czerny was a curious man, a sort of Sisyphus of the piano, and a butler to virtuosity. He had a childish pride in big numbers. As he wrote in a brief autobiographical account of his work as a composer: '. . . thus it is easy to see how the numbers of my compositions grew to 100, 200, 300 etc., not counting the equally numerous arrangements, which were never numbered.'[9] He almost made it to an Opus 800, and he left notebooks containing over ten thousand (!) themes and motifs. It is this naïve delight in sheer quantity that makes it hard to suppress a certain tone of mockery in any portrait of the man. But there is also something very touching about his industriousness and his determination to preserve the great tradition while at the same time keeping up with contemporary innovations. He worked hard, not just at his own compositions, but also to ensure that every sort of piano music was kept in print: he even re-published Bach's *The Art of the Fugue* as well as *The Well-Tempered Clavier*.

When Czerny died, on 15 June 1857, at the age of sixty-six, he left a fortune of 100,000 florins – certainly enough, in its modern equivalent, to make him a millionaire. A confirmed bachelor, he left a part of his fortune to his landlady and her brother – the rest went to charity. He had had a long and busy life – but was it really a life?

As a child he had once gone with his father Wenzel Czerny, also a piano teacher, on a visit that might have changed his life, had it not been so steeped in pedantry. It was in January 1801, an unforgettable experience: the day he met Beethoven.

Czerny's account is coloured by the familiar chaos that surrounded the great man: 'The room was a mess, papers and bits of clothing scattered everywhere . . . Beethoven himself was in a jacket of long haired dark-gray stuff and stockings of the same, so that he at once reminded me of Campe's picture of Robinson Crusoe . . . I also noticed, with the quick eye of a child, that in each ear he had a bit of cotton that seemed to be soaked in some yellow liquid . . . I had to play straight away.'[10]

Beethoven was impressed; he decided on the spot to take the boy on as a student: 'Send him to me a few times each week.' The ten-year-old was delighted with everything Beethoven taught him, above all about the art of playing legato, but then something happened that was entirely typical of the Czernys' petty bourgeois mentality. 'Since my father did not like to let me go alone into town and therefore always took me to Beethoven himself, which caused him to miss any number of lessons, and since Beethoven was often busy composing when we arrived and therefore excused himself, after a while my lessons were interrupted, and I was thrown back again on my own hard work.'[11]

Two years went by before Czerny met Beethoven again in Prince Lichnovsky's salon, on which occasion the great man roundly scolded his father for interrupting the boy's lessons. He declared that he was not impressed with the twelve-year-old's work: his father had obviously not been strict enough. Wenzel Czerny answered like a character in a melodrama: 'Ach, Herr von Beethoven, he is our only son.'[12]

Some ten years later the young Czerny himself was the famous teacher to whom ambitious fathers brought their hopeful sons. One of these visits turned out to be the second great encounter of Czerny's life.

Czerny wrote:

One morning in the year 1819 a man came to me with a little boy of about eight years and asked me to let the child play something for me on the fortepiano. He was a pale, weak-looking child, and while he played he swayed about on the stool as if drunk, so that I often feared he would fall to the floor. His playing was quite uneven, impure and muddled, and he had so little idea of fingering that he threw his hands across the keys quite arbitrarily. But despite all that I was astonished at the talent nature had given him. He played several things I gave him at sight, as a pure naturalist, but for that very reason in a way that made it all the more clear that nature herself had meant him to be a pianist. It was the same when I gave him a theme for improvisation, as his father requested. Without the least knowledge of harmonics he brought a certain sense of genius to his performance. The father told me . . . he was a low-ranking civil servant at the court of the Esterhazys, that he had so far instructed his son himself, and he begged me to take on his little Franzi . . .

Carl Czerny himself, for all the advice he gave as to how to make an entrance, how to bow, when to remove the white gloves, what sort of suit to wear, scarcely ever gave a concert, much less a concert tour. He had many reasons, above all this one: 'My performance always lacked the brilliant and well-prepared charlatan quality that is so necessary to most travelling virtuosos.'[13]

The little boy he took under his wing that day, little Franzi, had more than enough of that quality, and genius besides. So Carl Czerny, that shy performer, came to teach the most famous virtuoso of the century.

And now his solo entrance: Franz Liszt!

'Le concert, c'est moi!'
Franz Liszt and the Decade of Virtuosity

> The attraction of the virtuoso for the
> audience is rather like the attraction
> of the circus for the crowd. One keeps
> hoping that something sensational will
> happen – that Mr X will climb up onto
> Mr Y's shoulders to play his violin,
> or that Mr Z will conclude his recital
> by picking up the piano in his teeth.
> *Claude Debussy*

Berlioz called him the 'king of pianists'. Between 1838 and 1847 Franz Liszt gave some three thousand concerts all over Europe. From Paris to St Petersburg, London to Vienna, Berlin to Budapest – wherever Liszt could find an auditorium, be it national theatre or hotel lobby, opera house or university lecture hall, Liszt set up his piano and played. It was the age of the railway, and Liszt criss-crossed the continent in a luxurious 'Offenbach' carriage (parlour car, dining car and sleeper all in one). Music-lovers paid exorbitant prices for tickets to his concerts. Audiences showered him with flowers, jewels, even locks of ladies' hair. For a full decade Franz Liszt was the leading cultural phenomenon throughout Europe.

> I am the height of fashion. You will not believe how difficult it is for me to find a quarter-hour for myself. I can lock my door and hang a card on it signed by the doctor, but it's no use, my room is always full to bursting, it is quite unbearable. My life is magnificently monotonous: I am flattered and fêted by the whole world. In 24 hours they sold fifty copies of my portrait. Do not insult me by thinking that all this makes the least impression on me.[1]

Liszt earned a fortune with his playing. Sometimes he accepted

12,000 francs, but on one tour in Paris and Madrid he earned 20,000 francs per concert. He did have heavy financial responsibilities, however: he supported his mother and his mistress, the Countess d'Agoult, who spent enormous sums to maintain her position in Parisian high society. Then there were the three children attending the most expensive boarding schools in town. And everywhere he went he was besieged by fund-raisers for any number of worthy causes. Almost every second concert he gave was to benefit one charity or another. He played in aid of the Cologne cathedral and the Beethoven memorial in Bonn; he played to raise money for the poor people of Hamburg and the victims of flood in Budapest; he played for the Leipzig pension fund for poor musicians, for a Mozart foundation, and for the wounded survivors of the battle of Borodino. There were certain needy musicians, such as the Italian singer Pantaleoni, who seemed to hold a subscription to his good services. But Liszt never neglected his own pocket, nor his vanity.

'On Friday I played in the theatre in aid of the poor. The hall was full, a very rare thing in Preßburg. Again and again I was called back to the piano. The applause redoubled when I played the first chords of the Rakoczy march . . . I am convinced that you too would have been moved, for these people are no Viennese loudmouths, these are proud and generous souls.'[2]

Throughout Europe Liszt's fame went before him. Berlin critic Ludwig Rellstab described his triumphant departure from Berlin: 'He left not like a king but *as* a king . . .'[3] And a very royal arrogance was ascribed to him in any number of anecdotes. A Russian general was said to have asked him scornfully whether he had ever stood on a field of battle. Liszt was supposed to have answered: No, and had His Excellency ever played the piano? The piano was Liszt's battlefield, as Robert Schumann wrote: 'It is no longer a question of this or that style of playing but the pure expression of a bold nature determined to conquer fate not with dangerous weapons but by the peaceful means of art.'[4]

One young lady listener was beside herself with enthusiasm: 'His appearance at the piano is indescribable, he is submerged in the piano . . . His passion knows no bounds . . . Right at the start he broke three brass strings on the Conrad Graf . . . The missing bass note did not disturb him in the least – he must be used to it.'[5]

That young enthusiast grew up to become one of his great critics, full of scorn for all his imitators: her name was Clara Wieck-

Schumann. But Liszt never lacked for swooning admirers, among them many of the crowned heads of Europe – Czar Nicholas I, Queen Victoria, Isabella of Spain, the queen of Portugal and the king of Denmark. As for Louis Philippe, the bourgeois king in Paris, he knew Liszt well when he was just the Duke of Orléans, and 'petit Litz' himself a young unknown cosseted by the ladies at court. The great writers also came to his concerts – Victor Hugo, Balzac, Alexandre Dumas and George Sand, and sometimes even Heinrich Heine, scornful as he was of Liszt's excessive reputation. The composers came too – Meyerbeer, Mendelssohn and Schumann, Spohr, and of course his old teacher, Czerny. The cartoonists were always there: the vain virtuoso was a perfect victim for caricature. Liszt was lucky to have friends like Berlioz:

> . . . then there was supper. Most of the virtuosos, critics and culture-lovers in town were there . . . Liszt was unanimously elected to give a speech. For the first toast he spoke, in the name of the assembled company, for at least a quarter of an hour in my honour. Unfortunately he drank as much as he spoke . . . Belloni [Liszt's secretary] and I were fully occupied until two o'clock in the morning, marching him up and down the streets of Prague in an attempt to persuade him to wait till dawn before exchanging shots at two paces with some Bohemian who had bested him in the drinking bout. The next day he was due to play at noon. At half past eleven he was still asleep; woken at last, he got into the carriage, arrived at the concert hall, received three rounds of applause and played, in my opinion, better than he had ever played in his life. There is a god of pianists . . .[6]

From about the end of the 1830s Liszt refused to participate in the mixed concerts so popular at the time, for which the usual programme was a potpourri of orchestral overtures and vocal numbers, with the solo pianist squeezed in somewhere, and often only as accompanist. Liszt may not have invented the solo recital, but he was the first pianist who dared present himself unaccompanied not just in the intimacy of the music room, but in the great concert halls. The risk was social, musical, financial – and acoustic. On 4 June 1839 he wrote from Rome to the Princess Belgiojoso:

> Imagine that, wearied with warfare, not being able to put together a programme that would have common sense, I have ventured to give a

series of concerts all by myself, affecting the Louis XIV style, and saying cavalierly to the public, '*le concert, c'est moi.*' For the curiosity of the thing, I copy a programme of my soliloquies for you:

1. Overture to *William Tell*, performed by M. Liszt.
2. Fantasy on reminiscences of *I Puritani*, composed and performed by the above-named.
3. Studies and Fragments, composed and performed by same.
4. Improvisations on a given theme – still by same.[7]

Audiences came to expect to hear a selection of his more famous arrangements: his transcription of Beethoven's 'Pastorale'; his paraphrase of Schubert's 'Erlkönig' with dramatic emphasis on the ride to death; his fantasia on themes from Meyerbeer's opera *Robert der Teufel* or the variations on *Don Giovanni*. Liszt was not just a solo pianist: he refused to appear with an orchestra, but he none the less attempted to replace it with his solitary piano. No singer appeared on stage with him, but the piano was made to sing. He also loved to astound his audience by playing old-fashioned chromatic fugues by Bach, or Beethoven's impossible 'Hammerklavier' sonata. He was a showman, an adventurer, a born performer even when he was not playing.

> Should I tell you about Madame Pleyel? Why not? Some days before the concert she asked me whether I would give her my arm on Thursday, to introduce her to the audience . . . When the day came she sent for me a quarter of an hour before the concert and begged me again to do her the honour; so I introduce her to the audience, and the audience applauds and is beside itself with delight at my gallantry, my perfect manners (I wore a charming morning suit with gold buttons, patent leather shoes and an incomparable waistcoat!) . . . By the way I am spending a fortune on the tailor, I am unspeakably elegant these days.[8]

Liszt loved to dress himself up, appearing one night as penitent, the next as Bohemian, now the philosopher, now the snobbish dandy, now the half-caste gipsy, now the full-blooded Hungarian. He once entered his occupation and origins in a hotel register as follows: musician-philosopher, born on Parnassus, arrived from Doubt, bound for Truth. He was more pragmatic about the details of his wardrobe:

Send me via Erard: 1. the Hungarian coat with fur (it's called a séké) and include the wrapping for the coat; 2. the Hungarian nightshirt and the pair of blue Turkish trousers, along with another pair of morning trousers of the same sort in white (curious material); 3. my medallion of Bovy (do not forget the picture in the nightshirt and the statuette of Dantan, if possible); 4. my gray coat ... I am sending you the *Atheneum* by post, one of London's best newspapers. Have the article about me translated at once and send it to Specht, the editor of Schlesinger's *Revue Musicale*.[9]

Liszt would appear on stage like an exclamation point in black, a tall, gaunt, small-shouldered figure, long in the face as well as the nose, with dark hair down to his shoulders, long arms by his sides, and those famous long fingers. With the shadow of a smile on his pale, ascetic face he would bow ever so slightly, leaving the left hand on his narrow hip. There was an easy grace about him, a soothing elegance, as if it were his role to reassure the audience that all would be well.

'Yesterday morning, Sunday, received at home: Moscheles, Batta, Lord Burghesk, d'Orsay, Polez and about ten others. I played the Tarantella. Everyone delighted. Spent the evening at Lady Blessington's; she by the way said something pretty about me to Reeve, who introduced me on Friday evening – "What a pity to waste such a man on the piano!" '[10]

Then he would stride over to the piano, bow again, sit down, and sweep the hair from his brow behind his ears. It is a myth that he played with gloves on; he liked to take them off, slowly, and drop them on the floor. Liszt was a consummate performer: he played with his audience. Robert Schumann claimed that 'This power to subjugate an audience, to lift it, carry it and let it fall at will, was more pronounced in him than in any other artist, Paganini excepted.' Schumann added: 'He must be heard and seen as well; Liszt should not be allowed to play in the wings – a great part of his poetry would be lost thereby.'[11] Heine described the development of his performance technique over the years: 'In the old days, for example, when he played a stormy passage on the pianoforte, we would see the lightning flash across his face, his limbs rattling in the wind while his long hair streamed with imagined rain. Now he will play through the most violent thunderstorm like a traveller perched on the summit of an Alp, surveying the tempest in the valley below . . .'[12]

There is no doubt that Liszt's powers of suggestion as a pianist were a function of his showmanship, his instinct for dramatic gesture, as much as of his technical skill. He pulled faces; he leapt up and down the keyboard, sometimes kicking away the piano stool; he writhed like a python and moved his head back and forth like a man watching a game of tennis. But his hands were always the focus of attention (if the caricaturists are to be believed), flying like so many birds across the keys. He had little regard for the niceties of left and right, refusing to recognize the traditional divison of the keyboard: his right hand might commandeer whole passages in the bass, while the left crossed over to the descant. 'He does what he likes,' as Moscheles said, 'throws his hands high in the air – and yet it is astonishingly seldom that he hits a wrong note.'

It was the calculated passion of his performance that aroused the sympathy of his listeners: he flattered them with his openness, demanded their sympathy with his manifest emotion, and at the same time showed them how to respond to every note. As the Viennese critic Carl Kunt remarked, 'It is this magnificent tragic enthusiasm of Liszt's performance that is so exciting, so uplifting.'[13]

There were times when Liszt's enthusiasm bordered on the grostesque. He wrote:

A burlesque little incident all but jeopardized the success of the evening. Just before the Puritans motif a string snapped. The tuner appeared *subito*, intending to remove it, but did not manage to do so. As the string was not in my way, I went on playing, and as the tuner also went on fumbling for the string without success, I told him two or three times to go away and leave it. The good man did not hear me. In the end I gave him a heavy clap with one hand, while I continued to play with the other. The clap echoed around the hall. The tuner disappeared into the wings. Sensing his departure I stood up from the piano, turned to the audience, and commanded the tuner to take away the piano I had been playing on and bring out the one standing ready in reserve. When he later emerged to tune the new piano some members of the audience attempted to applaud him, but most of them whistled and jeered. The poor devil really had a hard time of it . . .[14]

He did seem to play as if the devil were in him. There is a story that one admirer, introduced to him after a concert, said: 'You are either Franz Liszt or the devil incarnate.' A very indicative anecdote, not so much for Liszt as for the popular conception that virtuosity and devilishness are somehow linked. The same story is told about Johann Sebastian Bach, heard at the organ – 'That is either Bach or the devil!' It is interesting that the devil is supposed to be the virtuoso, while God, in whose honour so much music is written and performed, is never accredited with that particular talent. Another of Liszt's admiring critics mentioned a possible pact with the devil: 'Now we have heard him, this extraordinary [pianist], who in a more superstitious century would surely have been condemned to death without mercy, on the grounds that such accomplishment must be inachievable without the aid of the Powers of Evil ... one need only consider the almost lugubrious and yet childlike visage – those sharp-hewn features, reminiscent of Paganini.'

Few critics failed to mention Liszt's resemblance to Paganini, who was himself suspected of evil associations. When Paganini died, Liszt did not hesitate to exhume the old clichés:

Paganini's fire is quenched ... and with it the world of art has lost a miraculous apparition such as it will never see again. His unspeakable genius could only be construed as the fruit of unspeakable deeds, and many admirers suspected he had sold his soul to the devil, and that every fourth string of the violin from which he coaxed such enchanting sound was made from the gut of his wife, whom he was said to have strangled with his own bare hands.[15]

As a young man Liszt had dreamed of becoming the Paganini of the piano, but when he attained his ambition he fought passionately to free himself of the inevitable comparison. Paganini seemed to follow him like a Mephisto; the unshakable association became a sort of existential Faustian drama for him. Which may explain why his obituary for Paganini begins to sound like a curse:

Every desire, every passion, even his own genius was alien to him; for what is genius but the priestly power revealing its godhead to the human soul? And Paganini's god was none other than his own dismally sorry soul! Art must not be seen as a convenient medium for selfish advantage and fruitless fame, but as a sympathetic power which brings men together and binds them to one another. In one's own life one must aspire to that ideal dignity that is the goal of all talent ... To control public opinion through an exemplary life, that is the task that every artist must set himself who aspires to be Paganini's heir. May the artist of the future joyfully renounce the vain, egotistical role which, as we hope, found its last representative in Paganini; may he set his goal within and not outside himself, and may virtuosity be his means, not his end. *Génie oblige*!

Virtuosity, in other words, was no exotic phenomenon but a blessing to mankind: clearly Liszt hoped to raise his own prestige by claiming a wider social significance for his talent. '*Génie oblige*!' is no expression of modesty; the last thing he intended was to renounce the narcissism of the virtuoso. Long since independent of generous patrons, he himself wished to be seen as a patron of the arts, a soloist and social authority in one, unreachable yet exemplary.

The transformation was made possible by Liszt's chosen instrument – the piano. No violinist could have assumed the role of the authoritative virtuoso, whose art 'brings men together and binds them to one another'. The solipsistic intimacy of the violin had to be replaced by the social range of the piano, the delicate husk of an instrument held closely to the body replaced by a thundering piece of furniture which the pianist could be said to play in the name of all those present. The violinist was an isolated phenomenon from another world of sound, while the pianist commanded a terrain familiar to virtually every listener. That made the latter more human – and doubly sensational.

As Liszt moved on to glory, even his piano-playing predecessors lost heart. Heine mourned their passing:

> The older pianists retreat to the shadows, and these poor, discarded invalids of fame suffer greatly for having been overestimated in their youth. Only Kalkbrenner holds his own to some extent. He performed again this summer; his lips gleam still with that same embalmed smile that we observed on the face of the Egyptian pharaoh whose mummy was unwrapped at the museum here recently. Henry Herz is remembered only for his concert hall; he is long since dead, and has recently married.[16]

One of Liszt's great ambitions was to play the unplayable. He reworked his early études, making them more orchestral, breaking up the fluency that betrayed Czerny's influence and introducing new difficulties, as if he himself were the only rival he had left. All the études were as yet unnamed, but sometime in the early 1840s he returned to the fourth one he had written as a young man, entitled it 'Mazeppa', dedicated it to Victor Hugo, and rewrote the finale. It is now the most famous, the most spectacular, and technically the most difficult of all his études. Mazeppa, Ivan Ivanovitch Mazeppa, was the lover of the wife of a Polish nobleman who (in Victor Hugo's version) strapped him to a horse and chased him out onto the steppe, where he was rescued and crowned a king. Mazeppa in fact was a great romantic hero, beloved of Byron as well as Hugo. Liszt played his own Mazeppa again and again.

Later Liszt reworked the études once more, tempering some of the most difficult passages and giving them names like 'Eroica', 'Feux Follets' (Will-o'-the-wisp), 'Harmonies du Soir', 'Recordanza', 'Paysage' and others. Then he gave the whole set a title calculated to preserve them from general usage, as if he wished to ensure an exclusive prerogative for the ultimate virtuoso: he called them his 'Etudes d'exécution transcendante'.

By which he meant that these works transcended the possibilities of human performance, perhaps even that they aspired to a sphere of utopian skill, where sound is vision. *D'éxécution transcendante* – a virtuoso's glissando, perhaps, towards a future truth. Liszt indicated something of the sort in a letter: 'The time has come for me . . . to throw down my butterfly mask of virtuosity and give free rein to my thoughts.'[17]

Franz Liszt gave his last public concert in Jelisawetgrad, Elizabeth-town, a small Russian garrison. Afterwards the Russian musician Alexander Nikolaievitch Serov, who had been in the audience, turned to his diary: 'It is now almost two hours since I left the concert hall. But I am still quite beside myself. Where am I? Where are we? Is this reality or is it a dream? Is it true, that I was permitted to hear Liszt?'[18]

CIVIL WAR AND THE WILD WEST
Gottschalk's Adventures in America

Louis Moreau Gottschalk, America's first world-famous pianist, lived for a time on the lip of an extinct volcano on Guadeloupe. He was tired of people, tired of women in particular, and he camped there on the crater like a monk. He had a small hut, perched high above the island, with a little terrace and a bit of ground beyond, dotted with thickets of bamboo and cactus. The last inhabitant had asked to be buried there, and a white stone marked his grave. Gottschalk enjoyed the scenery.

> Every evening I moved my piano out upon the terrace, and there, in view of the most beautiful scenery in the world, which was bathed by the serene and limpid atmosphere of the tropics, I played, *for myself alone*, everything that the scene opened before me inspired – and what a scene! Imagine a gigantic amphitheater, such as an army of Titans might have carved out in the mountains; to the right and left virgin forests filled with wild and distant harmonies that are like the voice of silence; before me sixty miles of country whose magic perspective is rendered more marvelous by the transparency of the atmosphere; over my head the azure of the sky; below the declivities, surmounted by the mountain, descending gradually toward the plain; farther on, the green savannas, then, lower, a gray point – it is the town; and farther on again the immensity of the ocean, whose line of deep blue forms the horizon . . . I let my fingers run over the keyboard, wrapped up in the contemplation of these marvels . . .[1]

Gottschalk, born in New Orleans in 1829, was the first American pianist to gain a reputation in Europe. Many of his compositions were clearly inspired by the Creole music of his home town. At the age of fifteen he went to Paris, to study first with Charles Hallé and then with Camille Stamaty, and he was soon a welcome guest in the fashionable salons of that city. Shortly after his sixteenth birthday, in April 1845, he gave his first public concert in the Salle Pleyel. Hector Berlioz was intrigued; Chopin is supposed to have hailed him as the future 'king of pianists'.

Success in Paris was followed by a tour through the concert halls of Europe. In Spain he was so popular that he stayed for two years. Then in the autumn of 1852 he sailed into New York harbour, and on 11 February 1853 he held his American début in the ballroom of Niblo's Garden. Phineas T. Barnum immediately offered him a year's contract for a spectacular tour around the country, but Gottschalk refused, preferring to stay in New York. In the winter of 1855–6 he gave eighty concerts there. That cured him of the big city for some time, and he set off on his lonely Caribbean adventure, not to return for six full years.

> I again began to live according to the custom of these primitive countries, which, if they are not strictly virtuous, are nonetheless terribly attractive ... In the depths of my conscience I sometimes heard a voice that recalled me to what I was, to what I ought to be, and imperiously commanded me to return to a healthy and active life. But ... the idea of again appearing before a polished audience seemed to me, very honestly, absurd.[2]

The life to which Gottschalk returned was certainly active, but by no means healthy. America was in the middle of its Civil War, and Moreau kept getting caught between the fronts. The following incident was typical of his life on tour:

> The other day in the car, there being no seat, I took refuge in the baggage car, and there I smoked for two hours, seated on the case of my piano, alongside of which, o human frailty! were two other cases also enclosing instruments, now mute, since the principle that made them vibrate, under a skillful touch, like a keyboard, has left them. They were the bodies of two young soldiers killed in one of the recent battles.[3]

Gottschalk's *Notes of a Pianist* are a curious mixture of wartime reportage, satirical social commentary and Wild West adventure – and at the same time they tell the quixotic tale of the triumphal march of the piano across North America. It was an eventful chapter in the nineteenth-century history of the instrument, a story full of tragic and comic episodes: the piano in the war, the piano in the Gold Rush, and the many pianos in the first of the monster concerts that were to lead, eventually, to the extravaganza at the opening of the Los Angeles

Olympics, which featured a thundering rendition of 'Rhapsody in Blue' as played on eighty pianos at once.

In the middle of June 1863 Gottschalk and his small troupe were on tour in Pennsylvania. The company included impresario Max Strakosch and Strakosch's wife, Amalia Patti (sister of the famous Patti), who was a singer. Sometimes a male singer travelled with them. The piano tuner always did. In Williamstown, still just within Unionist (i.e. Northern) territory, there were signs of mobilization as the troops prepared to make a stand against General Lee's secessionist Confederates. People on the streets were agitated; there were appeals for reinforcement from any able-bodied men; drums sounded in the night.

Strakosch had arranged a concert for the following evening in Harrisburg, the capital of Pennsylvania. Gottschalk urged him to cancel it, convinced that the city would be captured or at least besieged within the next few days. But Strakosch did not want to break the contract, and the following morning found them all in a train bound for Harrisburg, which may or may not have been taken by the time they reached it. Shortly before they arrived the train suddenly stopped, blocked by a pile-up of freight trains and extra cars of every sort, all of them packed full with goods hastily shipped out of the city in the hope that they would not fall into enemy hands.

As Gottschalk told it:

> The train stops in the middle of the bridge over the Susqehanna – why? The anxiety increases. Can you conceive anything more terrible than the expectation of some vague, unknown danger? Some passengers have sat upon the floor so as to be sheltered from bullets in case the train should be fired upon.
>
> One hour of anxiety . . . But the train standing in the middle of the bridge, the silence, the unknown, the solitude that surrounds us, the river whose deep and tremulous waves murmur beneath our feet, and, above all, our ignorance of what is taking place in front and what awaits us at the station – is not all this enough to worry us?[4]

So Louis Moreau Gottschalk and his companions took their fates in their hands and walked to the station, a distance of about twenty minutes on foot. Great mountains of trunks and cases blocked the tracks at the entrance to the freight station. One of the mountains had been pierced by a locomotive, which had tunnelled its way through.

Open suitcases disgorged their contents, and an elegantly-dressed pickpocket was busy inspecting the wreckage. Gottschalk made a cheering discovery:

> What luck! I have just caught a glimpse of my two pianos – the cowardly mastadons – (Chickering forgive me!) snugly lying in a corner and in perfect health. These two mastadons, which Chickering made expressly for me, follow me in all my peregrinations. The tails of these monster pianos measure three feet in width. Their length is ten feet; they have seven and a half octaves, and despite all this formidable appearance possess a charming and obedient docility to the least movement of my fingers.[5]

In the middle of a war zone he found time to praise his piano-maker, of Chickering & Sons in Boston, a firm employing five hundred workers with a production capacity of 42 pianos per week. The more recent models were certainly worthy of comparison with the established European makes. The enthusiastic pianist went on to apostrophize his instruments:

> Poor pianos! Perhaps tomorrow you will have lived! You will probably serve to feed the fine bivouac fire of some obscure Confederate soldier, who will see your harmonious bowels consumed with an indifferent eye, having no regard for the three hundred concerts that you have survived and the fidelity with which you have followed me in my Western campaigns.[6]

In those days the West meant everything to the west of the federal capital in Washington – places like Chicago, Detroit, and St Louis. It was by no means all wilderness, but the railway connections were so recent and often so hastily laid that derailments were routine occurrences. For a pianist the West began immediately outside New York; in much of the rest of the country musical culture was scarcely established, and in many places the Puritan tradition lingered on, disapproving. Latecomers to concerts would have considered it unmanly not to stomp down the aisles to their seats, and often enough the pianist had to beg back his stool from some weary member of the audience. There was never silence for the guest performer, except in those moments when he might have expected some applause: why clap when you might have spent the one-dollar admission on a much more exciting 'panorama' entertainment?

Abraham Lincoln himself was a Westerner; he attended one of Gottschalk's concerts in Washington.

Mrs Lincoln has a very ordinary countenance. Lincoln is remarkably ugly, but has an intelligent air, and his eyes have a remarkable expression of goodness and mildness ... Lincoln does not wear gloves.[7]

Touring in the West meant struggling through blizzards, mud and Siberian ice storms, sleeping rough on the floor of the local 'hotel', riding the railroad night and day. Gottschalk was proud of his Western adventures, and he deserved to be so. He certainly held the record as the most travelled pianist of the nineteenth century. He once firmly corrected a printing error in one of his travelogues: he had covered not 8000 but 80,000 miles in two years in North America – enough to have taken him round the world three times.

Gottschalk cheerfully described the attraction of those madcap concert tours.

Sometimes I find myself delayed on the road by some accident or unforeseen event. I then dispatch a telegram to my agent and the hour for the concert is postponed: but it also happens sometimes that the telegram arrives too late for him to publish it. The audience already assembled in the hall becomes agitated and restless at not seeing the artist appear. My telegraphic dispatch arrives, and Strakosch reads it to the audience, offering to return the money to those who don't have the patience to await my arrival. A telegram from Strakosch in answer to mine, which I generally receive at the next station, makes me aware of the audience's decision. Then, if it is willing to wait for me, I send, from station to station, a telegram, which my agent reads to the audience to keep it patient. This calms it. Soon there is established between us a sympathetic tie. It becomes interested in the unknown traveler whose thought traverses space to communicate with that of the crowd anxious to see him ... As the telegraphic dispatches follow each other, the enthusiasm increases. I am seen approaching more than twenty miles, no more than ten miles off, the last stations are generally passed amid the expectant enthusiasm of the whole hall. The excitement becomes so great they almost embrace each other ... Strakosch then appears and with tremulous voice says: "Ladies and gentlemen. I have the honor of announcing to you that Mr Gottschalk has just arrived."[8]

The truly Wild West of Gottschalk's day was California, the new El Dorado. The Gold Rush was on, and 'towns' sprang up overnight; many of them have long since disappeared from the map, mirages that they were, creations of mass delusion. In Virginia City Gottschalk decided that the only gold mine was the hotel, where a single room cost $35 a night, and the next morning the porter demanded a further $15 with no more explanation than this:

'I tell you that you must pay fifteen dollars, and that ends it; and if you are not satisfied, I will make you pay sixty dollars. Are you satisfied? God damn you!'[9]

On another occasion Gottschalk was due to give a concert in Dayton, near Nevada City. He sat waiting outside the hotel, puffing on a cigar. Suddenly he heard a great drumming sound. He asked what was happening and was told that people were being drummed up for his concert. On his way to the 'theatre' he was accosted by two drummers and a bell ringer determined to lead him there. Gottschalk turned tail and ran.

> Our audience consists of a few females, ten or twelve boys . . . The rest are miners in large flannel shirts, with pantaloons turned up over their large boots. Their large Californian hats are of gray felt with broad rims. Do not hasten to conclude from this that they were unruly. They listened attentively, and their decent and tranquil manner would cause shame to many audiences that pretend to the refinements of civilization. It is not, besides, the first time that I have had the opportunity of noting this in a Californian audience . . . It is true that I make my programs as simple as possible. It would be as absurd to play for them pieces very difficult to understand, or classical music, as to give beefsteaks to a newly born infant. They have never heard the piano, and of all instruments it is the most difficult to render comprehensible to an audience who have almost or never heard music. Every instrument that from its nature embraces multiple combinations of sounds, is obscure to an ear that is not accustomed to it. Scarcely is the concert ended when a young girl out of the audience mounts the platform and quietly turns out the only Argand that gave light, whether poorly or well, to this part of the performance. I suppose she is the daughter of the pro- prietor . . .[10]

On his return to the civilized world of San Francisco, Gottschalk began to pursue the idea of a monster concert, a simultaneous performance with a number of pianos. The idea seems to appeal to something in the American national character – something akin to the motto expressed by a Southern general in the Civil War, 'Get there firstest with the mostest'. Some fifty years before Gottschalk another American suggested a similar spectacle to the Parisian pianist Henri Herz, who undertook a tour of America that lasted several years. Herz was accompanied by a young man called Ullman, who dreamed of putting on a gigantic 'political concert', a military parade of virtuosity. He wanted forty pianos, eight hundred singers, five full orchestras. The programme was to include a choral 'Hommage à Washington', a 'Concerto de la Constitution', a grand triumphal march for all forty pianos and, as a finale, a 'Hail Columbia' performed by every military band available in and around Philadelphia. In 1984 Ullman might have had his way with the organizers of the Los Angeles Olympics, but in 1848 he found that Herz was unwilling to take on more than eight pianos at once.

Gottschalk began by leading a march from Wagner's *Tannhäuser* for fourteen pianos. The event was a success, and Gottschalk arranged a repeat performance, only to find that one of the other pianists had fallen ill, and that there were no more professional pianists in the whole of San Francisco. What to do? He was determined not to cancel, but to play with only thirteen pianos would sorely disappoint the public. Fourteen pianos had been announced, and fourteen pianos there would be. At the last minute Gottschalk heard about a child prodigy, son of a rich man about town, whose father liked to boast of his talent. Gottschalk, always sceptical about amateurs, asked the boy to play for him. His worst suspicions were confirmed.

The boy could not possibly perform, but it would have been difficult to refuse him, particularly if his rich and influential father had already announced the concert to his friends. Gottschalk's faithful tuner had a brilliant idea: he removed the inner mechanism of the piano marked out for the boy.

> Before going on the stage, I made my thirteen acolytes take notice, that, in order to produce the greatest effect, it was indispensable not to play any preludes, that thus the public might be more surprised on hearing all at once the fourteen pianos attack the flourish of trumpets with which the March from *Tannhäuser* commences ... One, two, three – we begin. It goes on marvelously. In the midst of the piece I looked at my

amateur: he is superb; he was sweating great drops; he was throwing his
eyes carelessly on the audience and performing with miraculous ease the
passages apparently the most difficult. His friends were in raptures . . .
We must repeat the piece. But at the moment of beginning the amateur
forgot my recommendation not to play an introduction, and could not
resist the temptation to play a little chromatic scale. I see him now! The
stupor that was printed on his countenance was inexpressible. He began
his scale again. Nothing. The piano was mute. For an instant he had the
idea that the ardor with which he had played had been fatal to the
strings, but, throwing a glance inside, he saw them all right . . . Then,
persuaded that the piano was just out of order, he strove to make me
understand that we could not begin the March again.

'Pst! pst!!' said he with a wild air, but I had seen the danger and
without loss of time I had given the signal and the March was
recommenced. My young man, to save appearances before the
audience, made the pantomime of the passages, but his countenance,
which I saw from below, was worth painting; it was a mixture of
discouragement and of spite. The fury with which he struck the poor
instrument, which could do nothing, was very funny.

'That was very well done, gentlemen,' I said, on entering the artists'
room, 'but the effect was less than the first time.'

'The mischief!' said my amateur to me, 'my piano broke down all at
once.' . . . Moral – beware of amateurs.[11]

Many years later Gottschalk gave a series of mammoth concerts in
Rio de Janeiro. He was not well, and the rehearsals alone exhausted
him (flags, gun salutes, trumpets, two orchestras and several choirs
were all part of the show) to such an extent that he could only groan:

'I go from one barracks to another. I am a symphonic, voltaic pile; a
steam engine become man. If I do not go mad, it will neither be my
fault nor that of my soldiers. My room is a Capernaum, my heart a
volcano, my head a chaos!'[12]

A few days after the biggest concert of the series, on 18 December
1869, Gottschalk was dead. Only one of his many works survived him:
the *Notes of a Pianist*, his diary.

13

A MAIDEN'S PRAYER

All that one can discuss with the
young ladies is the last sermon they
have heard, the last piano piece they
have learned, or the last dress they
have worn.

The Goncourt brothers

Play less piano, learn something!

Eduard Hanslick

Her name was Thekla von Badarzevska-Baranovska; she lived in
Warsaw, and in the course of her brief existence (1834–1861) she
achieved the most extraordinary and at the same time the most trivial
success in the history of the piano. With a single composition, a
melody that is little more than an octave sequence of three-part chords
encapsulated in just two sheets of music, she won herself an enormous
following in Europe, Asia, and the two Americas. The melody
remained popular for a good fifty years after its first publication in
Warsaw in 1856; in 1859 it was reprinted in the Parisian *Revue et
Gazette musicale*.

The name of the little song was 'Molitwa dziewicy', 'La prière d'une
vierge', 'Gebet einer Jungfrau', 'A Maiden's Prayer'. It was a miracle
of triviality that became the theme song of the century, because it
summed up the trivial tone of the period.

Franzpeter Goebels described the music with gentle irony:

The two fundamental elements of the composition, the virtuoso 'uplift',
handily developed in variations II and IV, and the fervently yielding
relapse, must be steadily cultivated, with new nuances coaxed from
them each time. The full breadth of feeling becomes apparent in the
central variation III, when correctly rendered. Piu Allegro (variation V)

marks the peak of fervour and must be played with true and soulful vibrato. While the left hand gently patters on, full attention may be given to the right. Not to be forgotten is the fact that the arpeggios, the vibrato and the crossing of the hands ... make a not insignificant impression on the audience. The motto of the whole performance should be: more appearance than reality![1]

However the true cunning of the piece lay not so much in the music, with its opportunities for pseudo-virtuosity, as in the title. It was in fact a very ambivalent title. Who was praying to whom? The rhythm alone made it clear that this was no Ave Maria.

What did a maiden pray for in those days? Did she pray that a flood of vague desire would not burst her little breast? Or that this very definite desire for one Lieutenant Miroslav von Zaborsky, he of the penetrating eyes, would not bring the blood to her cheeks at the next ball? Or was she secretly praying for Count Wenzel von Horvath, who was so deeply indebted to her father that he would soon have no choice but to shoot himself or take a wife? As long as he did not shoot himself!

If the music is any indication, it seems clear that the maiden in question was not a resolutely practical young lady making a profane prayer for material improvement. Horses, gold necklaces, silk shawls, the collected works of Sir Walter Scott, a Pleyel piano, a lace dress – these things she had in plenty. Yet the rhythm of her song is somehow reminiscent of a barcarole, and the theme with its rising plea and falling sob has something of a Capri fisherman's *bel canto*. There is a definite sense of nostalgia for the South in the lyrics as well, as if young Thekla von Badarzevska-Baranovska were yearning to set out on a tour of Italy with Mama and Papa, the footman, the chambermaid and the governess, there to meet, perhaps, an Italian grandee or an English lord. The blue grottos of Capri, the shimmering sea, Vesuvius and Pompeii – heaven on earth.

Islands in the sea, fishermen, boats, also woods and sylvan ecstasies feature heavily in the popular songs of the nineteenth century. Titles were expressive and sentimental, markings strongly emotive: 'Isola bella on the Lago Maggiore'; 'Bring Me Home to Die'; 'A Pale Young Maid is Waiting'; 'Convent Bells'; 'The Lion Awaking'; even 'My Heart, I Want to Ask You, What Is Love Then, Say?'

Music historians have little patience for that sort of music. Hans Christian Worbs noted that quality played an increasingly insignificant role in such compositions, commercial viability being the order of the day. 'In many sectors the musical work of art had become little more than a piece of merchandise, an industrial article produced by certain composers in accordance with certain clichés.'[2] Worbs further indicated a marked decline in quality around the middle of the century, when composers and critics increasingly denounced the sinking standards of the 'musical rabble' writing for amateurs.

Marcel Proust, that sensitive genius, answered the critics with the claim that 'bad music' embodies the dreams and despairs of ordinary men and women. 'Curse it as you may,' he wrote, 'you cannot condemn it; indeed a healthy respect for popular music indicates a sound knowledge of its social function.'[3]

Robert Schumann coined the phrase 'salon music' in 1838. He did not mean it as a term of contempt; he was merely describing the intimate nature of the genre. The decline of the expression and the music it described did not set in until about 1850 – just the time when the patrician salon was giving way to the parlour, that holy of holies in the middle-class household. 'A Maiden's Prayer' took its place firmly in the bourgeois front room, but even a song like Schubert's 'Du holde Kunst' ('You Fair Art') was written for that hour of musical refuge in a routine day of work.

The front parlour, after all, was a sanctum carefully shielded from the miseries of the world. Hans Salmen described it: 'In sharp contrast to the meagre workers' dwelling in grim ghetto districts people here surrounded themselves with plush furniture, oil paintings, artificial flowers, bric-à-brac, heavy curtains and busts of Beethoven . . .'[4] The enthusiastic décor was an unconscious bolster against any number of anxieties.

Furthermore, for the many thousands of new enthusiasts who flocked to the piano from the middle of the century, the term 'salon music' held a promise somehow ennobling. The function of salon music was surely to raise the front parlour to the level of a true salon.

Max Weber's succinct definition of the piano as 'a domestic instrument of the bourgeoisie' applies really only for the years after 1850 – and then only as long as the term is understood to include the petty bourgeoisie of artisans and low-ranking civil servants.[5] In 1855 Adolf Bernhard Marx published *The Music of the 19th Century* in which he wrote about 'domestic music', claiming that it was no longer a question of musical talent: 'In the so-called educated circles music was long since considered an imperative part of education; every family demanded it, wherever possible for every family member, with no particular regard for talent or inclination ... even among small traders and artisans precious time and money was diverted to secure, at least for the daughters, piano, sheet music, teachers and musical education, in the hope of thus being counted among the "educated".[6]

'At least for the daughters,' he said. It is certainly clear that if the piano was the 'domestic instrument of the bourgeoisie', it was the young girls who were destined to sit at it. As Walter Haacke wrote: 'The female preference for the piano as opposed to other instruments cannot be explained by the apparent ease with which it is played, nor by the fact that it allows the player to assume a seemly posture. There is much more to be said for the restriction of the piano to the home, where the woman is more fully realized than the man.'[7]

In September 1851 the American *Harper's Magazine* published the following advice for 'musical misses'.

> Sit in a simple, graceful, unconstrained posture. Never turn up the eyes or swing about the body; the expression you mean to give ... will never be understood by those foolish motions which are rarely resorted to but by those who do not really feel what they play ... However loud you wish to be, never thump ... Aim more at pleasing than astonishing ... Be above the vulgar folly of pretending that you cannot play for dancing; for it proves only that if not disobliging, you are stupid ... In performing simple airs, which very few people can do fit to be listened to, study the *style* of the different nations to which the tunes belong ... Although you must be strictly accurate as to time ... it should sometimes be relaxed to favor the expression of Irish and Scotch airs ... Never bore people with ugly music merely because it is the work of some famous composer, and do not let the pieces you perform before people not professedly scientific be too long.[8]

It seems reasonable to assume that this careful exegesis of piano etiquette was equally valid for the musical young ladies of England, France, Germany and Austria: the graceful posture, the pleasing style, the restrained expression, eyes firmly fixed on the music, which would not include Beethoven, but would include a full repertoire of socially acceptable three-minute salon pieces.

A certain level of accomplishment as a pianist and a singer was an investment for the future – a non-material dowry that none the less paid off in material terms. In order to ensure the musical education of marriageable young ladies, any number of boarding schools for girls were founded around 1850. Johanna Kinkel, one of the most intelligent women of her day, who corresponded regularly with Jacob Burckhardt and gave piano lessons herself, described the typical product of such establishments:

> It seems to me that we live in a period so predominantly musical that girls able to sing and play the piano enjoy an unfair advantage in comparison to their less musical sisters. From their earliest youth they are drawn into wider company, where they receive more attention and are more likely to marry than others, whose qualities often go unregarded. Girls of cold temperament often appear more soulful than others, because they express well-studied feelings, of which they are often entirely incapable, in beautifully melodic voices. Others, less practised at such artifice, may have deeper feelings, but their unmusical expression makes it seem a bitter irony.[9]

Johanna Kinkel would have liked to abolish the increasingly popular custom of musical performances in the home.

> I cannot understand why music of all things should have become such an exclusive social fashion. A cultured house in which there was no piano would be considered an impossibility . . . This habit of providing musical entertainment has a sour effect on any conversation. Just when one has had the luck to find a reasonable human being with whom one can discuss things of the greatest interest, one is interrupted in the middle of the most essential communication . . . In the end you lose all desire to give such a broken conversation the least attention, and you indolently allow it all to wash over you, chatter and tinkle, tea and cake, as it will.[10]

Even an emancipated woman like Johanna Kinkel, however, tailored her teaching methods to the needs of just such domestic music. She recommended a sort of times-table of basic harmonics, so that young ladies would be able to work out accompaniments and little pieces for themselves. She also warned, along with her most con-servative male colleagues, against overly ambitious instruction: '. . . the teacher must never fail to consider what a break marriage makes in the education of any woman. This consideration alone makes it necessary to set out certain stages for the dilettante, where she can so establish herself that she will not risk losing all that she has learnt.'[11]

Most women ambitious enough to pursue their musical interests and attempt a professional career risked the worst of all possible fates: lifelong servitude as a piano teacher. In the nineteenth century there was no such thing as a qualifying examination for piano teachers, so the field was wide open, and very bleak. Failed pianists, unmarried ladies, impoverished widows made up a musical proletariat, many of them much worse off than the visiting seamstress.

The most distinguished and determined women struggled vainly to succeed in the profession. Fanny Schindelmeisser opened what she called a *Musik-Unterrichts-Anstalt* ('Music-Teaching-Institute') in Berlin in 1835. Operating from her own home, she instructed a number of children simultaneously, at first without demanding any payment. She used paper keyboards to make up the necessary number of instruments. Her most significant and sensible ambition was to provide musical education for children during normal school hours, so that they would not have to devote their free time to piano lessons at the expense of other work.[12] Apparently it was this ambition that motivated her to petition any number of government agencies, from school governors to the Prussian ministry of health and education and the body administering trade and manufacture. The latter was responsible for issuing patents, and it summarily declared that it would be impossible to patent any method of teaching the piano, the success of such a method being dependent on the accomplishment of the student, which it felt would be a thing extremely difficult to judge.

After Fanny Schindelmeisser had failed in every one of her appeals for official recognition, a crafty colleague by the name of Bormann opened a royally sanctioned school for the teaching of the piano in Friedrichstadt. 'The possibility and the success of such a method of instruction for several students simultaneously has been proven here by the accomplishments of Frau Schindelmeisser . . . Those who wish to participate in the lessons of four hours per week will be asked to pay two thalers per month. Berlin, 12 September 1839. K. Bormann.'[13] Bormann intended to refine Fanny Schindelmeisser's concept in two respects: he meant to replace the paper keyboards with movable models, and of course his lessons would take place outside normal school hours, though on school grounds. Small wonder that Herr

Bormann and not Frau Schindelmeisser received the blessing of the
Prussian authorities.

To return for a moment to 'A Maiden's Prayer': whatever it was that
she so desired, she was apparently answered. Among the 24 further
works of Thekla von Badarzevska-Baranovska is one called 'La prière
exaucée', or 'The Answered Prayer'. We can all breathe more easily.

FOUR YEARS IN HIS OWN LABYRINTH
Brahms

> It does not just come to you! Do you
> think that any one of my few respectable
> Lieder came to me just like that?
> It was torture!
>
> *Johannes Brahms*

Aimez-vous Brahms? Do you like Brahms? The audience assembled in Leipzig's Gewandhaus on Thursday 27 January 1859 most certainly did not. They hissed and booed as the twenty-five-year-old composer rose after his performance of the Concerto for Piano and Orchestra No. 1 in D Minor, Op. 15. He had first performed the piece in Hannover just eight days previously. He scarcely managed to bow.

In a letter to his friend, the violinist Joseph Joachim, Brahms described 'how it came to pass that my concerto was a glorious and utter – failure . . . The first rehearsal passed unremarked by musicians and audience. At the second rehearsal there was no audience, and none of the musicians moved so much as a muscle in his face.' As for the actual concert:

> The first movement and the second were received in silence. At the end three pairs of hands slowly attempted to clap, whereupon a loud hissing from all sides forbad any such demonstration . . . This failure made no impression on me whatsoever, and any hint of bad temper soon fell away when I heard a C major symphony by Haydn . . . I believe it is the best thing that can happen to one; it forces one to collect one's thoughts and it bolsters one's courage. I am experimenting still after all. But surely the hissing was too much?[1]

Within days the critics were hissing in print. The first review appeared on 3 February in the magazine *Signale für die musikalische Welt*:

The fourteenth Gewandhaus concert was another occasion on which a new composition was ushered to its grave – the concerto by Mr Johannes Brahms . . . Leaving aside the earnestness of the attempt and the undeniable musical ability, there is nothing in it but bleak and barren waste . . . The ideas either limp by wearily or work themselves up to a fever pitch of excitement, only to collapse again all the more exhausted; in a word the whole feeling of the piece is unhealthy. The pale, schematic ideas are a sad sight in themselves, but the way in which they are used and abused makes the thing even more miserable . . . And one is expected to put up with this gasping and choking . . . for over three-quarters of an hour! One is expected to swallow this unchewed mass of sound and then top it off with a dessert of screamingly discordant notes! . . . Finally it must be said that as a pianist Mr. Brahms does not come up to the standards one has a right to expect of concert players in this day and age.[2]

Little wonder that Brahms always remembered the occasion as the greatest failure of his life.[3] The first scathing review was soon followed by a more considered critique, but the painful history of the piece itself made it difficult to accept such belated comfort. Four years' work, so it must have seemed to Brahms, had been destroyed in a single evening; four years of tortuous experimentation damned in that hissing of incomprehension. Few composers have wrestled as long and hard with a single work as Brahms wrestled with his first piano concerto.

But to say that he wrestled with it gives the reassuring but false impression that the work itself was already there in some form: if not as concrete as a sculptor's block of marble, still a solid idea in the composer's head. The fact is that for a long time Brahms was not at all sure what he was trying to compose: a sonata for two pianos, a symphony, possibly an oratorio, or indeed a concerto for piano and orchestra.

It all started on a walking tour, a young man's musical pilgrimage. At the age of ten Brahms gave his first public performance in Hamburg and was almost sent on a tour of America as an exotic child prodigy. By the time he was twenty he was an accomplished pianist with a natural desire to meet the greatest living proponent of his art: he walked to Altenburg, near Weimar, to visit Franz Liszt. Liszt received him cordially and even played a few Brahms' compositions at sight, since the young man was too shy to play for him. But Brahms did not feel comfortable in the solemn atmosphere of Liszt's home: 'I soon saw

that I did not belong there. I would have had to lie, and I could not.'[4]
Soon afterwards he decided to travel down the Rhine, again on foot.
The river was at the height of its popularity: source of so many
Romantic currents, it was crowded with sightseers and visionaries
from all over the world. On the banks of that mighty river the twenty-
year-old artist with the thin, pale but striking face framed by long
blonde hair was suddenly thrust into the public eye. He had been given
a letter of introduction to Clara and Robert Schumann, which
obviously meant little to him – it was only shortly before his visit that
he first heard Schumann's work.

It was hardly a mere visit: the Schumanns insisted he stay for the
whole of October 1853. Brahms could not have known what his host
wrote in his diary the day after the young man arrived: 'Visit from
Brahms (a genius)!'[5] It is unclear whether Brahms would have seen the
letter Robert Schumann wrote to music publishers Breitkopf and
Härtel in Leipzig just a week later: 'A young man has appeared here
who has moved us deeply with his wonderful music and who will, I am
convinced, stir up great changes in the musical world.'[6] There is no
doubt, however, that Brahms read the piece Schumann hastily wrote
over the next few days. 'Neue Bahnen' ('New Ground') was the title of
the piece, still considered 'the most famous Brahms article of all time'.[7]
Schumann had it published in his old forum, the *Neue Zeitschrift für
Musik* (which had long since thrown off his influence in allegiance to
the 'new German' circle around Liszt).

Schumann wrote that he had long awaited the sudden appearance of
an artist born

> to express the highest spirit of the age, a master needing no apprentice-
> ship, a Minerva who would spring upon us fully armed from the head of
> Cronus. And he is come, a young blood, watched over in his cradle by
> Graces and heroes. His name is Johannes Brahms, he came from
> Hamburg . . . He wore, even in his outward appearance, all the signs of
> a man with a calling. Seated at the piano he began to conjure up
> wondrous visions. We were drawn into ever more magical spheres. As a
> player too he was ingenious, transforming the piano into an orchestra of
> wailing and rejoicing voices. His sonatas were symphonies in
> disguise . . .[8]

Brahms was of course overwhelmed and enormously pleased,
particularly for his parents, who were bound to be delighted by such

praise. But he was also wary of the awesome implications of the
eulogy. 'The praise you have lavished upon me,' he wrote to
Schumann, 'will have raised public expectations to such an extent that I
do not know how I can do them justice.'[9] Breitkopf and Härtel
accepted him with alacrity: Brahms was able to publish his Sonatas in
C Major and F sharp Minor, his song cycle Op. 3, and the Scherzo in E
sharp Minor. There were other works which Schumann urged him to
publish, but Brahms refused. He was always a self-critical composer,
even at the height of his fame: he was forever burning drafts or
throwing sheets of music into the river. 'I have such respect for the
printer's ink,' he said as an old man.[10]

Brahms was in Hannover being fêted by friends when, at the
beginning of March 1854, news reached him of Robert Schumann's
suicidal leap into the Rhine and his subsequent descent into madness.
Without delay Brahms set out for Düsseldorf, arriving just a day
before Schumann was admitted to Dr Richarz's sanitorium in
Endenich. Clara noted gratefully: 'He said he had only come to cheer
me with music, if I so wished, that he wanted to stay here for now and
later devote himself entirely to Robert, when he is well enough to have
strangers about him.'[11] Clara Schumann – Clara of the glass coach –
was then thirty-four years old, the mother of six children with a
seventh on the way, and still very beautiful – or perhaps now
particularly so.

Brahms did manage to soothe her with his music. On 24 May Clara
wrote in her diary: 'At Klems I rehearsed with Brahms three
movements of a sonata of his for two pianos. Again it seemed to me a
colossal work, magnificent, and clearer than his earlier things. We
played it twice . . .'[12] Four days later there is another entry: 'Today I
played Brahms' sonata with Dietrich and then the same again with
Brahms. I played it again with the greatest interest and joy. – It is a
splendid work.'[13]

This is a significant entry, marking more or less the entrance to
Brahms' labyrinth. Albert Dietrich is the principal witness for the case
that this 'Sonata for Two Pianos in D Minor' is in fact a preliminary
version of the famous concerto, also written in D minor. Brahms'
biographer Max Kalbeck claims that Dietrich could never forget the
principal theme of that sonata, and that 'he later recognized it as the
beginning of the D minor concerto'.[14] According to Dietrich, Brahms
used another motif from the same sonata in his 'Deutsches Requiem':

the dance of death in that work, he claimed, was based on the second movement of the sonata, a slow scherzo. In the requiem words were set to the music: 'All flesh is grass; the grass withereth, the flower fadeth.'

The Biblical sentiment may have seemed well suited to the mood in the Schumann household at the time. But nineteenth-century interpreters went further, seeing a direct portrayal of the Schumann tragedy in the later work. 'The grandiose opening of the D minor concerto, with drumbeats punctuating the swirling effects on the organ and the first theme crouching for the dreadful leap as trills jerk through the whole orchestra like a shivering fit, is based on a vision of Schumann's attempted suicide.'[15] Brahms' student Gustav Jenner protested at this schematic interpretation, but contemporary music historians are suspicious even of Jenner's opinion 'that such a dreadful occurrence, overwhelming him with such force, could not fail to have an effect on Brahms that will have pressed him to artistic creation'.[16]

Let us stick to the letters, then. As early as the summer of 1854 Brahms seemed to suspect that the composition of this work would be a long and labyrinthine affair. On 19 June he wrote to Joseph Joachim: 'I would like to put my D minor sonata aside for some time. I have played the first three movements often with Mrs Schumann. [Scratched out] Actually even two pianos are not enough for me.'[17] Brahms began to rework the first movement as an orchestral piece. He was still unsure of himself with symphonic instrumentation and he sought advice from his friend Grimm, to whom he frequently sent drafts with requests for revision. He told Joachim: 'I also want to tell you that at the beginning I wanted to emphasize the low D, which is why I have the F–B flat in the clarinet and bassoon so faint. It has actually always pleased me that everything is so terse and short, but I do not know if that is right, particularly for orchestra . . . Do you encourage me to go to the other movements? I feel so insolent.'[18] Joachim did encourage him: 'I will cheer at the next movements!' But Brahms put him off: 'There is so much missing in the composition; I do not even entirely understand the instrumentation that is already there.' And he wrote to his old teacher from Hamburg, Eduard Marxsen, for further advice.

As drafts went back and forth through the post Brahms complicated and completed his own labyrinth. Gustav Jenner noted:

Brahms reworked the piece because two pianos were not enough for him. On the other hand the piano had formed the basis of the composition. A keenly critical artist like Brahms could hardly help feeling that it would be impossible to remove the discrepancy inherent in reworking a piano piece for an orchestra; the fact that he recognized this is a shining example of his tremendous talent and ability which foreshadows the greatness of his later symphonies. Because of this discrepancy the attempt to make a symphony out of the sonata was bound to fail, and it did fail.[19]

Brahms' dilemma was not purely his own: his difficulty was with the piano. It was not just a question of the instrumentation but also of the instrument itself, which is caught up in a continual balancing act. 'The pianoforte,' as Berlioz wrote, 'can be seen in two ways: as an orchestral instrument, or as a complete little orchestra in itself.' That definition pinpoints the dilemma in this case, which was that the two functions seemed to overlap even in Brahms' early work. The fact that he, as Schumann remarked, 'transformed the piano into an orchestra of wailing and rejoicing voices', that his sonatas 'were symphonies in disguise' means that Brahms must have felt torn between the two musical forms whenever he sat at the piano. On the other hand the version for two pianos is the classic form of the concerto conceived as a competition between two instruments, a game of question and answer. It was only logical that he should write to Clara in late January/early February 1855: 'Imagine what I dreamed last night. I had used my failed symphony for my piano concerto and I was playing it. The first movement, the scherzo and a finale, terribly heavy and grand. I was filled with enthusiasm.'[20]

Brahms could not have imagined all the labyrinthine digressions that would follow once he had decided on the concerto form. In the autumn of 1856 Clara wrote: 'Johannes has completed a magnificent first movement of a concerto – we played it several times on two pianos.'[21] It is strange that Clara Schumann failed to recognize the old D minor sonata, particularly as she was introduced to the concerto in an intimate version for two pianos. For that reason Carl Dahlhaus concluded that the reworking must have considerably changed the piece. On 1 October Clara considered this first movement completed. But Joseph Joachim, to whom Brahms had sent the music, wrote cautiously on 1 December: 'I am much occupied with your concerto – but I have certain reservations, much as I heartily enjoy and admire the work, which I can but imperfectly write down, whereas a discussion for and against could be wonderfully stimulating for us both. Can you not come to stay until Christmas, finish your concerto here, as you have no peace in Hamburg . . .'[22]

The first movement was not finished that Advent. Almost a year later, on 9 November 1857, Brahms wrote to Clara: 'These past few days I have been thinking over the first movement of my concerto. You cannot imagine what a worry for me. It is bungled through and through, that is the mark of dilettantism, how am I to get beyond it at last? I am pulling it around properly now and anything that does not work I will leave out, but there must be an end to it now.'[23] One Christmas later than the one Joachim had meant he received a proof of the first movement with a desperate note from Brahms asking him to say 'whether the effort was not entirely wasted'.

In the middle of his long struggle with the first movement Brahms conceived the second, an adagio. Again there is a puzzle: was this adagio based on the third movement of the original sonata (as Max Kalbeck is convinced it was), or was it an entirely new composition? A point in favour of the second argument is Brahms' letter to Clara dated 30 December 1856, in which he wrote: 'I am also painting a gentle portrait of you, which is to be an adagio.'[24] And to Joachim: 'Strangely enough here is an adagio as well. Will I ever be sure of a successful adagio! Write me exactly what you think of it. If you like it at all, then show it to our dear friend, otherwise do not.' A gentle portrait of the woman who was Brahms' (unrequited) passion for two full years? From whom he tore himself away, as Goethe did from his Lotte, just when she was ready to fall for him completely?

Music historians feel obliged to omit such personal details, but there is no reason for us to disregard the scene described by Brahms after his and Clara's last visit to the dying Schumann.

> I am sure I will never experience anything more moving than Robert and Clara's reunion.
>
> He lay there for some time with his eyes closed, and she kneeled before him, more quietly than one would have thought possible. He recognized her later, and also the following day.
>
> At one point he clearly wished to embrace her, threw one arm towards her.
>
> Of course he had not been able to speak for some time, one could only understand (or one thought one could understand) the occasional word.

He often refused the wine offered to him, then sometimes he would suck it from her finger so greedily and long and fervently, that one was convinced he knew the finger.[25]

For Brahms it was an unforgettable scene, a life experience. While Schumann lay dying, he killed something in himself – his hope of fulfilment in his love for Clara. By the middle of 1856, when they last visited Schumann, the two were indeed lovers in some sense. They often travelled together, and their letters grew increasingly tender; for two years it seemed as if only the shadow of the sick man in Endenich stood between them and their desire. 'We might have breathed more freely, that he had been released, and we could not believe it.'[26]

The result was not passion but a lifelong, forty-year friendship. Brahms fled from a situation he recognized. Soon afterwards he sent Clara a quartet, calling it 'an illustration for the last chapter about the man in the blue coat and yellow waistcoat'. Goethe's young hero Werther wore a blue coat and yellow waistcoat when he shot himself, and the combination was all the rage in Germany after the novel was published. Brahms' biographer Hans Gal wrote: 'The real puzzle with Brahms, as with the young Goethe, is his willingness to flee.'

Brahms had escaped from his existential labyrinth, and the concluding rondo of his piano concerto sounds like an equally determined attempt to free himself from his own composition, to put it behind him at last. The leitmotif of the rondo seems to say: *basta*! Joseph Joachim remarked on 'the robust and jaunty spirit of the first theme', and Carl Dahlhaus saw in the opening of the rondo a decided and almost violent attack.[27]

None the less the composition of the rondo was equally fraught with indecision and pleas for advice. 'So I am sending you the finale then, to be rid of it at last,'[28] Brahms wrote to Joachim in mid-December 1856. He added: 'But whether it will satisfy you! I doubt it very much. The ending was supposed to be good, but now it hardly seems so to me.' Joachim seemed slow to respond, so Brahms wrote again: 'I have been waiting so long for your overture and my rondo. When will I get them at last? Surely you are not afraid to mark up my rondo. I know it needs it.'[29]

In the middle of January 1857 he received a long letter from Joachim which opened with praise for the profoundly gentle accompanying

motif and complimented him on the majestic ending. But Joachim
went on to say: 'It is as if the motifs have been caught in the molten heat
of creation without having had time to cool and crystallize.' Furthermore: '. . . sometimes instead of developing a theme you introduce a
harmonic regression, which is doubly painful to me in a work of yours.
So for instance you . . . begin to play on the D minor phrase – one is
quite prepared to swim trustingly after you, I was expecting a most
courageous Brahmsiade – when all at once you throw the listener from
A minor and F major onto the sandbank of D minor . . .'[30]

Finally Joachim suggested that Brahms write 'another final
movement, for to rewrite a piece is often more effort than to create
afresh. But it would be a pity to lose so much that is significant in the
rondo, and perhaps you can persuade yourself to go at it with all the
impetuousness of the first time so as to recreate certain passages.'[31]

Brahms did not lose his nerve; he decided to rework the finale.
Months later he wrote: 'Here is the rondo for the second time . . .
Some of it has come out quite differently, hopefully better, some of it is
simply reworked.'[32] There followed repeated revisions, some in the
instrumentation. The first performance was delayed by almost a year.
On 25 March 1858 Brahms was booked to perform the concerto in
Hamburg's Musikverein, but plans were abandoned because Brahms
was not provided with an adequate instrument.

By the time he performed the piece in Leipzig Brahms felt he had
achieved all that one can achieve in a composition, 'the organization of
disparate elements'.[33] In the end he had not managed to escape from
the labyrinth, nor had he wanted to; instead he tried to draw the
audience in there with him. Is it any wonder that they lost their way
and began to hiss with impatience and anxiety? Now, 125 years later,
the concerto is recognized as a fascinating work of palatial splendour –
beyond the wildest dreams of that first letter to Clara, when he wrote:
'In spite of everything the concerto will please someone someday.'[34]

Reserved as he was, could Brahms really have been interested in the
plaudits of posterity? Perhaps his feelings were as contradictory as his
professed attitude to public honours: 'Decorations mean nothing to
me, I only want to have them.'[35]

THE WAR IN THE MUSIC ROOM (3)
Commercial Competition

> The great modern question is advertising;
> it is the god of trade and industry in our
> time. Without advertising, no salvation.
>
> *Guy de Maupassant*

There is a place in the nineteenth-century history of the piano for a letter sent from New York by the young Christian Carl Gottlieb, or Charles for short, to his youngest brother Theodor back in Brunswick. Charles advised the boy

> not to come here if you are still in a position to feed yourself properly by means of hard work and thrift, and that is the advice I give to everyone ... , for one must work more here than elsewhere and one is soon so accustomed to the better life that in the end one is convinced that our German potato soup tasted better in Germany than the roast one eats here every day. Of course America is a haven for anyone who wants to work and who had no work in Germany and had to struggle to make ends meet, but nothing is perfect and that is true even of the good life here in America. We had our worries in Germany, and here we have other worries. In Germany the doctor's bill for the whole year was only one thaler and here it is more than fifty. That is the worst thing for the Germans in general. Very few can bear the climate, most suffer from chest pains, and in general half the people here die of chest and lung complaints, for which one can only blame the climate ...[1]

In 1848, when he was barely twenty years old, Carl (Charles) had joined the revolutionary movement in Germany; the following year, when the reaction set in, he fled to America. A year after that the rest of his family, with the exception of Theodor, followed him in the *Helene Sloman*, an emigrant ship: his father Heinrich Engelhard Steinweg, his mother Juliane, and three further brothers, as well as three sisters.

They worked hard in New York because they had big plans; they intended to found a family company. Three years later they fulfilled their first ambition, opening a small factory at 82–88 Walker Street, New York. Charles' brother Johann Heinrich Engelhard was now Henry, and eighteen-year-old Johann Heinrich Wilhelm was William. The company name appears in gold on about 80 per cent of the concert pianos in use throughout the world today: Steinway & Sons.

The little family company had a long way to go on its road to international triumph. None the less, as music historian Cyril Ehrlich pointed out, the founding year of 1853 was something of an *annus mirabilis* in the history of the piano: the same year marked the opening of business for Bechstein in Berlin and Blüthner in Leipzig, as well as Steinway & Sons of New York.[2] There is of course some explanation for the remarkable coincidence, although it is certain that Bechstein, Blüthner and Steinway did not consult one another about their plans. For a start one must realize that these three companies were simply the best of hundreds of piano manufacturers founded about that time.

The coincidence begins to look even more plausible when one considers the birthplaces of the founders: Engelhard Steinweg came from Wolfshagen in the Harz region (he was already an accomplished organist before he began to make pianos, while still in Germany); Friedrich Wilhelm Carl Bechstein (a nephew of the legendary Bechstein) was born in Gotha; and Julius Ferdinand Blüthner came from Falkenhain near Merseburg. All of them came from the Thuringian–Saxon region of Germany, where the craft of instrument-making had been practised for so many centuries that the young people might be said to have had it in their blood. Engelhard Steinway may have been 56 in the famous founding year, but his son Charles (born in 1829) was very much of the same generation as Bechstein (1829) and Blüthner (1824): all three of them were still in their twenties when their companies first opened. These men, and other entertaining young founders like them, introduced a new epoch in instrument-making, responsive to all the technological innovations of the day, and determined to exploit a new commercial strategy of competitive marketing on a grand scale.

There had always been rivalry between piano manufacturers. One example was the eager pursuit of gold medals, mentioned by Mendelssohn, at trade fairs and particularly at world trade exhibitions.

There was also a tendency for early rivals in the piano market to build their own concert halls. One of the first of these belonged to Streicher, who had the clever idea of using a large hall in his Viennese factory for public concerts, with the audience treated to a display of his instruments. In Paris there was soon a Salle Erard and a Salle Pleyel, and Henri Herz too eventually built his own concert hall. It goes without saying that rival manufacturers' instruments never appeared in a company's private hall.

It was still a collegial business, however, and pianists maintained the upper hand in the first half of the century. Chopin for instance wrote of his last trip to London in 1848: 'Erard proved very obliging and has put one of his pianos at my disposal. Thus I have one instrument by Broadwood, another by Pleyel – three in all, though to what purpose, since I have no time to play.'[3] (He meant he had no time to play for himself.) In his public concerts he was obliged to use the Broadwood, as he was under contract to the company. They dictated the terms under which he gave private lessons – at the horrendous sum of 20 guineas. Altogether Broadwood took very good care of him, at one point arranging speedily and discreetly for new mattresses for his bed when he complained about the old ones. Later, when Chopin travelled by train to Scotland, the firm not only provided his ticket but also booked the seat opposite, so that the sickly and increasingly neurotic artist would not have to face a fellow passenger throughout the long journey.

Broadwood's advertising methods were of the old school: the firm still vaunted itself on its coup of 1817, when Beethoven sent his effusive letter of thanks for the instrument presented to him. That episode was presented as proof of particular distinction and quality (a claim indeed justified for many decades): a Broadwood was a Beethoven piano and every buyer could imagine himself the heir of the impetuous composer from Vienna. But the best advertising slogans always backfire in time: in the second half of the century the reference was more likely to create the impression that a Broadwood was an antiquated instrument. (Beethoven's letter is still reproduced in Broadwood catalogues to this day.)

The new piano-makers spoke a new language. Charles Steinway, for instance, wrote this enthusiastic letter about his new 'overstrung' piano with its significantly fuller and richer tone: 'If you read the musical papers you will soon get to read a terrific article about us and our business in the Berlin *Musik Zeitung* as well as in the Leipzig *Signalen*, for we are eager now to make our name known in Europe as it is absolutely necessary that the piano virtuosos who come here be made aware of our name, so that we can get them into our hands . . .'[4]

It was no coincidence that that letter was written in America. The Steinways simply followed the lead of the major Boston firm, Chickering & Sons, which had Louis Moreau Gottschalk under contract.

After one of his concerts Louis Moreau Gottschalk had had to defend himself against an attack in the press on a very sensitive point: the reviewer had faulted him for playing exclusively on Chickering pianos, and he thought it perfectly scandalous that the name of the manufacturer was prominently displayed on the side of the piano facing the audience. Gottschalk haughtily protested: 'This honest editor, who does not appear to be *au fait* in the matter of concerts, ought to know that no piano, here or in Europe, is placed upon the platform without having on it the name of its maker.'[5]

There could be no question of a commercial arrangement between artist and manufacturer: he, Gottschalk, preferred Chickering pianos not because all others were inferior, but because their fine, delicate and poetic tone suited his style of playing.

European pianists were often disconcerted by unabashed American advertising methods. Hans von Bülow, who was almost as famous for his arrogance and viciousness as for his distinction as a pianist and conductor, related the following incident. He had signed a contract with Chickering for a tour of America and then discovered, at an orchestral rehearsal in Baltimore, a great placard attached to the side of the piano, with CHICKERING written across it in big gold letters. Bülow leapt up, tore off the placard, threw it to the ground and shouted loud enough for every musician to hear: 'I am not a travelling advertisement!' As if that were not enough, he picked it up again during a break, laid it across the end of the piano and tried to fold it in two. Arthur Loesser, in *Men, Women and Pianos*, claims that such advertising placards were quite usual in America up to the 1920s.

At the same time Hans von Bülow was a prime example of a pianist closely bound to a particular manufacturer. In the first decade of

Bechstein's existence Bülow's relationship with the firm reeked of piano patriotism. In March 1860 he wrote to Bechstein in Berlin:

> When I asked my wife to suggest that you provide one of your lovely concert pianos for my performance in the philharmonic concert on 25 March in Vienna, I did so less for selfish purposes, but in the hope that I might produce a more brilliant effect on a 'Bechstein' than on a 'Bösendorfer' or a 'Streicher' . . . Far be it from me to deny that an instrument from your workshop is better suited to my small talent than any other instrument of German manufacture; on the other hand it will not have escaped you that by this action I will add the whole pack of Austrian piano manufacturers to the host of enemies I already possess in Vienna . . . My idea was to be of service to you in establishing a reputation throughout Germany, such as Streicher possessed some decades ago, or Erard in the whole world. My scheme was to demonstrate Prussian superiority in one area at least, the field of piano manufacture . . . [6]

Even such a dedicated fan of the Bechstein product was soon caught up in the brand-name competition, however. Three years after writing that letter Bülow published the following statement:

> The use by the undersigned of a concert piano from the factory of Steinway & S., in many ways an excellent instrument, in the first concert of the 'Gesellschaft der Musikfreunde' ('Society of Music Lovers') on 31 October . . . has given rise to any number of advertisements by overly enthusiastic friends of the company which are bound to confuse public opinion in the matter of my personal preference . . . On every occasion when I devote a concert programme exclusively to solo performance at the piano, I am as dependent for the exhaustive interpretation of my artistic intentions on the Bechstein 'colour piano', as I might – rather inadequately – call it, as I am on my ten fingers . . . Nonetheless as a 'committed pianist' I consider it my duty to sacrifice my personal preference when it is a question of encouraging another worthy and respectable industrial endeavour (thus for example the achievement of the Messrs Steinway) . . . This principle of justice and fairness I will continue to uphold whenever practicable; I wish however to be spared any hasty conclusions drawn from my well-meaning efforts at patronage. [7]

He then signed himself very formally as court pianist to His Majesty the King.

On another occasion Bülow approached Bechstein with a mixture of flattery and *fait accompli*. He was planning a tour of Russia when the owner of the distinguished Viennese firm of Bösendorfer, a make that is today one of the leading international brands, offered his services. Bülow wrote to Bechstein: 'Another offer has been made to me which is no small temptation. Our good Mr Bösendorfer would like to do the Russian tour with me, naturally on condition that I play his pianos, which are of course no serious competition for you, though they are for me, in that my touch and tonal colouring are less well served on his chessboards than they are on yours.'[8] In the end he agreed to do the Russian tour under the auspices of his Berlin 'inspirer', as he liked to call Bechstein, using his instruments and agents. But the tour was badly prepared, and a certain ill-feeling between them flared up into a (short-lived) row when Bülow again got ensnared in commercial rivalries while organizing a trip to America. 'Sir,' he wrote, 'you seem to have felt called upon to make improper use of a confidential communication on my part concerning the pianos I am to use in America . . . I must make clear to you my profound and fully justified indignation.'[9]

Only Franz Liszt was preserved from commercial pressures and temptations. He played every brand of piano, because he was overwhelmed with unsolicited donations; his homes looked more like salerooms. In 1861 he told music historian C. F. Weitzmann: 'As for the pianos in my possession, in Altenburg (near Weimar), there are the following instruments: 1 Erard in the reception room on the first floor, 1 Bechstein in the little salon next door – 1 Boisselot (Marseille) in my study and workroom . . . In the so-called music room (2nd floor) there are two Viennese grand pianos by Streicher and Bösendorfer, and in the other room there is a Hungarian one by Beregszay . . .' Fifteen years later he was asked the same question, and his answer reveals the changes in the market: 'In my present apartments (in the Hofgärtnerei) there is a magnificent Bechstein grand piano, and for my winter quarters in Budapest there are one or two Bösendorfer pianos . . . Chickering's piano, which I used in Rome, is now in Hungary, and the Steinway is often of service here for concerts.'[10]

Brand-name awareness, as we call it nowadays, took hold very swiftly, and any number of imitative names soon made their appearance. Once the original Bechstein was well established, instruments with labels like 'Beckstein', or 'Bachstein', 'Brechstein', 'Eckstein' and

'C. Rechstein' suddenly came onto the market in Germany. In America, Steinway & Sons found themselves competing with firms like 'Steinmay', 'Stannay', 'Steinmetz' and 'Stanley & Sons', while the Chickerings gained a rival called 'Pickering'.

The American market was further complicated by the stencil system, a legal form of brand-name piracy. Arthur Loesser has described the method used by the first mass-market producer of pianos, Joseph P. Hale, who bought in parts and set up something resembling an early assembly-line system, then sold the instruments indiscriminately.

> Thus, to invent a fictitious example – not therefore untrue in principle – let us suppose the thriving middle-sized town of Zoab, or Franklinsburg, in North-Southern Ohio, harbored two music stores: that of Hezekiah Hitchcock, and that of Benno Bimmelgieser & Son. Each would buy the same piano from Joseph P. Hale, differing possibly in the color of the varnish or in some detail of the leg carving; one, however, would have 'Hitchcock' and the other 'Bimmelgieser & Son' in gilt letters on the name board. Hitchcock, on the corner of Main Street and Broadway, would ask $350 for it, while Bimmelgieser & Son, housed in less glittering real estate, would sell it for $250 and still make a profit, since Hale sold these instruments indiscriminately for $160. Hitchcock's customers would be glad to pay the extra $100, feeling somehow that his nobler name and location were bound to make the piano better suited to their parlors. Or we can picture the hustling piano jobbers Twiddle & Bangs of Wampun city, the metropolis of Pennsyltucky. After making a reputation by selling Hale's pianos under their own stencil to small towns and villages, Twiddle & Bangs might want to clear out some remaining stock at a much lower price without injuring the prestige of 'their' product. They might then sell the same old Hale pianos at a reduction of fifty per cent, but restenciled 'Washington' or 'Mozart' or 'Rip van Winkle'.[11]

The success of the Steinway piano in the European market is visible in a caricature published at the time of the world trade exhibition in Paris in 1867. The drawing features a grand piano crowned with a sign proclaiming 'Pianos Steinway'; around the piano is a jostling crowd of onlookers in top hats and caps, all pushing their way forward with outstretched arms, desperate to touch the keyboard. The caption reads: 'At the sound of the admirable American Steinway pianos the exhibition public was seized to a man with a desire to play the instrument.'

The sudden rage for American pianos, however, meant the gradual decline of the established European manufacturers. Eduard Hanslick observed from London:

> English nationalism has recently turned to the question of piano manufacture. There are famous old English firms in the business; masters like Broadwood and Kirkman have led the trade since the pianoforte was first played publicly in London in 1767. Unfortunately the great English piano makers have not progressed with the times. Their instruments cannot compare with what Steinway displays in his London concert hall . . .[12]

On the whole, however, pianists still tended to use local instruments. Once, in London, Clara Schumann complained:

> The heaviness and high pitch of the instrument (a Broadwood) is causing me trouble again. For the last few days I have been practising at Broadwood's. – Recently Scharwenka played a Blüthner, a year ago Barth played a Bechstein, which hurt Broadwood considerably. I could not find it in me to do that to Broadwood by bringing a Steinweg (from Brunswick), but oh how happy I would be to have one, instead of struggling with this Broadwood.[13]

Clara Schumann's mention of Steinweg brings us to the story of the most curious and protracted feud in the history of the piano business. This particular war was carried on not in the concert hall but in courts and lawyers' offices on both sides of the Atlantic, to be resolved just a few years ago, in 1980, with a compromise that one newspaper announced under the headline 'Steinweg and Steinway reconciled'.

It was a family feud pursued through the provincial courts of Brunswick, Hamburg and Berlin for some forty years before it was taken to the national German court in the 1920s. Strictly it was not in fact a family feud at all: the 1926 decision of the Reichsgericht gives the history of the case.

> In the year 1865, after the deaths of two of his brothers in New York and at the behest of his relatives there, Theodor Steinweg emigrated to New York and entered his father's business . . . Before his emigration to

America he had sold his business in Brunswick in a contract dated 30 September 1865 for a price of 20,000 thalers to three of his employees, namely Wilh. Grotrian, Adolf Helfferich and H. O. W. Schulz ... with the authority to direct the company under the name 'C. F. Th. Steinweg Nachf. [Successors]' ... The new company was also authorized under the contract to continue to use the measures ... and models, although without the right to reproduce same, which Th. Steinweg had received from the American company for the same purpose. The latter, as well as Theodor Steinweg, retained the right to demand the return of these objects at any time. In the year 1869 the company name 'C. F. Theodor Steinweg Nachf.' was changed to the present company name 'Grotrian, Helfferich, Schulz, Th. Steinweg Nachf.' ...

In the year 1872 the commercial relationship between the company in Brunswick and the New York company was terminated ... There began a period of intense business rivalry and personal acrimony. In 1874 Theodore Steinway returned to Brunswick, changed his name back to Theodor Steinweg, and opened a sales operation under the name 'C. F. Th. Steinweg Europäisches Generaldepot von Steinway & Sons in New York'. In the year 1875 the company Steinway & Sons in New York opened a branch in London for the sale of their pianos, while Theodore Steinway founded a pianoforte factory under the name 'Steinways Pianofortefabrik' in the year 1880 in Hamburg ... In the year 1881, after the death of Schulz, the remaining two shareholders of the Brunswick company petitioned the commercial registry office in Brunswick for the removal of the names 'Grotrian', 'Helfferich' and 'Schulz' from their company name, so that the company could be called henceforth 'Th. Steinweg Nachf'.[14] [This petition was refused.]

One can see that the less Theodor(e) Steinway(weg) wanted to have to do with his former employees in Brunswick, the more fiercely they clung to his name. They went on petitioning the patent office with seemingly endless permutations of the company name, always under protest from the Steinways: 'Steinweg Nachf.', 'Steinweg Nachf. Grotrian Braunschweig', 'Grotrian-Steinweg Nachf.', 'Grotrian, Steinweg', 'Steinweg Successors', 'Grotrian Steinweg' and 'Grotrian-Steinweg' (hyphenated) were also among the names they tried. In 1919 the brothers Grotrian, who had inherited the business, changed their name by deed poll to Grotrian Steinweg. Such loyalty to the name of the founder!

The decision of the Reichsgericht in 1926 fell largely in favour of the

Brunswick brothers: it was judged that there was no danger of confusion on the part of the consumer, nor indeed of any confusion of business. A hyphen was however deemed necessary, so that Grotrian could not be taken as a forename: the instruments were to be labelled Grotrian-Steinweg.

But the Reichsgericht was not to have the last word in this bizarre case: the feud was revived after the Second World War. The Steinways went to the American courts; again the case was carried to the highest court; this time the American company won its argument, although the decision was valid only within the territory of the United States. At the end of February 1980 a compromise was finally reached in Frankfurt: it was agreed that both company names would continue to compete in the European market, 'Steinway & Sons' alongside 'Grotrian-Steinweg'; outside Europe, including of course in the United States, the German company would sell its instruments under a simple 'Grotrian' label.

One last note about that *annus mirabilis* 1853: all three of the great piano manufacturers founded in that year have now passed out of family hands. Bechstein was taken over by the American Baldwin Company, Blüthner was nationalized by the East German government in 1972, and Steinway now belongs to the American media conglomerate CBS.

DISCOVERED AT LAST
The Soul of the Piano

We now come to something like a Copernican revolution in the history of the piano: the discovery that the truth is not so obvious as it seems. The piano, in short, is a musical instrument played not with the fingers, nor with the arms, nor with the torso, nor even (as Gieseking and others have claimed) with the ear, but with the – feet. The true secret of the instrument has little to do with keys, strings, frame, or soundbox. As Anton Rubinstein boldly claimed: 'The pedal is the soul of the piano.'[1]

The *pedal*? *The* pedal? Surely the piano has two pedals, as a rule? Even a layman will soon realize which one Rubinstein meant: namely the right-hand or sustaining pedal that is the salvation of so many struggling dilettantes. A judicious application of the sustaining pedal will transform the clumsiest rendition into a smooth legato. Though of course that is not the sort of use Rubinstein meant to encourage. Any soul, however, is susceptible to evil, so the abuse of the pedal only strengthens Rubinstein's definition.

Even experienced theoreticians like Adolph Kullak are liable to wax enthusiastic when it comes to the pedal. In his *Aesthetik des Klavierspiels* (*Aesthetics of Piano Playing*) Kullak begins with an objective discussion of the first three functions of the pedal, these being (1) to facilitate elision between notes, (2) to multiply the number of notes sounding at any one time, and (3) to intensify the sound. Then he turns to the fourth function, namely 'to promote the poetic shading of the piece'. He explains:

> It is in the nature of the pedal to contribute a hovering quality to the tone. Even an isolated note, played with the pedal, will sound different from the same note played on its own. The softly chaotic humming of other strings wraps the note in a mysterious cloud of uncertainty which, as long as it remains subtle enough not to disturb the harmonic sense,

stimulates the imagination and the sensibility. Uncertainty is a prime
stimulant for the latter. – The same impression is markedly intensified if
the pedal is applied throughout a sequence of notes . . . Use of the pedal
in the treble range can elicit chords which are chromatic in themselves.
The sound is reminiscent of aeolian harps. The effect in the bass is of
organ pipes or bells. But it is not these instrumental echoes alone which
are so stimulating: the essential element is the listener's emotional
response to all that is sonorous, unusual, layered with meaning, in some
sense unclear . . . and evocative of mysterious or magical regions.[2]

The pedal is the soul of the piano – no other statement so concisely
expresses the refinement of the instrument and its music. No other part
of the piano has come quite so far in the process. The pedal in fact
began life as a perfectly mundane accessory, a cheap showman's
gimmick which long maintained the closest link to older instruments
like the harpsichord and the clavichord.

One way of picturing how the pedal was used in early forms of the
piano would be to imagine a street artist playing six instruments
simultaneously. He might have a mouth organ strapped around his
head, a fiddle clamped under his chin, with his left hand wielding the
bow while the right plucks at a zither, an accordion busily heaving
between his knees while one foot works a drum and the other a
triangle. The picture is by no means exaggerated: before 1830 it was
not at all unusual for an instrument to be fitted with up to eight pedals
(or stops).

As Rosamund T. Harding notes in her detailed study of the piano up
to 1851, some early instruments were even fitted with bassoons,
drums, triangles and cymbals. Harps and the old lute stop were still in
use. The chief purpose of the new pedals introduced from about 1800
was the imitation of Turkish music, with its characteristic chorus of
percussion and rhythm instruments. Thus there were bells, cymbals,
little drums, and even a big drum sound achieved by striking the
sounding-board with a stick.[3]

The pedal cannot be said to have become the soul of the piano until
the second half of the nineteenth century, when all these exotic
accoutrements fell away. The pianoforte had first to abandon the
foreign frippery and concentrate on its own sound, its own increasingly full and powerful, metallic and abstract sound, a far more
interesting field for experimental composition. With the introduction

of the full iron frame and the invention of cross-stringing, the pianoforte truly came into its own, and the pedal was free to reveal its true function – not as a source of additional sound, nor as a mere amplifier, but as a means of allowing the sound free rein. The powerful damper mechanism of the modern piano keeps the strings firmly in check: each damper is removed for the moment of striking, and only for the single note struck. The pedal however removes the whole damper mechanism, allowing the strings to resonate freely, rejoicing in the play of mathematics and harmony.

One of the earliest and most famous pedal pieces is the first movement from Beethoven's Sonata Op. 27, 2 in C sharp minor (the 'Moonlight Sonata'). Beethoven (along with Daniel Steibelt) was one of the first composers to include pedal markings in his work. Here, in the adagio sostenuto, he marked at the beginning: *'sempre pianissimo e senza sordini.'* The instruction was so revolutionary that it is often misunderstood to this day: an English footnote to an early edition explained that the pedal was *only* to be used when required by the harmony, and a common mistake is the conviction that the left (soft) pedal is to be used throughout.

There is one thing to be said for this interpretation, and that is that Beethoven did want the pedal used for the whole movement: *'senza sordini'* means 'without dampers'. (The trouble is that this instruction cannot be carried out to the letter on a modern piano, for the result would be not a cloud of sound but a full-scale smokescreen. How the pianist resolves the question, possibly by keeping the pedal halfway down, or releasing it every time the harmony changes, is one of those trade secrets that makes an 'easy' piece so difficult to perform.)

Chopin used the pedal above all for the play with overtones which is so characteristic of his work: the Nocturne in E sharp major is probably the most popular example. Interestingly, although he made precise and pointed use of the pedal in his compositions, he allowed his students to use it only very sparingly – this according to Debussy, who took lessons from a student of Chopin's. On occasion he even seemed to make double use of the pedal, for instance in the eighth prélude, when it is applied for groups of surging semiquavers the result is not just to produce a stardust of sound, but also to facilitate the performance, less pressure being required to strike the keys when the pedal is down. Soviet pianist Grigori Ginsburg pointed out a potential technical difficulty on this point: 'A passage played without the pedal is a much greater strain on the fingers, which are not just striking the keys but also lifting the dampers . . . For this reason an overly frequent change from pedal to no pedal puts the pianist in a difficult position: as he strikes one key with the dampers lifted, the next with the dampers down, his playing will be jerky and uneven.'[4]

Chopin said that the proper use of the pedal was 'the study of a lifetime'.[5] Robert Schumann however was the one to experiment, listening carefully for nuances of sound, muffling effects, overtones. Already at the end of the early 'Papillons' he used the pedal to extraordinary effect: there a six-toned chord is played with the pedal down, then one by one the keys are released, until the last note sounds alone through the veiled overtones of the other five. The use of the pedal at the end of the 'Paganini' passage in the *Carnaval* piece is just as striking: again marked 'ppp', the final chord is struck in semi-silence, then the pedal is pressed, creating the illusion, as pianist Charles Rosen described it, of a chord swelling in crescendo.[6]

The left or soft pedal is in some ways even more soulful than the 'Rubinstein' pedal to the right. In an upright instrument the softer effect is produced by shortening the distance from hammers to strings. In a grand piano however keyboard and hammers are actually shifted one or two millimetres to the side when the pedal is pressed, so that in the middle section (where there are three strings for every note) the hammers now strike only two strings. In older instruments the hammers were left striking only one string, whence the name '*una corda* pedal'. It will be obvious from this that the soft pedal not only muffles the tone but also changes the sound of the instrument: roughly speaking, it is rather like the difference between a full chorus and a chamber choir.

Adolph Kullak wrote of the soft pedal: 'Its main purpose is to allow the softest possible *piano* . . . All good piano teachers from Czerny to Riemann claim, with justification, that it is more of an achievement to play softly without the aid of the pedal . . . None the less the use of the pedal offers the undeniable advantage of a performance far more melodious than would be possible without it.'[7] Using both pedals at once results in a regular ecstasy of softness: 'The soft, hazy quality of the sound . . . makes a melancholy passage more brooding and inward-looking, a cheerful passage sweeter, a gentle passage more ethereal . . .'

Leaving aside the aesthetics of the matter we are left with the paradoxical fact that the softest sound is achieved by maximum mechanical effort, as a quarter of the 'machine' is moved from one place to another. It is time to consider, if only briefly, the miraculous mechanism of the piano.

If the greatest miracle of the piano is its sound, then the next greatest miracle is its soundlessness. Every note is brought into being by a long and secret process, conducted in utter silence. The key responds to pressure from headquarters (the finger, the hand, of the player) but is careful to avoid direct action itself, preferring to send out a special commando (the intermediate lever), while at the same time ensuring that the undercover expert (the damper arm) instructs the agent responsible (the damper head) to remove the intrusive material (damper felt) from the scene of action. Meanwhile, that is simultaneously, the commando will have activated its trusty adjutant (the escapement), while another man (the repetition lever) stands guard. But even he is only indirectly involved, his function being to arouse the 'sleeper' (hammer), who is of course ready and waiting to spring into action. At which point headquarters receives the message through its special channels (the ears): another mission accomplished.

The piano, in other words, is a highly complex machine. In one or two specific cases it has been calculated just how many mechanical movements are required to create a single piece of music: in one and a a half minutes playing Chopin's eighth prélude Pollini claimed to have caused eight thousand movements; Schumann's Toccata (Op. 7) required forty thousand in five minutes of play, according to Horowitz (who did not repeat the first part); and a mammoth work like the Hammerklavier Sonata demands almost a quarter of a million movements within the instrument.

The miraculous thing about all this movement – swinging, pushing, falling back, lifting, levering, striking – is that not a whirr nor a whine nor a rattle is to be heard, as long as the mechanism is in good condition. The parts responsible for this extraordinary discretion deserve a mention here: the leather and felt buffers on hammers and hammer rests, dampers and levers (and much more).

In the masterful development of this remarkable mechanism the piano is revealed as a child of the eighteenth century and a hero of the nineteenth. Rosamund T. Harding counted over a thousand patents filed up to 1851 alone. The piano stands as a monument to one and a half centuries of engineering genius. Tinkers and dreamers, carpenters and tanners, mechanics and musicians all played their part in this one small field of human endeavour. The piano incorporates all the ingenuity of the nineteenth century.

The ideology of piano playing begins with the use of the pedal. It is possible to tell what period and what school a pianist hails from by listening to how he uses the pedal. A period of intensive pedal usage (however individual styles may vary) is often followed by an era of new functionalism: Chopin is played coldly, Tchaikovsky without emotion, Mozart without subtlety. (There is a world of difference between Edwin Fischer's recording of the 'Well-Tempered Clavier' from the thirties and Glenn Gould's interpretation in the seventies, Fischer's lyricism contrasting sharply with Gould's almost spatial polyphony and clear constructivism.) The use of the pedal reflects the passage of generations.

THE NEW VIRTUOSITY

Jupiter of octaves, pope of scales,
knight of thirds, king of trills.
Hans von Bülow
(on some of his rivals)

The fact that Anton Rubinstein was responsible for that sensitive statement about the soul of the piano must have astonished all who saw him, much less heard him play. He was a giant of a man with a massive skull and a wild mane of hair: Rellstab called him the 'Hercules of the piano'. Many observers were reminded of Beethoven. For Liszt he was 'Van 2'.[1]

Much as Beethoven had burst into the closed world of Viennese society at the turn of the century, so Rubinstein stormed the musical citadel in central Europe, defying pianistic convention. His immediate reception was anything but warm. In 1862 Stephen Heller wrote: 'What exaggerations of the less salient points, and what negligence in the more important passages! One felt the boredom of those agile and powerful fingers that had nothing to put into them, as when they give the circus elephant an empty salad bowl to swallow.'[2] Clara Schumann was shocked the first time she heard him play: 'From the first chord he struck I was horrified by his hard touch and then I was not at all pleased with his prelude; it seemed so inartistic to chase up and down the keyboard in runs of sixths and thirds . . . His technique by the way is extraordinary.'[3]

It was not just that Rubinstein came from Russia: in pianistic terms he came from out of nowhere. He had his first lessons from his mother, who then entrusted him to Alexander Villoing, a teacher in Moscow. But Moscow was scarcely recognized in cultivated Europe; the least that was expected of anyone from the East was an apprenticeship with Henselt in St Petersburg. As Rubinstein reported: 'Villoing was my first teacher, after my mother, and, aside from the man who taught me music theory ... [he was] also my only teacher. When I was eight years old my lessons began and with my thirteenth year my musical education was complete. After Villoing – I repeat – I had no other teacher.'[4]

As a seventeen-year-old Rubinstein did seek an audience with Liszt in Vienna, but Liszt dismissed him with the advice that a capable person must expect to achieve everything alone, relying on no one's support. 'That put me off for a long time.' The truth of the matter is probably that Rubinstein caught Liszt too early, while the latter was still frequently on tour. In the last years of his life, as we will see, Liszt was happy to surround himself with any number of students, virtually holding court, with Rubinstein a familiar and forgiving guest.

Like Liszt, Rubinstein enjoyed a series of musical careers: the child prodigy grew up to become a prodigious pianist, then a super-virtuoso and finally a grand old man of the piano. Like Liszt he also composed, although very little survives but the schmaltzy 'Melody in F'. Like Liszt, too, he subscribed to the grand principle of *'génie oblige'*, remembering the social obligations of the successful artist: thus he became one of the moving forces behind the Russian Music Society in St Petersburg, where he also founded the Imperial Conservatory in 1862. He was director of the conservatory for five years.

He was never to forget an experience he had as a twenty-year-old in Moscow.

It was in the year 1850. I wanted to take Communion and I went to confession in the Kasan cathedral. When I went up to the table where the deacon was writing names in the book, he asked me to give my name, rank and profession.

'Rubinstein, artist,' I replied.

'You mean you are employed in the theatre?'

'No, I am not employed.'

'Then you must teach in an institute?'

Again I said no.

The deacon was embarrassed, and I was at a loss for words myself. Finally I broke the silence.

'Yes, I am a musician, an artist.'

'Now I understand! So you are employed?'

'I tell you I am not employed.'

'But who are you then? What am I to put in the book?'

So it went on for some minutes, and who knows how the scene may

have ended, had it not occurred to the confused deacon to ask me my
father's rank.

'He was a merchant in the second guild,' I said.

'Now we know,' the deacon triumphantly cried, 'who you are! You
are the son of a merchant of the second guild, and that is what we will
write in the book.'[5]

Later in life Rubinstein remarked that a certain price was paid for the
social accreditation of musicians, the recognized diplomas of
conservatory-trained pianists: '. . . the fervent love of music that
burned in us is no more.'[6] The delusion of an old man, perhaps, but it is
certainly true that the piano virtuoso was increasingly weighed down
with public honours and offices. Soon there would be professors of the
piano.

Back to the principle of 'génie oblige'. Rubinstein once gave a
charity concert in Berlin for which the list of beneficiaries survives.
The net proceeds amounted to 17,854 marks, which were distributed
as follows:

For the poor people of Berlin	5000	marks
For the Kaiser- and Kaiserin-Friedrich Hospital	1500	
For the children's holiday camps	1500	
For the children's sanatoriums	1500	
For the Society for the Feeding of Poor Children	500	
For the warming houses	500	
For the public kindergartens	500	
For the Fröbel Public Kindergarten	500	
For the Homeless Persons Refuge	500	
For the pension fund of the Philharmonic Orch.	1000	
For the support fund of the Association of Berlin Music Teachers	1000	
For the Russian community, to be distributed by Provost Maltzew	2000	
For the memorial to Haydn, Mozart, Beethoven	1000	
To anonymous recipients	854[7]	

In 1885–86 Rubinstein celebrated the end of his virtuoso career with a
series of 'historical concerts'. The idea of presenting an overview of the
whole development of piano music arose from the innate historicism of
the nineteenth century, and Rubinstein was not the first to attempt
such a thing. Between 1861 and 1863 Ernst Pauer (senior), an Austrian

pianist, had given a full programme of concerts which were intended to sum up the history of music for the piano and the harp from 1600 to the present day.

But Rubinstein's programme of historical concerts was more ambitious than anything previously attempted. His effort may be said to have heralded the beginning of the modern concert industry, which now routinely ensures that so much is on offer simultaneously throughout the world. He laid the precedent for the requirement that every virtuoso pianist be prepared to master a vast repertoire and to undertake a gigantic travel itinerary. He proudly reported

> full success in carrying out my plan. In Petersburg, Moscow, Vienna, Berlin, London, Paris and Leipzig respectively I gave a series of seven historical concerts, reducing the series to three concerts in Dresden and Brussels; in the aforementioned cities, furthermore, I gave my concerts twice, that is I repeated each concert the following day for music students ... Much of what I performed I had learned in my early youth. Everything that I performed for the first time in these concerts, which amounted to a good number of pieces, I had mastered in the course of one summer. I never used a prompter, which is in any case scarcely possible at the piano.[8]

The mammoth nature of the whole undertaking was matched by the length of each evening session, which must have amounted to four hours on average. The Beethoven programme for example included no less than all eight of the great sonatas. (Today it would be considered ambitious to perform just four of them at one sitting: the Waldstein sonata, the 'Appassionata', the sonata Op. 90 and Op. 111.) At about the same time Hans von Bülow gave a series of Beethoven concerts of similar dimensions, though the task he set himself was arguably even more difficult: in one evening he played the five last piano sonatas.

It is interesting to note that while Rubinstein began his historical programme with William Byrd, he then dealt with three whole centuries of music in the course of the first evening, covering Bach and Handel, Haydn and Mozart. This means that the following six concerts (24 hours *in toto*) were devoted to the nineteenth century. Rubinstein's programme, in other words, implicitly proclaimed the pianoforte and its music to be a nineteenth-century matter – a proclamation which coincides with our thesis here. The true work for the piano arises from the interplay of secular attitude, individual genius and explosive sound. The heavy bias of the programme, with whole evenings devoted to Chopin and Schumann respectively, reveals the performer's personal predilections. Rubinstein once declared that 'Everything that excited us in music, everything we loved about it – all that died with Chopin and Schumann.'[9]

Rubinstein paid a price for his ambition. During one of his mammoth concerts, in Paris, he slumped over the keyboard in a dead faint.

Rubinstein was the most impetuous representative of what could be called the third wave of nineteenth-century virtuosity, if Kalkbrenner, Herz, Hummel and company may be said to make up a first wave, with the Liszt decade standing alone as a second. By the time Rubinstein was in his heyday, Liszt had retired from active touring to instruct at least two generations of successors. Nowadays one would speak of master classes or summer academies or piano workshops. Every year for three decades, the master spent some months surrounded by worshipping young pianists eager to learn the secrets of genius. For half a century the concert halls of the world were supplied with pianists who could describe themselves as students of Liszt. Eugene d'Albert, one of the last and most famous of them all, counted Frenchmen, Turks, Poles, Russians, Americans, Dutch and a few Germans among the host of disciples. Some, according to d'Albert, played very well, others very badly, but in any case he felt he learned a great deal, since Liszt largely taught by example.[10]

At first these teach-ins took place in Altenburg castle near Weimar, later in the old Hofgärtnerei. In the Altenburg period Liszt was still at the height of his fame, and still touring, but later he became more and more of a living legend, a cult figure of the piano. Max Kalbeck described the atmosphere at Altenburg, to which he was by no means immune: 'Altenburg castle with its two storeys and countless rooms combined kitchen and boudoir, throne room and library, hotel and home, display cabinet and workshop. The whole presented itself as a magnificent Liszt museum in which the most remarkable object was the owner himself, and the permanent collection of every honour Liszt had ever received was a standing source of flattery for the master of the house.'

The most famous Altenburg alumnus, after Hans von Bülow, was Carl Tausig, who died when he was just thirty years old. His father,

Aloys Tausig, also a renowned pianist, had taken lessons with Liszt's one-time rival Sigismund Thalberg. According to those who had the good fortune to hear him play, the younger Tausig was of all nineteenth-century pianists the one who came closest to Chopin's style. Lenz, who himself knew Chopin well, said of Tausig: 'He played like Chopin, he felt as he did, he *was* Chopin at the piano.'[11] Rubinstein, who was never too particular about wrong notes, called him 'the infallible'. In 1865 Tausig founded a School of Higher Piano-Playing in Berlin, which he directed for five years. He recorded his preferred exercises in a much-published study on 'How to Practise the Piano'. On the other hand he was apparently given to such unhelpful comments as 'Terrible! Shocking! Dreadful! Oh God! Oh God!'[12]

Tausig also shared Chopin's aversion to public performance. Amy Fay, an American who studied with both Liszt and Tausig, reported that he once withdrew from a series of four concerts, already announced in the newspapers, on the grounds that his nerves were too frail.[13] C. F. Weitzmann called him 'the last of the virtuosos'; certainly he appears to have been one of the last of the breed whose subtle art was linked to a feeble constitution. After his death in 1871 the stage was seized by a phalanx of more robust talents, many of them born within a few years of one another: Emil Sauer and Conrad Asorge (1862), Alfred Reisenauer (1863), Eugene d'Albert (1864) and Frederic Lamond (1868).

Liszt was always happy to let his favourite students follow him from one of his princely establishments to the next – even when he descended on 'Villa Wahnfried' in Bayreuth, which he did with unwelcome regularity. D'Albert was once witness to a heated family row in that house. The episode is worth noting if only to provide a passing glimpse of the one nineteenth-century composer who had little patience for the piano: Richard Wagner. Wagner used the piano only in his very earliest works: his Op. 1 is a piano sonata (in B flat major); Op. 2 is a Polonaise for four hands; apparently there was an earlier sonata in A major, and later on 'A Sonata for the Album of Mrs M. W.' (Mathilde Wesendonk). He also made various arrangements for the piano, including one of Beethoven's 9th Symphony, one of Mozart's *Don Giovanni* and another of Palestrina's 'Stabat Mater'. Otherwise the piano was something of an alien element in the Wahnfried establishment, all the more so when a crowd of strangers were fooling with it. One of the more understandable of Wagner's rigid household rules was the arrangement he made with his father-in-law Liszt: the latter was to receive his students only in Wagner's absence, and work was to be abandoned as soon as Wagner returned home. Liszt therefore, according to d'Albert, spent a large part of each lesson peering out the window for his son-in-law. But one day he was so absorbed in explaining something to d'Albert that he forgot himself, until suddenly the door sprang open to reveal Wagner in high dudgeon. D'Albert apparently rushed out, leaving Liszt to his fate.[14]

Liszt would not have been Liszt had he not collected a chorus of talented and enthusiastic disciples. All his life he was surrounded by an entourage of devoted beauties, and his female students included Martha Remmert, Anna Mehlig, Amy Fay, Adele aus der Ohe and the most famous of them all, Sophie Menter.

A piano lesson should be an occasion for rigorous musical discipline and solid training, but at the same time it can be a romantic encounter. Theodor Leschetitzky, whose renown as a teacher rivalled Liszt's own, is a prime example of the devoted pedagogue. Leschetitzky spent some years teaching at the conservatory Rubinstein had founded in St Petersburg before moving to Vienna in 1878 to set himself up as a private instructor, having studied there himself under Czerny. With one marriage already behind him, Leschetitzky proceeded to marry three of his students in succession: Annette Essipoff, Eugenia Donnemourska and Marie Gabrielle Rosborska.

Leschetitzky's most famous student was Ignacy Paderewski, whose later career turned from the piano to politics. In 1918 Paderewski was sent to Washington as ambassador for Poland, then recalled the following year to serve as prime minister and foreign minister in the newly founded Polish state. In 1922 he took up the piano again, but in 1940, after the German occupation of Poland, he was elected president of the parliament in exile. As a young man he was extremely popular with the ladies: on one American tour he was all but crushed to death by crowds of admirers, and in three months he earned no less than $300,000. Paderewski also appears to have been the first professional pianist to insure his hands – for $100,000.

Clara Schumann was another famous teacher of the piano; in later years she made a home for herself at the newly founded Raff Conservatory in Frankfurt am Main. Unlike Liszt and Leschetitzky, however, her influence seems to have been short-lived. Of her many students, only three women managed to make names for themselves: Nathalie Janotha, Fanny Davies and Ilona Eibenschütz (whom a young George Bernard Shaw once applauded for her sensitive rendition of Schumann's Symphonic Etudes).

Clara herself continued to give concerts, and her account of a performance in the presence of Queen Victoria seems as good a way as any to take our leave of her.

> That was an incredible concert . . . Mad. [*sic*] Neruda, Frl. Regan, a few gentlemen and myself all contributed. The room was very pleasant for music but not very large – 700 people were invited (for 5–7 in the evening), and there were some 100 people in the hall, for the most part *standing* behind empty seats . . . The queen did not greet us but sat half turned into the room, talking throughout, stopping only to hear the last measures of each piece and then to applaud . . . All the while one heard the steady murmur of the other 600 guests in the adjoining rooms. The most incredible thing happened after the first half: the queen stood up to take tea and for the interval first the royal band played a sort of potpourri and then two bagpipers let fly. I did not know what to think, did not at first understand what it was, until Mad. Neruda told me that this is the queen's favourite music! . . . I was beside myself, only wanted to run away. Then it was time for the second half and the queen had already taken her seat when it seemed to occur to her that she ought to say something to us. So she came up, began with a slight bow in my direction and the words 'very nicely played' . . . , moved her gaze round the circle and then returned to her seat . . . when it was all over she said not a word of thanks – I have never known such a thing in all my life . . . this queen will never see *me* again, *that much I know*![15]

Clara was by this time well on her way to becoming a sort of Queen Victoria of the piano. There are a number of striking biographical coincidences: she was born in the same year as the English queen, 1819; she married in the same year, 1840; in the course of her brief marriage she was the more famous, one could say the 'reigning' partner; and like the queen she survived her husband by forty years. She also guarded the memory of her beloved Robert Schumann as fervently as Victoria mourned her Albert.

There is one more name that stands out from the crowd of nineteenth-century pianists, and that is Ferruccio Busoni. Born in Empoli, near Florence, in 1866, he was another child prodigy. By his early twenties he was teaching in the conservatories of Helsinki, Moscow and Boston, already a true cosmopolitan. Berlin was the city he seemed to consider his home: he lived there for three long stretches of his life, first around the turn of the century, then in the years before the First World War and finally through the last years of his life in the early twenties (he died in 1924).

Alfred Brendel, in an early essay which he later retracted in part, hailed Busoni as the man who perfected the art of piano-playing. For all Brendel's later reservations he did concisely sum up the genius of this extraordinary man.

As an all-embracing spirit Busoni has no equal in the history of music: world-famous phenomenal pianist, conductor of new orchestral works, composer of important stage and instrumental music the true value of which has not yet been recognized, influential teacher, extraordinarily cultivated man of letters, admirer of the theatre as sublimated life and of conscious life as applied theatre, world citizen, child of his controversial times and prophet of a music of the future free from the constraints of law-givers.[16]

As a pianist Busoni was a thinker, a sorcerer and an explorer all at once; it was he who wrote that 'the piano is the best actor in the company of instruments.' No other pianist of his generation had his sense of the plasticity of the instrument. He once wrote to his wife: 'Bach is the foundation of piano-playing, Liszt the culmination. Study both and Beethoven becomes possible.'[17] Busoni reveals himself there as the dialectician of the piano.

Busoni's style both as pianist and composer is best demonstrated by comparing his transcription of Bach's 'Chaconne for Solo Violin' with Johannes Brahms' version of the same work. Bach's Chaconne was an unheard-of experiment in its time: the solitary violin standing in for a whole orchestra, moving from harmonic fugue to lyric chorale to operatic pathos, now contemplative, now thrilling to the dance – all on a mere four strings. Brahms saw the whole work as an act of asceticism, an orchestra or a choir or both compressed into the narrow span of the one small instrument. His transcription for the piano was consequently reductive, written for the left hand alone; he meant to recreate the solitude of the lone violinist. Busoni on the other hand responded to the magnificent power of the original piece. He therefore used the piano as Bach had used the violin, calling on all its resources in one of the most subtle and difficult works ever written for the keyboard. In the hands of certain contemporary pianists the work can appear overdone; but in this one composition Busoni truly succeeded in uniting Bach and Liszt. Busoni was by the way so well known for his transcriptions of Bach that one young pianist who had studied under him was described by a contemporary critic as a Bach–Busoni student.

Busoni himself never studied under Liszt, but in his time he was hailed as Liszt's true successor. His admiration for Liszt never stopped him from denouncing slavish imitators.

> Pose is the order of the day. There is a pianist here called Friedheim, a pupil of Liszt, with long hair and a face that looks half severe, half bored. When he plays he comes forward and bows in such a way that his hair covers his face; then he throws his head back to tidy his mane. Then he sits down with a great deal of fuss, and looks around waiting until the audience is quiet; then he seizes the keys 'as the wild beast seizes his prey', to quote Hanslick. But the loveliest thing is to see him during the *tuttis* of the orchestra. There he has room to show off all his tricks. He examines his nails, considers the audience, thrusts his hands into his hair, and does other silly things.[18]

Busoni himself seems to have been quite free of such mannerisms, or else he was too vain to be vain. At the time of his début in London he did not hesitate to write home to his Swedish wife about the empty halls and indifferent reviews, quoting liberally from the papers: 'A young pianist – a new pianist – a pianist simply named Busoni, yet unknown – that's how they all begin.'[19] He was delighted to discover what he thought must be the origin of his name in a French Larousse: 'Figurative: *Homme stupide* (!!) What a sad celebrity my name has attained! So when one says: *Quelle espèce de buson, que celui-la*! it means: What a fool he is!'[20]

Dialectical, demonic, disciplined – the three Ds of Busoni's style (and personality). For all his fame and consequent wealth, Busoni never allowed his discipline to slip. Soviet pianist Alexander Goldenweiser recorded this characteristic incident:

> I took the sleeper to Petersburg, as it was then called; that same day

Busoni had given a concert in Moscow and he was due to repeat the
performance the following day in Petersburg. When I entered the
sleeping car I found Busoni already there. As luck would have it we
were both booked into the same hotel in Petersburg, the 'Astoria' – and
our rooms were on the same floor. Half an hour went by and then I
heard Busoni begin to play; I left my room and sat down in the corridor
to hear how he practised; he worked for three and a half hours. Busoni
was one of the greatest pianists of his time; he had played the same
programme the previous evening in Moscow. He was technically
impeccable, having performed the same works a thousand times, most
recently the very day before – but instead of contenting himself with
half-an-hour's warm-up before going out for a walk Busoni went
through the entire programme from the first note to the last.[21]

It was as if Busoni mistrusted his own technique as well as the
chameleon quality of his instrument. Above all he seems to have been
always uneasily conscious of his many virtuoso rivals. As he once
wrote: 'It is (at first sight) astonishing when another succeeds in doing
what only one could do before; but as soon as there are whole hosts of
others it becomes sheer Darwinism.'[22]

THE AGENT

We artists are a luxury of the bourgeoisie.
Frank Wedekind

Which do you prefer: making music
or selling pork?
Erik Satie

In the last two decades of the nineteenth century Europe seemed to be teeming with great pianists, and audience enthusiasm reached fever pitch. The piano was at the peak of its development and its fame, and scores of pianists achieved international renown (and often great wealth) virtually overnight. Were I to attempt to list all their names this book would begin to resemble a telephone directory.

The commercial success of the professional pianist spawned a hitherto unknown breed of entrepreneur: the concert agent. The travelling impresario was replaced by an established man of business dealing not in stocks and shares but in new musical talent. The most successful concert agent in Europe before the turn of the century was undoubtedly Hermann Wolff of Berlin, who was blessed with musical sensitivity, commercial ingenuity and a quick wit. Liszt once summed him up in a remark to Hans von Bülow: 'You see, dear Hans, he is the great zoo-keeper and he has all you lions in his cage,' whereupon Wolff retorted, 'The difference being that the lions feed me rather than I the lions.'[1]

Like the travelling impresario before him Wolff still played the role of escort and confidant, always ready to call the doctor, turn down the bed, make the camomile tea. He preferred to stay in the background, but when he did move out from the wings it was to act as patron, discoverer and champion. He moved in, for instance, at the time of Eugene d'Albert's inglorious début in Berlin, as his daughter later remembered:

... [d'Albert's] first appearance in a big charity concert in the Viktoria-Theater was a complete failure ... There was no proper programme, rather a mixture of musical ingredients thrown together for the benefit of an uninitiated audience. ... and the expectant crowd listened with growing impatience to the performance of Schumann's 'Symphonic Etudes' by an utterly unknown young pianist. They began to laugh and talk, and there were even cries of 'Stop!'. The unfortunate d'Albert left the stage fully demoralised. Backstage however was someone who, unmoved by this unpleasant exhibition on the part of an ignorant audience, recognized the genius of the player. Trusting his infallible instincts my father ... offered to take over the business management of his concerts, and even guaranteed the astonished d'Albert a minimum annual stipend.[2]

Unlike certain American impresarios such as Bernard Ullman or Max Strakosch, Wolff had a solid and well-rounded education behind him. Born in Cologne in 1845, he moved to Berlin at the age of ten and attended the Friedrich-Werder Gymnasium, where he did business training but also studied the piano and music theory, so that in later life he was able to play at sight and accompany songs. He was also a music critic. As a young man he wrote up a typical day's schedule: 'Morning at Bote & Bock, midday at the Exchange, meal at 4 o'clock, back to Bote & Bock. I rarely get home to our summer house before 10.30 in the evening, and never to bed before midnight. I have taken on the task, on behalf of our music journals, of collating and editing musical news from every possible English, German, French and Italian paper.'[3]

In 1880 Wolff founded his own business, Konzertdirektion Hermann Wolff. In 1882 he was instrumental in the founding of the Berlin Philharmonic Orchestra and the Philharmonic Society. A former skating rink was rebuilt as a concert hall, the new 'Philharmonie', and Berlin was soon established as a national centre for music. Not a little was due to the initiative of Hermann Wolff.

The company letterhead shows how broad its interests were: 'Konzertdirektion Hermann Wolff, Management of the Philharmonic Concerts, the Stern Choral Society, the Philharmonic Chorus, London Symphony Concerts ..., Chatelet Concerts in Paris ..., Philharmonic Concerts in Copenhagen ..., European Representation of Abbey Schöffel and Maurice Grau in New York ...'[4] There follow the names of various singers, violinists, conductors, and at least ten pianists. Among the assets of the company, aside from the artists themselves, was an early duplicating machine.

New virtuosos continued to join Wolff's stable, some of them as eccentric as they were sublime. Vladimir Pachmann, for instance, a Pole famous for his renditions of Chopin, attracted audiences with his extravagant mannerisms as much as with his music. At the end of a particularly difficult passage he would kiss his own hand or reprimand himself ('You fluffed it, Pachmann!').[5] He once told Marcella Sembrich, a singer with whom he had appeared for a concert in Breslau: 'I killed two singers recently. But I can't kill you.'[6]

Pachmann liked to think of himself as the greatest pianist of his time ('I play like a god!' he is supposed to have said), but he was soon obliged to applaud the next generation in the form of ten-year-old Josef Hofmann, who appeared one day in Wolff's parlour. Pachmann played the boy a few pieces, ending with Mendelssohn's 'Rondo capriccioso'. Then, according to their hostess, the boy sat down, saying '*Moi, je joue ça comme ça*', and proceeded to play the same piece 'in the same tempo, perhaps with less finesse, but with great genius. We were all flabbergasted, Pachmann most of all . . . Pachmann was so overcome that he told Papa Hoffmann: "In ten years' time we will all be sitting at his feet, for he is Chopin and Liszt in one." '

Handling artists is not really like taming lions, of course, but rather like juggling raw eggs. However powerful Wolff became he was still at the mercy of the virtuosos he himself discovered. If he put himself out for one artist, accompanying him on tour for instance, one of the others was bound to feel neglected; if he gave them all equal attention, they were all sure to complain. Wolff was a master at a very tricky business, but he sometimes came close to despair in his dealings with Hans von Bülow. As he once wrote to his wife: 'It takes patience, self-control, a thorough understanding of his character and pity, to stay on his good side. Quick to love . . . , quick to hate, as full of certain prejudices as he is free of others, he is one of the most extraordinary selfless-egotistical characters whom Nature, that most original of all inventors, has possibly ever created.'[7]

Hans von Bülow was the first great pianist to fulfil an ambition to conduct. Barenboim, Ashkenazy, Eschenbach, Pollini are now familiar figures on the podium, but at the end of the nineteenth century it was still an unusual career. Mozart and Beethoven both occasionally conducted, of course; Mendelssohn and Schumann both had their own orchestras; Brahms would have liked to compose from the podium. But Bülow was the first professional pianist to become a renowned conductor. His desire to do so may have sprung from a pianist's impatience with inadequate accompaniment, or it may have had to do with the increasingly popular habit of orchestrating music written for the piano. Then of course Bülow will have felt a natural urge to move on to a bigger 'instrument', having mastered the grand piano. Certainly he seems to have been attracted by the rhetorical possibilities of the podium.

Hermann Wolff may have been the man who introduced the critical concert programme, with notes and comments on each piece to be performed, but Bülow was the inventor of the concert speech. His were liable to be vicious. No friend of the director of the Königliches Theatre, whose name was Hülsen, Bülow once introduced the coronation march from Meyerbeer's *Prophet* with these words: 'Ladies and gentlemen! We will now play the piece as the composer wrote it, and not as performed by the Hülsen Circus.'[8] This was shortly after a disastrous production of the opera under Hülsen's direction. Some time later Bülow was finally banned from the Königliches Theatre.

Bülow's most famous speech was given on 28 March 1892 at the end of his fiftieth concert in the Berlin Philharmonie. It was to be his last concert, or so it had been advertised, and the audience refused to let him go without some comment. As he lowered his baton after the final chord of Beethoven's 'Eroica', there was a chorus of calls from the floor: 'Bülow, speech!'

So Bülow spoke. He spoke at length, having obviously prepared his words. The text of the speech has survived. Very well then, he began, for one last time he would invoke Article 27 of the constitution (the right to free speech) and say a few words about Beethoven. Hähnel, sculptor of the Beethoven memorial in Bonn, had ascribed the nine symphonies to the nine Muses. He, Bülow, had a different image, a theatrical image: he saw the symphonies grouped in threes as the three acts of a drama, the climax of each act being the celebration of an ideal – the Hero, Nature and Mankind respectively. 'Let us look more closely at these ideals, starting with the second: Nature. Now Nature, thank God, is no ideal but a solid reality that we will soon be enjoying in preference to this polluted city.' Then, typically scornful: 'Mankind is really an abstraction, a phantom ... Yes, what is this Mankind in actual fact? Nothing but an assortment of Tom, Dick and Harry. So Mankind is really just a pretty dream, or rather a dangerous dream that has borne enough bad fruit ...'[9]

Like so many sceptics Hans von Bülow was a progressive in his dislikes but a conservative in his preferences, a contradiction he revealed as he proceeded to re-dedicate the 'Eroica', Beethoven's celebration, as he saw it, of the Hero. Beethoven himself had torn up the original dedication to Napoleon when the latter donned the mask of 'a mad Caesar', but no musician, according to Bülow, had ever been convinced by the subsequent dedication to Prince Lobkovitz. So Bülow declared he would re-dedicate the work, and the name he chose to honour made this a highly controversial speech at the time.

Two years previously, in 1890, the young Kaiser Wilhelm II had forced his Chancellor to retire. In 1892 Berlin was still torn between devotion to Bismarck and loyalty to the Kaiser. Bülow boldly took his stand: 'We musicians ... hereby dedicate Beethoven's heroic symphony to the greatest spiritual hero to have seen the light of the world since Beethoven himself. We dedicate this symphony to Beethoven's brother, to the Beethoven of German politics, Prince Bismarck! Prince Bismarck – all hail!'

Whereupon the hall was filled with a clashing chorus of noise, wild applause on the one part competing with boos and hisses from the court party and its supporters. Bülow came out again and again, clearly enjoying the tumult. Finally he came forward to the edge of the stage, pulled out his handkerchief, bent over and silently wiped his shoes – a mimed response to the Kaiser's comment that anyone who did not like the way things were going could shake the dust from his feet and leave the country.

The public response to Bülow's dramatic departure was summed up in a poem by a young female admirer:

Wie Bismarck eisern standst du da
Im Nest des Servilismus!
Drum: sein ist die Eroica,
Doch dein der Heroismus!

(Like Bismarck you stood steadfast
In the den of servility!

Therefore: his is the Eroica,
But yours the Heroism!)[10]

Hermann Wolff's house was the meeting place of a glittering musical
circle. As an old man Brahms would stop in after a concert in Berlin to
be regaled with his favourite dish (or what his hostess believed was his
favourite dish): humble pork and beans. Brahms' lifelong friend
Joseph Joachim was also a frequent guest, as were Saint-Saëns and
Edvard Grieg. Rubinstein was often treated to a lavish meal after one
of his concerts, while d'Albert would be served a vegetarian dish.

It was at the Wolffs' that Eugene d'Albert met Teresa Carreño, the
famous South American pianist. He had recently heard her play and
was so taken with her that he dreamed of a lifelong duet. But who was
Teresa Carreño? Born in Caracas in 1853, she gave her first public
performance there in 1861. In 1862 her parents took her to New York
where she studied under Gottschalk. At the age of ten she played for
President Lincoln in the White House. As a teenager she toured
Europe, winning herself international acclaim and the acquaintance of
the entire musical elite of the continent. By 1890 she had survived two
unfortunate marriages; disappointed in love, she devoted all her
passion to the piano. In Germany she was called 'the Valkyrie'.

Carreño was not overly impressed with d'Albert when she first met
him in the Wolffs' home in 1891. 'The first impression Teresa had of
her rival was decidedly unpleasant,' according to fellow Venezuelan
Israel Pena. 'D'Albert looked to her like a sort of mustachioed dwarf,
badly groomed and careless in his dress. Teresa was very cool to him,
while he enthusiastically congratulated her on her rendition of Grieg's
A minor concerto. Her coolness and indifference pricked Eugene in
the core of his male vanity.'[11] Her first impression must have been
rapidly revised, for she soon afterwards agreed to take part in a public
recital with d'Albert, in which he played Beethoven's G major
concerto. Then the pair began to appear regularly in concerts for two
pianos, and they were married in London within the year.

Louise Wolff described the two of them in her diary: '. . . the most
unlikely pair in the world. He thirty – she forty-three. He quiet,
indecisive, effeminate, she bold, enterprising, energetic, a fiery,
unbridled nature. "Américaine du Sud", as she always says. A beauty
well known to generations, highly talented, but somewhat wild.
D'Albert is her third husband, she his second wife.'[12]

The first child arrived, then the second, and then the crisis: d'Albert allegedly told Teresa just days after the birth that he wanted a divorce. She refused to agree, exhausted and bewildered as she was, and eventually turned to Mrs Wolff for advice. The Wolffs' daughter Edith Stargardt-Wolff told the tale:

> We children could hear her impassioned pleas and accusations, all conducted in French, without leaving our rooms. While Mrs Carreño sought comfort and advice from my mother, d'Albert went to my father, and often they were there at the same time in adjoining rooms. D'Albert insisted that he must have his freedom, he was by far the younger of the pair and he had his life before him, while Teresa's best years were behind her . . .[13]

Throughout the marital dispute the two continued to appear together, and Carreño even gave the début performance of d'Albert's E major concerto. Eduard Hanslick may or may not have been deceived by this show of solidarity:

> D'Albert is on to a good thing: he can choose to play his most difficult pieces himself or leave them to his beautiful wife, whose strength and bravura rival his own. Mrs. d'Albert, whom we have had ample opportunity to admire in her unmarried state as Teresa Carreño, performed the new concerto entrusted to her with astonishing virtuosity. Whether her performance was as heartwarming as it was brilliant it is difficult to say after this one hearing. I failed to perceive the 'innermost feeling' prescribed by the composer for the single solo part at the beginning of the adagio.[14]

Their ways parted soon afterwards, in public as in private. The children they divided between them. Hermann Wolff, however, continued to handle both parents.

ACCOMPLICE IN CATASTROPHE
The Piano in the Novel of the Nineteenth Century

> He has the Buddenbrook hands . . . The
> Buddenbrooks can span all the ninths and
> tenths.
>
> *Thomas Mann*

It is the most horrible scene. The man takes off his boots and tiptoes to the wall where his knives and guns are hung above the sofa. He selects a dagger and pulls it out of its sheath. He shruggs off his coat – having only just rushed back from the country – and creeps to the door of the salon, listens a moment, then bursts into the room where two people are sitting over a late meal. They are visibly shocked to see him. One of them recovers enough to smile and say they had just been at their music, only to be silenced by a furious glare from the newcomer. The latter then turns to the woman, who is his wife, and thrusts his elbow into her face, causing her to cry out and fall back on the sofa. Then she sees the knife and stammers: 'Nothing has occurred between him and me, nothing. I swear it to you.' In her husband's view this amounts to a confession, and he grabs her round the throat with his left hand. When she tries to pull away he rams the knife under her ribs. Then he pulls it out again, allowing her to leap up and shout for the children's nurse. The nurse runs in and cries 'Good God!' as the wife collapses on the floor.

Pozdnisheff is the name of the murderer. His motive is the classic one of jealousy, but in an extreme and unusual form. He has murdered his wife – why? Because she played the piano with another man. Years later, when he has served his sentence, he explains to a fellow traveller in a train what her playing meant to him. 'Two persons are cultivating the noblest of arts – music – together; this needs a certain proximity in which there is nothing indecent, and nobody except a silly, jealous husband could find anything blameworthy in it. And yet everyone knows perfectly well that it's owing to these very occupations, especially musical studies, engaged in together, that by far the greatest amount of wickedness happens in our society.'[1]

Pozdnisheff is possessed by the *idée fixe* that the whole purpose of the piano is to encourage illicit romance, and that piano music is designed to arouse the passions.

> 'Ah!' he cried, 'it's a strange piece of music, that Sonata, especially the first part. Music generally is a strange thing . . . Music, they say, acts on us by elevating the soul. That's absurd . . . It neither elevates nor depresses the soul, but provokes it . . . It is meant to be played and then to be followed by the deeds for which it nerves one; but to call forth the energy of a sentiment which is not about to manifest itself in any deed, how can that be otherwise than harmful?'[2]

The piece in question is Beethoven's 'Kreutzer' sonata, which inspired Tolstoy to write his short novel of that name. Published in 1900, his tale of misguided jealousy was the climax in a literary cult of the piano that had been building up over the century.

It all began quite innocently with Jane Austen. Young Frank Churchill of Austen's *Emma* bears no resemblance to the brutish Pozdnisheff; as if to prove it he sends his (secret) beloved a Broadwood – this being the first recorded use of the piano as a gallant gift, a grandiose substitute for chocolates and flowers.

> Mrs Cole was telling that she had been calling on Miss Bates, and as soon as she entered the room had been struck by the sight of a pianoforte – a very elegant-looking instrument – not a grand, but a large-sized square pianoforte; and the substance of the story, the end of all the dialogue which ensued of surprize [*sic*], and inquiry, and congratulations on her side, and explanation on Miss Bates's, was that this pianoforte had arrived from Broadwood's the day before, to the great astonishment of both aunt and niece . . .[3]

Even in the genteel world of Jane Austen, however, the piano can be a catalyst for malicious comment and more or less open tension. In *Pride and Prejudice* Elizabeth and Mary Bennet use the piano as much as a monument to girlish vanity as a musical instrument. But the dramatic possibilities of the instrument come truly to the fore when the scheming Lady Catherine, who sees accomplishment at the piano as a sign of social inferiority, lectures Elizabeth Bennet on the subject:

I often tell young ladies that no excellence in music is to be acquired without constant practise. I have told Miss Bennet several times, that she will never play really well unless she practises more; and though Mrs. Collins has no instrument, she is very welcome, as I have often told her, to come to Rosings every day, and play on the pianoforte in Mrs Jenkinson's room. She would be in nobody's way, you know, in that part of the house.[4]

A proper young lady, in other words, would be sure to practise diligently, though without disturbing the household, so as to have something to offer society – although of course the very fact that she could play would prove that she was not a lady in the truest sense. That is how matters stood at the beginning of the century, and thus they were reflected in the novels of the time.

In fact virtually every nineteenth-century heroine could and did play the piano, from Elizabeth Bennet in Austen's *Pride and Prejudice* to Charlotte Brontë's *Jane Eyre*, from Ottilie in Goethe's *Wahlver-wandtschaften* [*Elective Affinities*] to Fontaine's *Effi Briest*, from Flaubert's *Madame Bovary* to the Goncourt brothers' *Renée Mauperin*. In Thackeray's *Vanity Fair* the piano is no longer an entirely innocent pursuit: somehow, along with the excessive use of powder and paint, too many petticoats and extravagant hats, it has become a mark of coquettishness. Amelia Sedley, the positive heroine, can play, but only just. Becky Sharp on the other hand, with her green eyes and half-French artistic heritage, is an accomplished pianist; little wonder that she is destined to lose her virtue. Dexterity implies frivolity; skill in performance implies shamelessness. Anyone who can play the piano that well is surely not to be trusted. By the middle of the nineteenth century the piano had come a long way.

Wilkie Collins exploited this notion of innocence and immorality at the keyboard to considerable effect. In *The Woman in White*, which T. S. Eliot called the first and best modern English detective story, Laura Fairlie plays Mozart with extraordinary feeling. Forced to marry the ruined and ruinous Sir Percival, she spends her last evening with the man she loves playing her farewell to him and to her music.

She kept her place at the piano; and I kept mine at the card table. She played unintermittingly – played as if the music was her only refuge from herself. Sometimes, her fingers touched the notes with a lingering fondness, a soft, plaintive, dying tenderness, unutterably beautiful and mournful to hear – sometimes, they faltered and failed her, or hurried over the instrument mechanically as if their task was a burden to them. But still, change and waver as they might in the expression they imparted to the music, their resolution to play never faltered. She only rose from the piano when we all rose to say goodnight.[5]

After that, through the following five hundred pages of the novel, Laura scarcely sits down to play again – an indication of the dramatic shift in her fortunes which is reversed only at the very end of the book.

When the good pianist retires, however, the evil principle incarnate takes possession of the keyboard in the form of the inscrutible Conte Fosco. Needless to say he never plays Mozart, only overtures to Italian operas and Neopolitan street songs. He uses his accomplishment not to entertain society but to enthral his victims. The intelligent Marian Halcombe is held captive by his playing for a full half hour while Fosco's wife carries out a devilish scheme: the piano has become an instrument of social blackmail.

> Again he stopped me – this time, by going back to the piano, and suddenly appealing to me on a musical question . . . 'Had I heard *Moses in Egypt*? Would I listen to this, and this, and this, and say if anything more sublimely sacred and grand had ever been composed by mortal man?' – And, without waiting for a word of assent or dissent on my part, looking me hard in the face all the time, he began thundering on the piano . . . There was something horrible – something fierce and devilish, in the outburst of his delight at his own singing and playing, and in the triumph with which he watched its effect upon me, as I shrank nearer and nearer to the door. I was released at last . . .[6]

Flaubert was the first great novelist to realize the full dramatic potential of the piano. In *Madame Bovary* he uses it as a seismograph of the soul, an indicator of his heroine's progress and fall. Emma Bovary's piano is the accomplice of her dreams and desires.

Right at the beginning of the novel we learn that the heroine is an excellent pianist, carefully trained at her convent school for well-bred if not wealthy young ladies. In the first weeks of his marriage to her Charles Bovary is allowed to enjoy her accomplishment: 'The quicker her hands moved when she played the piano, the greater his surprise. She struck the notes with a sure touch, and could run down the keyboard from treble to bass without a moment's pause. Thus shaken from its slumbers, the old instrument with its jangling strings could be heard at the other end of the village . . .'[7]

Flaubert then uses the piano to mark the decline of the marriage. 'She gave up her music. What was the point of playing? Who was there to hear? Since she would never sit in a concert hall in a short-sleeved dress of black velvet, letting her fingers ripple over the ivory keys of the Erard grand, and hearing murmurs of ecstatic appreciation blow round her like a breeze, what was the point of subjecting herself to all the boredom of practising?' Emma Bovary, country doctor's wife, as a concert pianist – what a triumph that would have been, at least for her. As it is, the untouched piano stands in silent accusation of Charles's self-satisfied dullness, the empty nights in his bed, the miserable marriage in a miserable village, the constraints imposed by society.

Then all of a sudden Emma begins to play again, seized with an inexplicable urge at the start of yet another winter. She plays the same piece four times through, complaining at her clumsiness. Could it be that she is dreaming of that imaginary concert hall when she breaks off in the middle of a piece to sigh: ' "It's no use! I ought to take lessons, but . . ." '[8]

When Bovary then, well-meaning as ever, offers to arrange lessons for her locally, he is rewarded with a cry of dismay and a sarcastic suggestion that they might as well sell the instrument then and there. Nothing will do for Madame Bovary but weekly lessons with the costly and glamorous Mademoiselle Lempereur in the big city of Rouen. Does this mean that Emma has set her sights on a real career?

In fact of course this sudden enthusiasm for the piano is just an exercise in camouflage. Emma never goes to Mademoiselle Lempereur but spends the precious hours on a mahogany bed at the Hôtel de Boulogne with her lover Léon. The piano, if not an active accomplice in her crime, is at least a pawn of passion, as much deceived as Charles himself.

In so many of Flaubert's novels the piano functions as a focus for romance and drama, passion and pain. *L'Education sentimentale* is full of pianos; even the hero Frédéric Moreau 'hired a piano and composed German waltzes'. But the most important piano in the book belongs to Marie Arnoux, the lovely lady Frédéric could never quite win. It is the sight of her piano being sold at auction that at last marks the end of a hopeless affair: 'The assistant had opened a piano – her piano! Still standing up, he played a scale with his right hand and offered the instrument at twelve hundred francs; then he came down to a thousand, eight hundred, seven hundred ... Mme Dambreuse playfully described it as an old tin kettle.'⁹

Vanity Fair also features a piano auction, held when Amelia's father John Sedley goes bankrupt and the contents of his house and cellar are put up for sale. Becky Sharp is astonished to see Amelia's little Broadwood piano sold for 25 guineas. Later Amelia manages to buy back her piano, which has somehow transformed itself into a Stodart –a clear question of poetic licence.

We come to another remarkable scene. Two brothers sit opposite one another in a small apartment in Rome, Via Argentina number 34, writing for all they are worth. The elder of the two is already a successful writer at the age of twenty-six; the younger, just twenty-two, has so far produced nothing longer than a short story but is now hard at work on a novel. The sibling rivalry is almost more than the younger man can bear. Sitting now at the piano, he breaks off suddenly to turn to his brother: '*In inimicos!*' – in other words, he declares his enmity.

This episode took place in fact, not fiction: twenty-five years later Heinrich Mann recalled the scene to his younger brother Thomas.

It is hardly surprising to find Thomas Mann drawing confidence and a militant sort of courage from the keyboard. At around the same time the character of little Hanno Buddenbrook was taking shape in Mann's imagination. The boy was to have been the solitary hero of the novel that grew to a family epic: *Die Buddenbrooks*. Published in 1900, Mann's first great work includes a scene that is the culmination of a century of literary fascination with the piano. In describing how Hanno plays for his guests on the occasion of his eighth birthday party, Mann goes straight to the musical and psychological core of the player's childish rhapsody.

Then came the finale, Hanno's beloved finale, which crowned the elevated simplicity of the whole piece. Soft and clear as a bell sounded the E minor chord, tremolo pianissimo, amid the purling, flowing notes of the violin. It swelled, it broadened, it slowly, slowly rose: suddenly, in the forte, he introduced the discord C sharp, which led back to the original key, and the Stradivarius ornamented it with its swelling and singing. He dwelt on the dissonance until it became fortissimo. But he denied himself and his audience the resolution; he kept it back. What would it be, this resolution, this enchanting, satisfying absorption into the B major chord? A joy beyond compare, a gratification of overpowering sweetness. Peace! Bliss! The kingdom of heaven: only not yet – not yet! A moment more of striving, hesitation, suspense, that must become well-nigh intolerable in order to heighten the ultimate moment of joy.[10]

Eight-year-old Hanno is a sensual pianist, savouring the anticipation of a delayed musical orgasm. Elizabeth Bennet and Jane Eyre played out of a sense of duty; Emma Bovary and Conte Fosco used the piano as an unwitting accomplice in crime; Pozdnisheff condemned it as an instrument of the devil. But Hanno's piano is not just the vehicle of tragedy; it is a metaphor for the tragedy itself – the early death of a brilliant but obsessive boy. Later, when Hanno is in secondary school, his dear friend Kai Count Mölln urges him to give up his music.

Hanno ignores his advice and sits down to play again, belabouring a simple melody into the small hours of the morning – clearly now inviting death.

The fanatical worship of this worthless trifle, this scrap of melody, this brief, childish harmonic invention only a bar and a half in length, had about it something stupid and gross, and at the same time something ascetic and religious – something that contained the essence of faith and renunciation . . . there was a sort of cynical joy, a yielding to desire, in the way the last drop of sweetness was, as it were, extracted from the melody, till exhaustion, disgust and satiety supervened.

The final yielding comes just three weeks later, as the doctor attempting to treat the boy for typhoid fever wonders . . .

whether this illness, which he calls typhoid, is an unfortunate accident, the disagreeable consequence of an infection which might perhaps have been avoided, and which can be combated with the resources of medical science; or whether it is, quite simply, a form of dissolution, the garment, as it were, of death. And then, whether death chose to assume this form or another is all the same – against him there is no remedy.[11]

Death in another form – for instance the seductive guise of music, with the keyboard its fixed and fatal grin.

A two-line scene from Zola's *Nana* may serve as an afterword:

'"Well I never!" Tatan Néné exclaimed on seeing this happen. "Why on earth is he putting champagne into the piano?"

'"Really, my dear girl, you don't know that?" replied Labordette solemnly. "There's nothing so good as champagne for pianos. It gives them sound."'[12]

> ... the main reason why I decided many
> years ago (1908) to say farewell to
> the piano was that I thought it madness
> to refuse the mercy of the goddess
> Intelligence ...
>
> *Alberto Savinio*

> I woke up one April morning, I no longer
> know which one, and said to myself,
> no more piano. And I never touched
> the instrument again.
>
> *Thomas Bernhard*

In 1900 the world was full of pianos – just as today it is full of cars. The market was saturated. In some places it was declared illegal to play a piano near an open window. Composers – with the exception of Debussy – abandoned the instrument. The popularity of the piano was its own undoing. *Les jeux sont faits, rien ne va plus.*

Scene: 1904, New Jersey. The piano dealers of America had assembled for their annual convention. They were agreed as never before: business was dreadful – there were far too many pianos already. In 1900 alone 171,000 pianos were manufactured in the United States, and that number did not include harmoniums and pianolas. What to do? A national campaign must be set in motion, from New England to California, from the Canadian border to New Orleans, exhorting people to throw out their antiquated instruments. All the old rubbish must be burned. The delegates decided to set an example. They got hold of two dilapidated pianos, built a funeral pyre for them and set fire to the lot. They made speeches over the flames, waved little flags, banged daringly on the burning keyboards, threw metronomes at each other and ducked the bursting strings. It was a grand old party.[1]

Statistics, c.1900: London, then the world's biggest city with a population of 7 million, boasted 175 piano factories and 500 shops selling musical instruments. Paris, with a population of around 3½ million, had 50 factories and about 250 dealers in musical instruments. New York, then a city of 'only' 3.7 million, had 130 piano factories and about 200 retail outlets. (These figures do not include specialist factories producing mechanical pianos.) But the world capital of piano manufacture at the time was Berlin, a city less than one-third the size of London, but with just as many piano-makers.[2]

Scene, c.1900: Berlin, Reichenberger Straße. This street was the assembly line of Berlin's piano manufacturing industry (the Köpenicker Straße was a close rival). The enormous factory at numbers 122–124 set the tone. Ferdinand Manthey worked right next door and rented out his first floor to Aloys Becker, a smaller enterprise. At number 142 Mörs & Co shared the workshop with Paul & Co, while A. Pöschel worked away at number 160, Ernst Krause at number 57, and the firm of Seidel Nachfolger at number 65. The major suppliers were not far away: there was a specialist in metal fittings (number 134), another for nameplates (number 135), and on the fourth floor of number 142 R. Wittwer Nachfl. produced 'decorative piano parts'.[3]

There were any number of subsidiary suppliers in the piano industry at the turn of the century. You could make a fortune in piano covers alone – those silk or velvet, embroidered and betasselled throws that would transform a piano into a decorative piece of furniture, much to the detriment of the acoustic effect. Then there were canvas and felt cloths required for transport, also an excellent source of income. Manufacturers of candlesticks did very good business, each piano requiring two special fittings. This still left room for makers of music stands, medallions, marquetry work and all sorts of little extras. Even sculptors and plasterers profited from the piano boom, selling busts of Beethoven, Mozart or, latterly, Wagner, to hordes of eager amateurs.

Statistics: A company specializing in the production of black keys put out this advertisement: '2.8 million half-tones made and sold last year'. A composer who worked as a pianist in a Paris cabaret wrote a short piece called 'Vexations' with the indication that it should be repeated 840 times. Another young musician, bandleader in a cabaret in Berlin, began to experiment with a technique of composition based not on tonality but on the free combination of the twelve notes of the chromatic scale. He later identified a problem in his system, which lacks any zero: 'There is not enough nothing in it.'[4] A conductor said: 'Our sense of hearing is logarithmic, so that when, for example, we hear an A followed by an E, we do not hear it as the frequency ratio 3:2 but rather as the logarithm of this ratio, which determines the interval between the two notes.'[5] This is the twentieth century.

This century has shown itself increasingly impatient with the piano, incarnation that it is of the semitonal tradition. Scriabin experimented with quarter-tonal music using two pianos. Stravinsky used the piano lid for a crashing finale forzato. Boulez and others worked with sound clusters. Yet others have been known to reach in and pluck the strings like harpists. Arch-innovator John Cage took to decorating the piano like a Christmas tree: screws, rubber bands, eggspoons, hairpins and other carefully specified bits and pieces he would set between or on the strings to produce a 'prepared piano', showing little respect for an instrument so revered in the nineteenth century. On the other hand the piano as we know it is the result of incessant experimentation: few instruments have invited so much fiddling.

For all the impatience of this twentieth century, the piano has survived – and triumphed. As a concert instrument it is no less popular than ever, and the great pianists of our day are worshipped as cult figures. In 1900 piano-lovers and profiteers may have feared the end was nigh, but their fears have proved unjustified.

Two more statistics: the tension exerted on the frame of a modern concert piano is 20 tons, while 20 tons of thrust are required to lift a modern jet aircraft into the sky. The piano, therefore, is an introverted jet. It cannot fly, but it can uplift an audience. What Mozart once said of Vienna might now be said of the whole world: 'This is certainly the land of the piano.'[6]

APPENDIX

ACKNOWLEDGEMENTS

I would like to thank the Staatliches Institut für Musikforschung (Berlin) in the Stiftung Preußischer Kulturbesitz, and in particular Jutta March, one of those rare librarians who is as helpful, encouraging and hospitable as she is efficient and reliable. I am also very grateful to Gudrun Schwinger of the Sender Freies Berlin, who let me use her music library as a sort of personal reference library; I am indebted to a source she suggested for the chapter on concert agents. I would also like to thank the authors whose books accompanied me through two and a half years of research, and whom I would like to mention here in place of a bibliography: first of all Harold C. Schonberg with his book on *The Great Pianists*, then Berthold Litzmann with his three volumes on Clara (and Robert) Schumann, which in fact amount to a far-reaching cultural history of the nineteenth century, and finally Carl Dahlhaus with his great study of *Die Musik des 19. Jahrhunderts* (*The Music of the Nineteenth Century*), although in the end I relied on his work less than I admired it. The following notes are intended not to suggest any academic pretensions, only to allow the interested reader to follow up this or that lead.

NOTES

TRANSLATOR'S NOTE

Where reference is made to works in the original German, the extracts quoted have been translated directly for this edition.

PRELUDE

1. H. Sahling (ed.), *Notate zur Pianistik* (VEB Deutscher Verlag für Musik, Leipzig, 1976), p. 163.
2. A. Rubinstein in ibid., p. 63.
3. H. Neupert, 'Vom Musikstab zum modernen Klavier' in H. Junghanns, *Der Piano- und Flügelbau* (Frankfurt, 1971), p. 46.
4. H. Neuhaus, *Die Kunst des Klavierspiels* (Cologne, 1977), p. 53.
5. M. Schneider, *Schubert* (Reinbek, 1958, vol. 19), p. 55.
6. M. Weber, *Die rationalen und soziologischen Grundlagen der Musik* (Tübingen, 1972), p. 77.
7. Sahling, *Notate*, p. 25.
8. H. C. Schonberg, *The Great Pianists* (London, 1964), p. 18.
9. H. Heine, *Zeitungsberichte über Musik und Malerei*, edited by M. Mann (Frankfurt, 1964), p. 142.
10. E. Hanslick, *Aus neuer und neuester Zeit: Musikalische Kritiken und Schilderungen* (Berlin, 1900), pp. 105–18.
11. Quoted in A. Boucourichliev, *Schumann* (Hamburg, 1958), vol. 6, p. 98; this is probably from a letter written in 1839 to Heinrich Dorn in which Schumann complains of the piano being too 'cramped' for his purposes.

CHAPTER 1

1. Quoted in K. Schönewolf, *Beethoven in der Zeitenwende* (Halle Salle, 1953), vol. I, p. 91.
2. Ibid., p. 98.
3. Ibid.
4. C. Czerny quoting Gelinek in ibid., p. 63.

5. St. Ley, *Beethovens Leben in authentischen Bildern und Texten* (Berlin, 1925), pp. 79f.
6. F. G. Wegeler and F. Ries, *Biographische Notizen über Ludwig van Beethoven* (Coblenz, 1838), p. 141.
7. Seyfried, quoted in Ley, *Beethovens Leben*, p. 137.
8. Wegeler and Ries, *Biographische Notizen*, p. 156.
9. Ibid., pp. 143f.
10. Quoted in *Grosse Kulturepochen: Biedermeier* (Hueber, München), p. 259.
11. In P. Schleuning, *Der Burger erhebt sich*, Reihe Geschichte der Musik in Deutschland, das achtzehnte Jahrhundert (Hamburg, 1984), pp. 47f.
12. Ibid.
13. Wegeler and Ries, *Biographische Notizen*, pp. 110f.
14. Lakanal, in Schönewolf, *Beethoven*, vol. I, p. 132.
15. C. Dahlhaus, *Die Musik des 19. Jahrhunderts: Neues Handbuch der Musikwissenschaft* (Athenaion, Wiesbaden, 1980), vol. 6, p. 35.
16. Ibid., p. 118.
17. W. H. Wackenroder, *Schriften* (Reinbek, 1958), p. 169.
18. Ibid., p. 91.
19. Th. W. Adorno, *Einführung in die Musiksoziologie* (Ges. Schriften 11, Frankfurt, 1973), p. 411.
20. Seyfried, quoted in Schönewolf, *Beethoven*, vol. I, p. 336.
21. Ibid.
22. Ibid.
23. Ibid.
24. Ibid.
25. Ibid.
26. Wegeler and Ries, *Biographische Notizen*, pp. 96f.
27. Ibid.
28. Ibid.
29. Schönewolf, *Beethoven*, vol. I, p. 653.
30. Tomaschek, quoted in ibid., p. 653, footnote.

CHAPTER 2

1. In J. N. Forkel, *Über Johann Sebastian Bach Leben, Kunst und Kunstwerke* (Kassel, 1942; facsimile of first edn, 1802), p. 45.
2. *Johann Sebastian Bach, Leben und Werk*, dtv dokumente (München, 1984), p. 136.
3. Ibid., p. 139.
4. Ibid., p. 138.

5. Ibid., p. 137.
6. Quoted in R. Kirkpatrick, *Domenico Scarlatti* (Princeton, 1953), pp. 30–1.
7. Ibid., p. 31.
8. Forkel, *Über Johann Sebastian Bach*, p. 47.
9. Dtv dokumente, p. 136.
10. Schonberg, *The Great Pianists*, pp. 45ff.
11. Ibid.
12. Ibid.
13. Quoted in E. Forbes (ed.), *Thayer's Life of Beethoven* (Princeton, 1964), vol. I, p. 417.

CHAPTER 3

1. Quoted in Forbes, *Thayer's Life*, vol. II, p. 694.
2. Ibid.
3. Hanslick, *Musikalische Kritiken*, p. 111.
4. J. Mattheson, *Critica musica* (1725; repr. Amsterdam, 1964), pp. 335ff.
5. Schonberg, *The Great Pianists*, pp. 19–20.
6. As translated in Forbes, *Thayer's Life*, vol. II, p. 694.
7. As translated in E. Anderson, *The Letters of Beethoven* (London, 1961), pp. 659–60.
8. Forbes, *Thayer's Life*, vol. II, p. 668.
9. Anderson, *Letters*, p. 657.
10. Viennese newspaper, 9 July 1824, facsimile (Graz, 1983).
11. M. Butor, *Dialogue avec 33 variations de Ludwig van Beethoven sur une valse de Diabelli* (Paris, 1971), p. 15.
12. Ibid., p. 137.
13. Ibid., p. 141.
14. A. B. Marx, *Ludwig van Beethoven, Leben und Schaffen* (Berlin, 1884), vol. II, p. 373.

CHAPTER 4

1. J. F. Cooper, *The Last of the Mohicans* (London, 1832), p. 386.
2. Quoted in O. E. Deutsch (ed.), *Franz Schubert, Briefe und Schriften* (Vienna, 1954), p. 209.
3. Franz Schubert, *Die Texte seiner einstimmig komponierten Lieder* (Heidelberg/New York, 1974), vol. II, p. 209.
4. Quoted in H. J. Frölich, *Schubert* (München, 1978), p. 165.
5. Ibid., pp. 106ff.

6. Ibid., p. 152.
7. A. Brendel, *Nachdenken über Musik* (München, 1984, Serie Piper no. 265), p. 99.
8. B. Massin, *Franz Schubert* (Paris, 1978), p. 1282.
9. Frölich, *Schubert*, p. 44.
10. R. Schumann, 'Das Komische in der Musik' in Schumann (ed.), *Gesammelte Schriften über Musik und Musiker* (Leipzig, 1974), p. 67.
11. Deutsch, *Franz Schubert*, p. 207.
12. J. F. Cooper, *The Pioneers* (London, 1832), pp. 423–4.

CHAPTER 5

1. B. Litzmann, *Clara Schumann, Ein Künstlerleben* (Leipzig, 1906), vol. I, pp. 14f.
2. Ibid., p. 1.
3. Ibid., p. 20.
4. Ibid., p. 27.
5. Ibid., pp. 28ff.
6. Ibid.
7. Ibid.
8. Quoted in H. E. Jacob, *Felix Mendelssohn und seine Beit* (Frankfurt, 1959), p. 46.
9. L. Rellstab in W. Reich (ed.), *Felix Mendelssohn im Spiegel eigener Aussagen und zeitgenössischer Dokumente* (Zürich, 1970), pp. 26ff.
10. Ibid.
11. Ibid.
12. Litzmann, *Clara Schumann*, vol. I, p. 30.
13. Ibid., vol. III, p. 434.
14. Sahling, *Notate*, p. 21.
15. Ibid.
16. G. Wehmeyer, *Carl Czerny oder die Einzelhaft am Klavier* (Kassel, Basel, 1983), p. 163.
17. Litzmann, *Clara Schumann*, vol. I, pp. 44ff.
18. *The Works of Heinrich Heine*, transl. by C. G. Leland, vol. VII, 'French Affairs: Letters from Paris' (vol. I, Article VI) (London, 1893), pp. 165–7.

CHAPTER 6

1. Letter of 12 December 1831 to Titus Woyciechowski; this is a synthesis of several translations.

2. *Reisebriefe von Felix Mendelssohn aus den Jahren 1830–1832* (Leipzig, 1862), pp. 302ff.

3. G. Flaubert, *Sentimental Education*, transl. by A. Goldsmith (London, 1941), p. 64.

4. Stendhal, *Lucien Leewen* (Berlin, 1951), p. 260.

5. *Reisebriefe*, p. 323.

6. Lauglé and Vanderbusch, *Louis et le Saint-Simonien* (1832), quoted in W. Benjamin, *Illuminationem, Ausgewahlte Schriften* (Frankfurt, 1961), p. 190.

7. W. Georgij, *Klavierspielbuchlein* (Zurich/Freiburg, 1978), pp. 66–7.

8. *Reisebriefe*, p. 323.

9. Benjamin, *Illuminationem*, p. 186.

10. *Reisebriefe*, p. 135.

11. K. Kobylanska (ed.), *Frédéric Chopin, Briefe*, transl. into German by C. Rymarowicz (Frankfurt, 1984), p. 133.

12. Ibid., p. 132.

13. Ibid., p. 126.

14. Ibid., p. 133.

CHAPTER 7

1. Kobylanska, *Briefe*, p. 158.

2. C. Bourniquel, *Chopin* (Reinbek, 1959, vol. 25), p. 8.

3. Ibid., p. 66.

4. Ibid., p. 68.

5. A. Cortot, *In Search of Chopin*, transl. C. and R. Clarke (London, 1951), p. 91.

6. Kobylanska, *Briefe*, p. 58.

7. Ibid., p. 75.

8. Cortoot, *In Search of Chopin*, p. 108.

9. Ibid., p. 112.

10. Ibid., p. 22.

11. Bourniquel, *Chopin*, p. 155.

12. Cortot, *In Search of Chopin*, pp. 85–6.

13. Kobylanska, *Briefe*, p. 143.

14. Chopin's unfinished notes on teaching the piano, transcribed in Cortot, *In Search of Chopin*, pp. 40–7. Cortot is wrong to dismiss these notes as a 'puzzle made up of the most commonplace clichés'.

15. Ibid.

16. Ibid.

17. Ibid., p. 22.

18. Ibid., pp. 40–7.
19. Quoted in H. Kinzler, *Chopin, Über den Zusammenhang von Satztechnik und Klavierspiel* (München/Salzburg, 1977), p. 87, footnote 195.
20. O. Bie, *Das Klavier* (Berlin, 1911), p. 196.
21. Ibid., p. 204.
22. Rellstab in *Iris*, issue dated 1834, pp. 18f.
23. *Frédéric Chopin, Briefe und Dokumente* (Zürich Manesse, 1959), p. 216.
24. Kinzler, *Chopin*, p. 103.
25. Schumann, *Gesammelte Schriften*, p. 107.
26. Kobylanska, *Briefe*, p. 170.
27. Bie, *Das Klavier*, p. 200.

CHAPTER 8

1. Quoted in Schonberg, *The Great Pianists*, p. 163.
2. H. Heine, *Zeitungsberichte*, from *Heines Werke in fünf Bänden* (Weimar, 1959), p. 148.
3. C. P. E. Bach, *Über die wahre Art, das Klavier zu spielen* (Leipzig, 1981, reissue), p. 17.
4. D. G. Türk, *Clavier Schule*.
5. L. Ramann, *Franz Liszt, Gesammelte Schriften* (reprinted Hildesheim/New York, 1978), p. 72.
6. Ibid., p. 80.
7. Ibid., pp. 95f.
8. Ibid.
9. Quoted in Litzmann, *Clara Schumann*, vol. I, pp. 201ff.
10. L. Ramann, *Franz Liszt als Künstler und Mensch* (Leipzig, 1880), vol. I, p. 435.
11. Ibid., p. 137.
12. Ibid., p. 437.
13. Schonberg, *The Great Pianists*, p. 163.

CHAPTER 9

1. R. Schumann, *Tagebücher*, edited by G. Eismann (Leipzig, 1971), vol. I, p. 342.
2. Ibid., p. 344.
3. Ibid., p. 339.
4. Ibid., p. 344.
5. Schumann, *Gesammelte Schriften*, p. 11.

6. Ibid.
7. Schumann, *Tagebücher*, p. 391.
8. Schumann, *Gesammelte Schriften*, p. 33.
9. H. Eggebrecht, 'Töne sind höhere Worte' in *Musik-Konzepte, Sonderbande Robert Schumann*, edition text und kritik (Frankfurt), vol. I, p. 105.
10. Schumann, *Gesammelte Schriften*, p. 10.
11. Ibid., p. 66.
12. Ibid., p. 143.
13. Schnebel, 'Rückungen- Ver-rückungen, Psychoanalytische Betrachtungen zu Schumanns Leben und Werk' in *Musik-Konzepte*, vol. I, p. 38.
14. Ibid., p. 29.
15. Litzmann, *Clara Schumann*, vol. I, p. 169.
16. Ibid., p. 179
17. R. Barthes, 'Rasch', *L'obvie et L'obtus: Essais critiques III* (Paris, 1982), p. 266; transl. here direct from the French.
18. Ibid., pp. 268–9.
19. E. Hanslick, *Aus meinem Leben*, quoted in U. Molsen, *Die Geschichte des Klavierspiels in historischen Zitaten* (Balingen, 1982), p. 143.
20. Ibid., p. 133.

CHAPTER 10

1. Wehmeyer, *Carl Czerny*, p. 132.
2. Ibid., p. 133.
3. Ibid., p. 132.
4. Schonberg, *The Great Pianists*, p. 55.
5. E. Hanslick, *Geschichte des Concertwesens in Wien* (2 vols bound as one; reprinted Hildesheim/New York, 1979), vol. II, p. 226.
6. Litzmann, *Clara Schumann*, vol. I, p. 107.
7. Weymeyer, *Carl Czerny*, p. 173.
8. Ibid., p. 176.
9. C. Czerny, *Erinnerungen aus meinem Leben, mit Werkverzeichnes*, edited by W. Kolneder (Straßburg/Baden-Baden, n. d.), p. 27.
10. Ibid., p. 13.
11. Ibid., p. 14.
12. Ibid., p. 27.
13. Ibid., p. 23.

CHAPTER 11

1. Franz Liszt, *Briefe an Marie Gräfin d'Agoult* (Berlin, 1933), pp. 201, 278.
2. Ibid., p. 302.
3. Ramann, *Franz Liszt als Künstler*, vol. I, p. 173.
4. Schumann, *Gesammelte Schriften*, p. 183.
5. Litzmann, *Clara Schumann*, vol. I, p. 199.
6. H. Berlioz, *Lebenserinnerungen* (München, 1914), p. 444.
7. Schonberg, *The Great Pianists*, pp. 121–2.
8. Liszt, *Briefe*, pp. 295f.
9. Ibid., p. 392.
10. Ibid., p. 387.
11. Schumann, *Gesammelte Schriften*, p. 181.
12. Heine, *Zeitungsberichte*, p. 115.
13. Hanslick, *Concertwesens*, vol. I, p. 335, footnote 1.
14. Liszt, *Briefe*, p. 252.
15. Ramann, *Liszt, Gesammelte Schriften*, vol. II, pp. 108ff.
16. Heine, *Zeitungsberichte*, p. 147.
17. *Briefwechsel zwischen Franz Liszt und Carl Alexander, Großherz von Sachsen* (Leipzig, 1909), p. 8.
18. *Franz Liszt, Sein Leben in Bildern* (Kassel/Basel, 1967), p. 97.

CHAPTER 12

1. Louis Moreau Gottschalk, *Notes of a Pianist: Edited, with a Prelude, a Postlude, and Explanatory Notes, by Jeanne Behrend* (New York, 1964), pp. 41–2.
2. Ibid., p. 42.
3. Ibid., p. 261.
4. Ibid., pp. 133–4.
5. Ibid., p. 236.
6. Ibid., p. 236.
7. Ibid., p. 171.
8. Ibid., p. 218.
9. Ibid., p. 311.
10. Ibid., pp. 309–10.
11. Ibid., pp. 302–3.
12. Ibid., pp. 403–4.

CHAPTER 13

1. F. Goebels in *Aspekte bürgerlicher Musikkultur, Reihe Musik im 19. Jahrhundert* (Stuttgart, 1981), p. 15.
2. Ibid., p. 18.
3. Ibid., p. 19.
4. Ibid., p. 20
5. Weber, *Grundlagen der Musik*, p. 77.
6. A. B. Marx, 'Die Musik des 19. Jahrhunderts und ihre Pflege' in Goebels, *Aspekte*, p. 21.
7. W. Haacke, *Am Klavier, Werke europäischer Meister aus sechs Jahrhunderten* (Königten, 1958), p. 17.
8. A. Loesser, *Men, Women and Pianos, a Social History* (London, 1955), p. 509.
9. J. Kinkel, 'Musik als Mode' in *Frau und Musik, Die Frau in der Gesellschaft, Frühre Texte*, edited by E. Reiger (Frankfurt, 1980), p. 50.
10. Ibid., p. 48.
11. Ibid., p. 55.
12. F. Schindelmeisser, 'Ein Wort über meine Musik-Unterrichts-Anstalt' (1840) in Reiger, *Frau und Musik*, p. 225.
13. Ibid.

CHAPTER 14

1. A. Moser (ed.), *Brahms im Briefwechsel mit Joseph Joachim* (Berlin, 1912), vol. I, pp. 233–4.
2. *Musik gedeutet und bewertet, Dokumente zur Rezeptionsgeschichte von Musik*, dtv dokumente no. 2937 (München/Kassel), pp. 119–20.
3. H. Gal in a comment in his edition of Brahms' letters (Frankfurt, 1979, Fischer Taschenbuch no. 2139), p. 25.
4. In H. A. Neunzig, *Brahms* (Reinbek, 1973, vol. 197), p. 23.
5. Litzmann, *Clara Schumann*, vol. II, p. 80.
6. Neunzig, *Brahms*, p. 29.
7. Ibid.
8. Schumann, *Gesammelte Schriften*, p. 226.
9. Gal, *Brahms*, p. 13.
10. Neunzig, *Brahms*, p. 33.
11. Litzmann, *Clara Schumann*, vol. II, p. 302.
12. Ibid., p. 316.
13. Ibid., p. 318.
14. *Musik gedeutet*, p. 125.

15. Ibid., p. 126.
16. Ibid., p. 130.
17. Moser, *Briefwechsel*, pp. 46–7.
18. Ibid., p. 56.
19. *Musik gedeutet*, p. 134.
20. Quoted in C. Dahlhaus, *Johannes Brahms, Klavierkonzert no. 1 d-moll Op. 15* (München, 1965), p. 4.
21. Ibid.
22. Ibid.
23. Ibid., p. 5.
24. Ibid.
25. Neunzig, *Brahms*, p. 39.
26. Ibid.
27. Dahlhaus, *Klavierkonzert*, p. 25.
28. Ibid., p. 5.
29. Ibid.
30. Ibid., pp. 25–6.
31. Ibid.
32. Ibid., p. 6.
33. Quoted in M Kagel, 'Die mißbrauchte Empfindsamkeit, zum 150. Geburtstag von Brahms', *Frankfurter Allgemeine Zeitung*, 7 May 1983.
34. Moser, *Briefwechsel*, vol. I, p. 234.
35. Quoted in L. Finscher, 'Der Grundton der Melancholie', *Frankfurter Allgemeine Zeitung*, 7 May 1983.

CHAPTER 15

1. T. Steinway, *People and Pianos* (New York, 1961), p. 16. Facsimile letter in original German, transl. here by H. Goodman.
2. C. Ehrlich quoted in D. Wainwright, *Broadwood by Appointment* (London, 1982), p. 290.
3. Kobylanska, *Briefe*, p. 290.
4. Steinway, *People and Pianos*, p. 21.
5. Gottschalk, *Notes*, p. 243.
6. H. von Bülow, *Neue Briefe*, edited by R. Graf du Moulin Eckart (München, 1927), p. 30.
7. *Eine Chronik des Hauses Bechstein: Festschrift zum 125jährigen Jubiläum im Jahre 1978*, p. 33.
8. Bülow, *Briefe*, p. 328.
9. Ibid., p. 367.
10. Liszt letters quoted in C. F. Weitzmann, *Geschichte des Clavierspiels* (Stuttgart, 1897), pp. 294–5.

11. Loesser, *Men, Women and Pianos*, p. 527.
12. E. Hanslick, *Musikalisches Skizzenbuch*, quoted in Molsen, *Die Geschichte des Klavierspiels*, p. 82.
13. Litzmann, *Clara Schumann*, p. 425.
14. Quoted in *Unsere Abwehr* (Grotian-Steinweg, Braunschweig, 1926), pp. 9ff.; see also *Frankfurter Allgemeine Zeitung*, 22 March 1980.

CHAPTER 16

1. Sahling, *Notate*, pp. 49, 109.
2. A. Kullack/Niemann, *Aesthetik des Klavierspiels* (Berlin, 1916), p. 342.
3. R. T. Harding, *The Pianoforte, Its History Traced to the Great Exhibition of 1851* (Surrey, 1978), p. 133.
4. Sahling, *Notate*, p. 111.
5. *Chopin, Briefe und Dokumente*, p. 216.
6. C. Rosen, 'Das romantische Pedal' in *Das Große Buch vom Klavier* (Freiburg, 1983), p. 113.
7. Kullack, *Aesthetik*, p. 347.

CHAPTER 17

1. Schonberg, *The Great Pianists*, pp. 258, 253.
2. Ibid., p. 257.
3. Litzmann, *Clara Schumann*, vol. III, pp. 19–20.
4. A. Rubinstein, *Erinnerungen aus fünfzig Jahren*, transl. from the Russian by E. Kretzschmann (Leipzig, 1893), p. 9.
5. Ibid., pp. 78–9.
6. Ibid., p. 81.
7. From E. Stargardt-Wolff, *Wegbereiter großer Musiker* (Berlin, 1954).
8. Rubinstein, *Erinnerungen*, pp. 110–11.
9. Ibid., p. 104.
10. C. Pangels, *Eugene d'Albert, Wunderpianist und Komponist* (Zürich/Freiburg, 1981), p. 38.
11. Schonberg, *The Great Pianists*, p. 244.
12. Quoted in ibid.
13. Ibid.
14. Pangels, *Eugene d'Albert*, p. 43.
15. Litzmann, *Clara Schumann*, vol. III, p. 274.

16. A. Brendel, 'Vollender des Klavierspiels: Zum 30. Todestag von Ferruccio Busoni', in Brendel, *Nachdenken über Musik* (München/Zürich, 1984, Serie Piper 265), p. 149; the retraction is in 'Nachtrage zu Busoni', ibid., pp. 160–1.

17. Busoni, *Briefe an seine Frau*, edited by F. Schnapp (Zürich/ Leipzig, 1935), p. 21.

18. Schonberg, *The Great Pianists*, p. 305.

19. Busoni, *Briefe*, p. 15.

20. Ibid., p. 30

21. Sahling, *Notate*, p. 59.

22. F. Busoni, *Von der Einheit der Musik, Verstreute Aufzeichnungen* (Berlin, 1922), p. 183.

CHAPTER 18

1. Stargardt-Wolff, *Wegbereiter*, p. 14.

2. Ibid., p. 47.

3. Ibid., pp. 47–8.

4. Ibid., p. 52.

5. Ibid., p. 115.

6. Ibid.

7. Ibid., p. 80.

8. Ibid., p. 72.

9. H. von Bülow, *Briefe und Schriften*, vol. II, pp. 447–8.

10. Stargardt-Wolff, *Wegbereiter*, p. 78.

11. I. Pena, *Teresa Carreño*, quoted in Pangels, *Eugene d'Albert*, p. 118.

12. Stargardt-Wolff, *Wegbereiter*, p. 128.

13. Ibid., p. 129.

14. Pangels, *Eugene d'Albert*, p. 137.

CHAPTER 19

1. N. Tolstoy, *The Kreutzer Sonata*, transl. by I. Lepinski (London, n.d.), p. 179.

2. Ibid., pp. 194–7.

3. J. Austen, *Emma* (London, 1930), pp. 161–2.

4. J. Austen, *Pride and Prejudice* (London, 1949), pp. 171–2.

5. W. Collins, *The Woman in White* (London, 1926), p. 118.

6. Ibid., p. 314.

7. G. Flaubert, *Madame Bovary*, transl. by G. Hopkins (London, 1948), p. 49.

8. Ibid., p. 315.

9. G. Flaubert, *Sentimental Education*, transl. by A. Goldsmith (London, 1941), p. 384.

10. T. Mann, *Buddenbrooks*, transl. by H. T. Lowe Porter (London, 1956), p. 413.

11. Ibid., p. 599.

12. E. Zola, *Nana*, transl. by C. Duff (London, 1953), p. 114.

EPILOGUE

1. *Das Große Buch vom Klavier*, p. 182.

2. *Weltadreßbuch der gesamten Musikinstrumenten-Industrie* (Leipzig, 1906).

3. Ibid.

4. J. Cage, 'Erik Satie', in *Musik-Konzepte 11, Erik Satie*, edition text und kritik (Frankfurt), p. 33.

5. E. Ansermet and J.-C. Piguet, *Gespräche über Musik* (München, 1985, Serie Piper 74), p. 65.

6. Wolfgang Amadeus Mozart, *Briefe und Aufzeichnungen* (Kassel, 1963), vol. III, no. 602.

INDEX